UNCONDITIONAL LIFE

UNCONDITIONAL LIFE

The Postwar International Law Settlement

YORIKO OTOMO

OXFORD
UNIVERSITY PRESS

OXFORD
UNIVERSITY PRESS

Great Clarendon Street, Oxford, OX2 6DP,
United Kingdom

Oxford University Press is a department of the University of Oxford.
It furthers the University's objective of excellence in research, scholarship,
and education by publishing worldwide. Oxford is a registered trade mark of
Oxford University Press in the UK and in certain other countries

First Edition published in 2016

Published in the United States of America by Oxford University Press
198 Madison Avenue, New York, NY 10016, United States of America

British Library Cataloguing in Publication Data
Data available

Library of Congress Control Number: 2016936873

ISBN 978–0–19–873381–2

For Ted and Oscar

ACKNOWLEDGEMENTS

I acknowledge the elders, families, and forebears of the Wurundieri tribe of the Kulin Nation, traditional custodians of the land upon which I have carried out much of my work, from whom I have demanded an impossible hospitality. The institutional support for this research has come from the University of Melbourne, Melbourne Law School, and the Institute for International Law and the Humanities. I am grateful to all the administrative staff members who have made my doctoral experience a smooth one. It would not have been possible to undertake three years of full-time research without the support of a Fay Marles scholarship, whose namesake was the first woman Chancellor of my alma mater. I have benefited from the hospitality of many other institutions, in particular the Department of Law at the London School of Economics and Political Science and the School of Law at Birkbeck College, University of London, at which I undertook visiting fellowships.

Previous iterations of the ideas in this book have been published in articles the following articles and book chapters that I have written: 'On Mimicry and Madness: Speculations on the State' 28 *Australian Feminist Law Journal* 2008; 'Endgame: Feminist Lawyers and the Revolutionary Body' 31 *Australian Feminist Law Journal* 2009 (Special Issue Victoria Sentas and Jessica Whyte, eds); 'The Decision not to Prosecute the Emperor' in *Beyond Victor's Justice? The Tokyo War Crimes Trial Revisited* (Tim McCormack, Yuki Tanaka, and Gerry Simpson, eds) Martinus Nijhoff, International Humanitarian Law Series (2010); 'Blind Spots and Hook Turns: Searching for Virtue in International Law' in *Between Resistance and Compliance? Feminist Perspectives on International Law in an Era of Anxiety and Terror* (Sari Kuovo and Zoe Pearson, eds) (2011); and 'Her Proper Name: A Revisionist Account of International Law' 2(1) *London Review of International Law* 2014. I am grateful to all of my editors and anonymous reviewers for their generous comments.

This work has been developed through many discussions in seminars, workshops, and conferences that I have attended during my PhD candidature including (among others) the annual international *Melbourne Legal Theory Workshop* (which I attended in 2006, 2007, and 2009); the *Critical Legal Conference*, Birkbeck College (2007) and the *LLM Special Seminar Series*, London School of Economics and Political Science (2007); the *Seminar Series on Religion and the State*, University of Tokyo Center for Philosophy (2008); a week-long workshop at Queen Mary College with Luce Irigaray (2008); *Between Resistance and Compliance*, the Oñati Institute for the Sociology of Law (2008); the *Tokyo War Crimes Trial Conference*, Melbourne Law School (2008); and the *International Global Law and Policy Workshop*, Harvard Law School (2010). I would like to thank the organizers of those events for facilitating my participation and those participants who enriched those forums with their engagement. The people I met at those occasions and to whom I am indebted for their support include Peter Fitzpatrick, Christine Chinkin, Hilary Charlesworth, and Martti Koskenniemi.

I would like to thank faculty members at Melbourne Law School for their guidance, in particular Gerry Simpson, Lee Godden, and Sundhya Pahuja. My PhD writing group, Jothie Rajah, Daniel Muriu, and Eve Lester made it possible for me to imagine that I would one day complete this book. Many happy hours have also been passed with fellow researchers Marc Trabsky, Connal Parsley, Cressida Limon, Ed Mussawir, Olivia Barr, Michael Ho Foui Sang, Virginie Tassin, Olivera Simic, Angus Firth, Debbie Whitehall, Takele Bulto, James Parker, Victoria Ridler, and Rose Parfitt. Other friends and colleagues from around the university include Judith Grbich, Ian Duncanson, and Marc Hiatt. Special thanks go to Luis Eslava for his constant care and intellectual companionship. The company of Anthony Nicholas, Katsu Suganuma, Naomi Langdon, Makiko Ryujin, and James Wilkes has seen me through the most difficult occasions. My friend Vanessa Bleyer has been an inspirational figure for many years. I am grateful for her long-standing mentorship and material support. Thanks to Judith Grbich, Stephen Humphreys, Louise Arimatsu, and Matthew Nicholson for their comments on this text in its form as a final draft of a PhD thesis. This book would not be the same without Luce Irigaray, whose work and friendship has opened up new ways of reading and writing for me. Thanks go to my mother, whose copy of Luce Irigaray's *Speculum of the Other Woman* I am yet to return, and to my grandmother.

My patient supervisors have had the most formative influence on this work. Jenny Beard supervised me in my first year of the PhD. Anne Orford taught me in my first year at university and has led me over many intellectual and institutional hurdles since then. Shaun McVeigh is a friend and mentor whose generosity has made an otherwise difficult task a pleasure. To Jenny, Anne, and Shaun I owe deep thanks, as well as to my PhD examiners, Gregor Noll and Maria Drakopoulou. I am grateful to Merel Alstein and Emma Endean at Oxford University Press for their extraordinary efficiency and support, and to my anonymous reviewers for their comments on the original manuscript.

TABLE OF CONTENTS

INTRODUCTION

With nuclear weapons, humanity is living on a kind of suspended sentence. For half a century now these terrifying weapons of mass destruction have formed part of the human condition...life on earth has taken on the aspect of what the Koran calls 'a long nocturnal journey', like a nightmare whose end [we] cannot yet foresee. Although endowed with reason, man has never been so unreasonable; his destiny is uncertain; his conscience is confused; his vision is clouded and his ethical co-ordinates are being shed, like dead leaves from the tree of life.[1]

Bedjaoui J, President of the ICJ for the 1996 Advisory Opinion, *Legality of the Threat or Use of Nuclear Weapons*

What does it mean to be human in today's globalized world, a century after the First World War when we are still living with a 'suspended sentence'? Technology has the power to annihilate human life and yet, it remains central to our conception of ourselves as human. This is because it is technology—taken here to mean the expression of our capacity to invent—that we imagine distinguishes us from other living beings. It is important precisely because it makes us more than animal—it makes us human, and more than human.

We live amidst nuclear weapons and in a world where violent conflict—both legal and illegal—proliferate. This nightmare is compounded by other global catastrophes: climate change, ecosystem collapse, and mass migration. It has been we humans—particularly since the Second World War—who have created technologies that pose 'systemic, unpredictable, uncertain and infinite'[2] risks, unbounded in time and space. These risks pose the threat of spectacular and visceral biological

[1] ICJ Reports, 8 July 1996, p 226, para 2-3.

[2] Bernard Stiegler, *Technics and Time, 1: The Fault of Epimetheus* (George Collins and Richard Beardsworth trans, 1998 ed) [trans of: *La technique et le temps, 1: La faute d'Épiméthée*, 1994] 140. My thanks go to Cressida Limon for drawing attention to this text.

destruction: 'exceptional hazards'[3] that now unleash irreparable damage on a global scale. Since the end of the First World War, we have witnessed the deliberate detonation of nuclear weapons and accidental radiation fallouts; countless global wars and proxy wars; the continued production of small arms and massive weapons; overfishing; overhunting; urbanization, and desertification: these are large-scale problems that are compounded by anthropogenic climate change.

In response to this destruction caused largely by our technological power, we turn to technological invention. Or specifically, we invest in the *idea* of invention, of our capacity to create, as the solution to technological risk—witness the endless technologies proposed for climate change: carbon capture and storage, electric cars, nuclear energy. And this creative capacity relies in turn on a post-war settlement that has harnessed laws of war and trade so as to enable technologies of war and trade to drive the global economy.

Created for the most part in the first half of the twentieth century, such phenomena have emerged as a vision of a domain that is inter-national, held together by the authority of a global law. One of my premises (explained at length later in the book) is that this law, like nuclear power or genetic science, can itself be considered a technology (or *technē,* in the original Greek, meaning art or artifice). If we are to understand the term 'technology' in a broad sense—as the art of animating something material to make it functional—then harnessing nuclear reactions to produce energy, and harnessing human force to produce an international authority, can indeed both be described as technologies.

[3] Barbara Adam and Joost Van Loon, 'Repositioning Risk: The Challenge for Social Theory' in Barbara Adam, Ulrich Beck, and Joost Van Loon (eds), *The Risk Society and Beyond: Critical Issues for Social Theory* (2000) 1, 2. As pointed out by Pat O'Malley (in 'Governmentality and the Risk Society' 28(1) *Economy and Society* 1999, 138–48) and other scholars, Beck's description of risk as epiphenomena can be nuanced with reference to the allocation of risk by government policy, and focused with reference to the development of governmentality through the management of risk (i.e. the use of risk as a structuring framework for governance). The argument in this book does not engage with the extensive literature on Foucaldian governmentality, but certainly resonates with it.

Since technology—both in the rhetorical and representational sense—has been a touchstone of the twentieth century, this book examines how technological invention manifests as a precondition of living as humans in today's globalized world. In doing so I seek to problematize the ways in which international law, as well as two other post-war technologies (GMOs and nuclear weapons), are used to provide evidence of a universal human*ness* (the qualities or attributes of being human), and examine the tensions between them.

When I ask, then, what it means to be human today in a globalized world, it becomes apparent that the question of technology forms part of an answer, as does the role of international law. In investigating the significance of technology for thinking about international law today, the book analyses the ways in which various jurists, philosophers, and heads of state have since the Second World War deployed a public language of the 'international' (sphere, space, domain) in discussions about technological risk. The tensions that emerge in this public language are highlighted in two international law cases dealing with questions of technology and risk from the end of the twentieth century: the *Nuclear Weapons* Advisory Opinion from which the opening quote derives (where the International Court of Justice is called upon to decide on the legality of the 'threat or use' of nuclear weapons), and the *EC–Biotech* dispute (where the World Trade Organization's Dispute Settlement Body is called upon to determine the legality of the European Union's moratorium on genetically modified organisms). These case studies have been chosen because they both grapple head-on with the key themes I am interested in, emerging after the Second World War, and because they also take place at a turning point in global history: the rise of the Internet age, a geopolitical order shifting away from the 'West', and a growing realization of the limits of the earth's carrying capacity. There are of course many other international law cases and moments that could also be fruitfully analysed within this rubric, and I turn to some of these at the end of the book.

Chapter 1, 'Reading International Law' explains how this book sits among a broader set of investigations by international law scholars who draw on critical theory. It does so by giving a succinct account of how international law problems are expressed in terms of three philosophical concerns: (1) international law's crisis of authority as a problem of metaphysics; (2) international law's crisis of judgment as a problem of aesthetics; and (3) international law's end of virtue as a problem of ethics. These three concerns (metaphysics, aesthetics, and ethics) have driven Continental philosophy over the past century, and have functioned as theoretical anchors for critical jurisprudence. Chapter 2, 'Risk, Technology, and the State' opens my investigation proper by discussing the two cases, *Nuclear Weapons* and *EC–Biotech*, which exemplify the jurisprudential concerns outlined in Chapter 1. The chapter gives an account of these cases with a view to opening them up to theoretical analyses, describing for example how they are beset by deliberations continuing for years, opinions running to thousands of pages, emotionally charged dissents, and judges deciding not to decide. I suggest that these phenomena are akin to hysteria. The text of these two cases is 'hysteric' in that it appears in turn as a torrent (in the form of endless deliberations), and as silence (a withholding or deferral of judgment). What becomes evident in Chapter 2 is that this hysteric response (understood in psychoanalytic terms) has something to do with international law's inability to contain the destructive force (and simultaneous 'saving power', a term I will elaborate later) of technology.

Chapter 3, 'Where the Danger Is, Grows the Saving Power Also' then looks at how post-war thinkers have thematized the role of technology in their determinations of what it means to be human in a globalizing world. Looking at Martin Heidegger's discussion of these themes (in his post-war essay 'The Question Concerning Technology') and Bernard Stiegler's 1994 work on technology ('Technics and Time: The Fault of Epimetheus'), I suggest that these thinkers provide an interesting set of stories about technology, human life, and the international domain, resonating closely with the public language of international law jurists and commentators. Moreover, this public language can then be understood in terms of the broader theological concerns that drive the work of the post-war philosophers, in particular the difficulty of creating and maintaining an affective, human, community that will be the subject of a universal authority. The second part of Chapter 3 discusses feminist critiques (by philosophers Luce Irigaray, Julia Kristeva, and Adriana Cavarero) of the Western metaphysical cosmology that shapes the foregoing discussions, looking in particular at how the human body that is taken as the template for the modern body politic is coded as a masculine body. It is this gendered metaphysics of post-war philosophical ideas and political discourse that creates, I argue, a deep structural problem that manifests as crisis in the two international law cases that I introduce in Chapter 2.

Chapter 4, 'Atomic Age' offers a commentary on how this gendered metaphysics is also reflected in post-war discourse. Examples from the wartime speeches and declarations by officials and the heads of state of the United States, Germany, and Japan, as well as from international law documents such as the *United Nations Charter*, give us a sense of the discursive world of international law at the time. Reading across these texts, we can see how they invented a new domain in which (they claim) a universal humanity or humanness will be secured independently of the Church's jurisdiction. This new universal authority is established by means of a masculine global economy made up of a brotherhood of states: to this economy the former imperial powers of Japan and Germany are forced to submit: in the case of Japan, by giving up the authorizing force of its feminine goddess.

At this point let me briefly explain the work that the term 'unconditional' does in this book. I linger on this strange word as it appears in several guises in international law—and a close examination of the word reveals that in each instance it is used to gloss over incommensurability in the stories that international lawyers tell themselves. The demand by the Allied forces to Japan (and Germany) after the war is a demand for unconditional surrender—that is, a total existential, military, and economic surrender to the conditions of the new global society. The future survival of Germany and Japan in this sense is therefore of course *entirely conditional* upon the substitution by those states of their former law for the law of the new brotherhood, and of the acceptance by those states of the international law rules that govern trade and war. I will suggest that this demand is, in fact, impossible. Its impossible demand is foregrounded in the paradoxical logic of 'unconditional sovereignty' that founds international law's authority (as explained in Chapter 3), and illustrated by the performative 'fragmentation' of the Japanese emperor's two bodies in his metamorphosis from a divine authority to a secular one. The unconditionality of 'unconditional sovereignty' and 'unconditional surrender' thus denotes a fantasy: in the first instance, that it is possible for state bodies to be self-authorizing and self-contained; in the second, that it is possible for a state to substitute one cosmology for another without remainder. The 'unconditionality' that appears in these two phrases, is in fact a political claim releasing the state from the jurisdiction of the Church: a secular separation from the authority of the Church and a declaration of self-authorization. In the world imagined by international law, it is the universalization of a particular state-form itself that guarantees the 'protection' of humanity. I therefore take this term, 'unconditional', to describe the more general fantasy at work in the structure and rhetoric of international law: a fantasy that the self-authorizing (but mutually recognizing) brotherhood of states will guarantee the humanness of life lived within that political economy; a fantasy that this life does not need any divine authority or material condition, but exists purely within a symbolic realm.

This analysis and the discussion about the two cases (*Nuclear Weapons* and *EC-Biotech*) at the beginning of the book are brought together in Chapter 5, 'Unconditional Life'. In this chapter, I show how the risks (to humanity) associated with the nuclear and genetic technologies in the cases are counterpoised to the 'unconditional' sovereignty of the states that develop and wield them. Judge Weeramantry in *Nuclear Weapons* states, for example, that '[n]uclear weapons, the ultimate evil, destabilize humanitarian law which is the law of the lesser evil' and that the existence of nuclear weapons is a 'major challenge to the very existence of humanitarian law'. The court's struggle is framed in terms of a contest for existence between nuclear weapons and international law. The decision is riven with a drama that plays out the attempt and the failure by judges to make commensurable what is incommensurable. And what becomes clear at this point is that the court cannot choose between the mutually constitutive bodies of the sovereign state and the biological human, nor between international law and other technologies that have a similarly saving and destroying power vis-à-vis human life. The opposition between risk and unconditionality in these two cases thus exposes a tension inherent in modern, secular, globalized political life. The relation between international law and nuclear/genetic technologies emerges—in a domain without God—as one of *competition between technologies* that seek, in vain, to guarantee the reproduction of humanness. These technologies (international law, sovereign statehood, nuclear weapons, genetic technologies, and so on) assume an unconditional life to which they are beholden, which they claim to protect yet to which they also pose an existential risk.

Chapter 6, 'The Human's Bodies', returns to the framework set out in Chapter 1 to think about the implications of the analysis in the foregoing chapters. Specifically, the first half of the chapter looks at how we can think otherwise about international law in terms of metaphysics, aesthetics, and ethics. If international law indeed manifests crises because it is required to perform an impossible task (to dictate what is right and good and reveal truth) on the basis that it is an expression of transcendent human authority, then it may be time to change our conception of what international law is, and what it should do. The second half of the chapter looks at how reimagining international law will help us to better respond to problems of trade, war, and the environment in the twenty-first century.

To reiterate the opening question of this book: what does it mean to be human in today's globalized world? Twentieth century public discourse on technology, the human, and the international domain imagines technology (including the technology of international law) as being a condition of modern life. It does this insofar as the idea of a secular human world is supported by a capacity to control the existential boundaries of that world with nuclear weapons, genetic technologies, and a political formation called the state. The question of how to *live* with this technological capacity is a far more difficult one. The public language of international law entrenches the idea that securing human life in an international domain is a masculine preserve. It also presents 'humanness' to be a way of transcending the material constraints of becoming and living in a finite world. For those of us invested in thinking about international law, the challenge then may be to think about what a humanness that does not rely on this fantasy of unconditional life would look like.

1

READING INTERNATIONAL LAW

This chapter describes the theoretical frames that I use for reading international law. To recapitulate the focus of this book: there are three themes—technology, human life (or humanness), and the international domain—that I examine in the International Court of Justice's Advisory Opinion *Nuclear Weapons* and the WTO's decision *EC–Biotech* cases; these themes reappear in public discourse throughout the twentieth century. As well as tracing the ways in which the themes are treated in *Nuclear Weapons* and *EC–Biotech*, I look at how the relationship between the themes is conceptualized by European post-war philosophers, and how those themes are in turn reflected in international public discourse (exemplified in the Second World War surrender documents, treaties, and post-Cold War speeches) throughout the second half of the twentieth century. I offer a commentary on the themes as they move across the above texts. Framed in terms of the question, 'Is technological invention a condition of human life in the international domain?', Chapters 2 to 4 of the book show how the idea of 'humanness' has, over the course of the twentieth century, become dependent upon a particular vision of the international domain and upon a certain relation between humanness and technological invention. Chapter 5 brings this analysis back to a reading of the two cases, to examine its significance for understanding international law today.

And so, turning to the question of method: there is sometimes an aversion among lawyers who work as legal researchers or scholars, to stating jurisprudential problems in the lexicons of what have in recent times been designated as 'other' disciplines. This is presumably due to an anxiety over the preservation of disciplinary jurisdiction. Nonetheless, in thinking about international law and its relation to the world, I find it useful to frame the problem in terms of three philosophical concerns: (1) international law's crisis of authority as a problem of metaphysics; (2) international law's crisis of judgment as a problem of aesthetics; and (3) international law's end of virtue as a problem of ethics. These three concerns (metaphysics, aesthetics, and ethics) have driven Continental philosophy over the past century,[1] and have effectively been theoretical anchors for critical jurisprudence. I will explain each of these three frames one by one, in terms of their relevance for thinking about international law and the central question. As will become evident, the three frames loosely track the order of the chapters. Together they are also helpful in thinking more broadly about my commentary on the texts in each chapter.

1.1 INTERNATIONAL LAW'S CRISIS OF AUTHORITY AS A PROBLEM OF METAPHYSICS

In using the phrase 'crisis of authority' I refer to the examples of the ICJ's *Nuclear Weapons* Advisory Opinion and the *EC–Biotech* finding of the World Trade Organization ('WTO') Dispute Settlement Body ('DSB'). In these cases (discussed at some length in the following chapter) the jurists involved are unable to calculate and mitigate the risks posed by the technologies at issue, and appear to become trapped between the emancipatory claims of technologies that promise to save human life (by securing the state) and the destructive power of technological production (i.e. the uncontrolled proliferation of nuclear weapons and genetically modified organisms). This inability to calculate future risk is reflected in the jurists' writings in those cases, which demonstrate what I call a 'hysteric' quality, in their form and style. In the case of *Nuclear Weapons*, this inability is also reflected in their polarized opinions (for and against the legalization of the use of nuclear

[1] 'Continental philosophy' is a relatively recent term used within the English-speaking world to distinguish post-Kantian philosophy that differs from the empiricism of the analytic tradition of philosophy. The 'Continental' tradition includes German idealism, phenomenology, existentialism, hermeneutics, structuralism and post-structuralism, French feminism, and theorists of Marxism and psychoanalysis. For a helpful exposition of these traditions, see Matthew Calarco and Peter Atterton (eds), *The Continental Ethics Reader* (2003). While it is beyond the scope of this book to discuss these traditions on their own terms, it may be helpful here to note that in the past few decades there has been an enthusiastic uptake of these theories within the legal academy: see for example Nick Smith (ed.), 'Introduction to the Special Issue on Continental Philosophy of Law' 42(1) *Continental Philosophy Review* 2009, 1–4.

weapons) and in *EC–Biotech* it is also reflected in the delayed and lengthy findings of the DSB. It can be argued that this hysteric writing constitutes resistance, of a kind, to the clear, unanimous, and authoritative decision-making that a global public would expect of a legal order that presents itself as ubiquitous.

If this resistance is evidence of a 'crisis of authority' for international law, what does it mean to describe it as a 'problem of metaphysics'? I find that it is helpful to think about the idea, institutions, and discursive influence of international law in terms of its material (such as territories, bodies, etc.) and immaterial (such as jurisdictional claims, ideologies, etc.) aspects. Throughout this book I will claim that international law is driven by a desire to produce and guarantee 'unconditional life': what I describe later as human life that is not predicated on the existence of God, that is nonetheless somehow infinite, and immortal. The human body is different to every other body: such is the received wisdom. Moreover, while each individual human body is different from every other human body, they are all nonetheless the same: all share the quality of a human*ness* that is invisible, immanent, and universal. This quality is what ensures the continuation of human life beyond death, in a figure that has two imagined bodies: one that is material, and the other that is part of a social symbolic order that reproduces itself, *in perpetuum*.

Who or what brings this human into the world? Who or what continues to recognize such a being, not only as a differentiated entity but also as something more than the sum of its parts? Who or what guarantees this being into the future, beyond the individual human's end? Within Christian culture these questions have traditionally been referred to the authorizing force of God, the ritual exchange of words (through confession and mass), and the consumption of Christ's body that transubstantiates the divine into the material.[2] In my reading, once this Christian mythology is challenged in the post-Reformation entry into secular (or 'late') modernity, international law plays a crucial role in taking on this

[2] For an excellent account of how early Christian concepts continue to influence Western ontology (and particularly, how the promise of salvation is retained in international law discourse today), see Jennifer Beard, *The Political Economy of Desire* (2006).

authorizing function. It does so by positing the individual human as part of a community across space (evidence of which is an identifiable mass called 'humanity') and time (evidence of which is a certain background quality of 'humanness').

Speaking in terms of historical epochs, we can borrow the term 'late modernity'—defined by the global organization of capitalist economies driven by technological change—to describe the ideological paradigm of international law.[3] Furthermore, as a project of late modernity we can make sense of international law as it has been used (through treaty-making and jurisprudence) to produce competing claims to human life in the international domain, against religious jurisdiction. International law's crisis of authority can therefore be described as a problem of metaphysics if we understand the difficulty that jurists have in guaranteeing humanness to be a difficulty tied up with the theology they are bound to draw upon when dealing with questions concerning technology. In other words, while attempting to produce an immanent human order,[4] international law as a project of late modernity is always already captured by theological frames of reference.[5]

[3] There is much debate among historians as to whether it is helpful or not to think about the past in terms of 'epochs'. It is Heidegger's radical historicization of the theological question, 'What is an entity?' in his later work that departs from the fundamentalist and universalist ontological claim that previous (Kantian) metaphysics had striven towards. If we think of metaphysics as providing 'each historical "epoch" of intelligibility with its ontological bedrock' (or in other words, enabling for the purposes of my analysis an ontological historicization of legal text), then such a categorization becomes necessary: Iain Thomson, *Heidegger on Ontotheology: Technology and the Politics of Education* (2005) 8.

[4] In this book I use the term 'immanent' in the Spinozist sense, which is that the process of life production is self-contained, not requiring any transcendent or external cause. See Antonio Negri, *The Savage Anomaly: The Power of Spinoza's Metaphysics and Politics* (Michael Hardt trans., 1991 edn) [trans. of: *L'Anomalia selvaggia: Saggio su potere e Potenza in Baruch Spinoza*, 1981].

[5] Heidegger argues that any thinking of this modern secularization is always already captured by theological frames of reference. He uses the term 'ontotheology' to describe this: *Identity and Difference* (Joan Stambaugh trans., 2002 edn) [trans. of: *Identitat und Differenz*, 1957]. See also Iain Thomson, above n 3, and the discussion in Jacques Derrida, *Of Spirit: Heidegger and the Question* (Geoffrey Bennington and Rachel Bowlby trans., 1991 edn) [trans. of: *De l'esprit*, 1987].

Jacques Derrida calls these frames of reference 'unavowed theologemes': hidden forms of logic or myths tracked in some way by modern ideas.[6] They become evident when we look—in Chapter 3 in some detail—at how post-war thinkers have responded to questions concerning technology, vis-à-vis human life. The thinkers whose work I look at in the first part of the chapter include Sigmund Freud, Walter Benjamin, Carl Schmitt, Martin Heidegger, and Bernard Stiegler. Let me give two examples of why the ideas of these thinkers are so crucial to making sense of the relation between international law, technological invention, and human life. Heidegger, for example, is concerned with what he calls the problem of 'ontology', as the question of how to conceptualize 'Being'.[7] For Heidegger, time constitutes a transcendental horizon that guarantees human existence, and this horizon is projected by singular beings themselves, and towards themselves, through their power of invention. In his later work he describes this invention as being first and foremost *technological*.[8] He argues that technology should be understood as a process of representing the world through law—which he regards as a kind of master technology—and that such a process of self-invention simultaneously poses the freedom and the destruction of an essential humanness. The human is freed by achieving his inner human potential; however, the human risks destruction through the instrumentalization of himself and the world.

Bernard Stiegler takes up this line of thought to argue that not only is technology a saving or destructive force, but that it is the only way in which we know ourselves to be human—as a form of life that has the capacity to invent itself into material (corporeal) and metaphysical (communal) existence.[9] Human history,

[6] Jacques Derrida, *Voyous* (2003) 155.

[7] Albert Hofstadter, 'Introduction' in Martin Heidegger, *The Basic Problems of Phenomenology* (Albert Hofstadter trans., 1988) xviii; Martin Heidegger, *Being and Time* (John Macquarrie and Edward Robinson trans., 1978 edn) [trans. of: *Sein und Zeit* 1953; originally published 1927].

[8] Martin Heidegger, *The Question Concerning Technology and Other Essays* (William Lovitt trans., 1977 edn) [trans. of: *Die Frage nach der Technik*, 1954].

[9] Bernard Stiegler, *Technics and Time, 1: The Fault of Epimetheus* (George Collins and Richard Beardsworth trans., 1998 edn) [trans. of: *La technique et le temps, 1: La faute d'Épiméthée*, 1994]. While he does not comment on law in particular, he does draw a parallel between technology and law, remarking for example that in

in other words, is only guaranteed by technological prostheses (which allow us to imagine ourselves to be whole, complete), creating a mythic origin and projecting an infinite future towards which we travel. This account is particularly apt for describing international law *as a technology or human invention*, competing against other technologies and religious orders[10] to secure human existence—and, like those other technologies, failing, inevitably, to do so.

These philosophers' accounts of technology are essentially eschatological—by which I mean they share a theologically grounded concern with a (real or posited) trajectory of humankind as such, to the end of time. Their accounts all refer to an intractable bind that we face in our quest to reproduce (invent and guarantee) our own humanness, whereby any attempt to do so will elude control and—on the accounts of these philosophers—lead instead to our dissolution within the instrumental logic of technology. Most interestingly, these eschatological accounts of technology are not confined to the writings of the philosophers I mention here, but also drive much of the public discourse produced in international institutions and by heads of state during and after the Second World War.

In the second half of the chapter, I look at counter-narratives of technology by feminist philosophers writing in the same broad post-war period. Luce Irigaray and Adriana Cavarero (on whose work I focus) argue (in different ways) that our public discourse of humanness relies on a privileged idea of masculinity, and they reassert the creative capacity of the human in terms of a maternal feminine corporeality. They show how gendered public (philosophical) discourse produces a polis and politics that is then (I argue) reflected in international law. While post-war accounts of technology and human life by Heidegger and Stiegler thus give

'modern society' '*legitimation is dominated by technical and scientific rationality, which progressively spreads across all areas of life ...*' at 11.

[10] The 'God of Scripture' has, of course, retained traction with religious communities, but can no longer account for the corporeal–territorial integrity of the human polis. The 'God of Scripture' as a medium for revelation is distinguished by the theologian Jean-Luc Marion from the 'God of Philosophy', which is metaphysical as opposed to scriptural: Jean-Luc Marion, *God without Being* (Thomas Carlson trans., 1995 edn) [trans. of: *Dieu sans l'etre*, 1983].

us a very good idea of the underlying logic of public discourse in this period, the feminist accounts enable us to further the analysis and critique of that very logic, as well as to imagine a different trajectory for our thinking into the future.

The struggle faced by jurists in *Nuclear Weapons* and *EC–Biotech* is thus symptomatic of a broader problem that international law inherits from the Church's prior claim to a universal jurisdiction. Trying to make sense of public discourse in terms of a theological heritage in post-war philosophy is limited in that it does not offer a way of critiquing the given structure. Viewed from the perspective of international law, I propose that it is more useful to think of this problem (the struggle to authorize human existence) in terms of nihilism, rather than in terms of eschatology.

By 'nihilism', I am of course referring to a problem that has a long history of philosophical debate, beginning with Friedrich Jacobi's criticism of the *idealism* proposed by Immanuel Kant.[11] Nietzsche engages extensively with this historico-ontological problem, and Martin Heidegger frames it in terms of a metanarrative of collapse in Western metaphysics. Friedrich Nietzsche provided not the first but certainly the most well-known formulation of nihilism in his classic text *Will to Power*: 'What does nihilism mean? That the highest values devalue themselves. The aim is lacking; the "why" receives no answer.' For Martin Heidegger, Nietzsche's nihilism 'presents a metanarrative of the formation and collapse of Western metaphysics and the opening up or chance of a "new beginning"'.[12] The problem of modern nihilism, whether understood as a historical collapse of the idea of transcendence, or as signifying a sociological crisis of legitimacy, is often dismissed within philosophy as being an intractable and hence rather unpromising one, and in legal theory is rarely addressed. Taking the problem seriously, however, is crucial to

[11] Introduction to: Friedrich Nietzsche, *Will to Power* (Walter Kaufmann and R.J. Hollingdale trans., 1968 edn) [trans. of: *Der Wille zur Macht*] 9. I owe a heavy intellectual debt to Sara Beardsworth for her work, which has clarified for me the relation between psychoanalysis and sociology by couching it in terms of the philosophical problem of nihilism: Sara Beardsworth, *Julia Kristeva: Psychoanalysis and Modernity* (2004) 2–12.

[12] Beardsworth, n 11, 4.

imagining any future work of international law. Whether understood as signifying the historical collapse of the metaphysical notion of transcendence or a sociological crisis of legitimacy and rationality in a 'disenchanted' world,[13] nihilism provides a helpful frame for my problem in this book, because international law is fundamentally concerned with the construction and anchoring of value.[14]

I also undertake a close reading of post-war texts.[15] What we find is that international law's 'crisis of authority' manifested in its inability to account for technological risk is driven by a deeper problem of metaphysics: a valuing of one sex and gender over all others. Following on from the feminist critique in Chapter 3, what becomes apparent is that the humanism grounding the idea of secular jurisdiction is deeply gendered. In short, the sovereign body politic is imagined as 'a *masculine* body that reflects fantasies about the value and capacities of that body'.[16]

The recognition of sameness in international law takes place in the language of recognition and fraternity: a band of brothers without fathers or mothers. International law's purported authority, therefore, comes into crisis because of its reliance on a metaphysics that recognizes one gendered attribute (masculinity) as the defining characteristic of humanness in the international domain, to the detriment of a 'feminine' (or any other kind of) materiality.

[13] See Max Weber, 'Science as a Vocation' in *From Max Weber: Essays in Sociology* (1946) (H.H. Gerth and Wright Mills trans., 2009 edn) [trans. of: *Gesammelte Aufsätze zur Soziologie und Sozialpolitik*, 1924], and Theodor Adorno and Max Horkheimer, *Dialectic of Enlightenment* (Ian Cumming trans., 1998) [trans. of: *Dialektik der Aufklarung*, 1979].

[14] In the late 1980s and early 1990s there was some limited discussion of nihilism within a jurisprudential context: see for example Peter Goodrich, *Reading the Law: A Critical Introduction to Legal Method and Techniques* (1986) 213–14. See also Necati Polat, 'The Same and the Similar: Nihilism and Mimetic Hostility' 5(2) *Law and Critique* 1994.

[15] For this, I rely on techniques from critical discourse analysis: see for example Norman Fairclough, *Critical Discourse Analysis: The Critical Study of Language* (1995), and Michelle Lazar (ed), *Feminist Critical Discourse Analysis: Gender, Power and Ideology in Discourse* (2005).

[16] Moira Gatens, 'Corporeal Representation in/and the Body Politic' in Rosalyn Diprose and Robyn Ferrell (eds), *Cartographies* (1991) 43, 84.

1.2 INTERNATIONAL LAW'S CRISIS OF JUDGMENT AS A PROBLEM OF AESTHETICS

I use the phrase 'crisis of judgment' in reference to the reasoning and writing style demonstrated by jurists in the *EC–Biotech* and *Nuclear Weapons* cases. By describing this as a 'problem of aesthetics' I refer to the implicit idea of law having a power that art has, to reveal truth. This power of revelation attributed to law is placed at risk when the jurists are asked to articulate the right relation between technology and human life, and the material human body and the figurative body of the state.

The implication of thinking about judgment as problem of aesthetics—an act that has the power to reveal a truth—is discussed in Chapter 6. For now, some initial thoughts on the work of judgment: to begin with, the legal decision takes place during a suspension of disbelief. This suspension enables judgment to take place: a falling in love with the fantasy that the law returns life to its origin, and fulfils an originary loss. It is the fantasy that ordering various elements into a perfect form will enact a human transcendence. This is law in its aesthetic emanation. The performativity of law and its ability to transform verbal judgment—its symbolic taste—into a material outcome is an instance of the word made flesh.[17] This procedure of transubstantation is vital to maintaining the ties between a socio-symbolic order and a material one.

The fact that both judges in the *Nuclear Weapons* case and the Panel in *EC–Biotech* determined that they preferred *not to decide* reflects a failure to stage this procedure. It also reflects an acknowledgement that international law's capacity to reveal truth about the world through its technological capacity is undermined by its very existential premise. No artifice, in other words, can produce a human body that preceded the body of the state. As proposed in the Introduction, international law produces a vision of human life that comes into being *ex nihilo*. This vision portrays

[17] Marco Iacoboni, *Mirroring People: The New Science of How We Connect with Others* (2008) 95 describes along these lines how '[o]ur language faculty is intrinsically tied to the flesh …'.

life produced by masculine (incorporeal) technologies, such as law, sovereign states, nuclear weapons, and genetically modified organisms. And yet, this vision, this fantasy of unconditional life, disrupts international law's imagined role.

Supposing—following on from the analysis in this book—that there were indeed still a place for international law in a world of globalized risk, we would need to change the way in which we think about the work of judgment. In particular, we would need to think about *how* the work of revelation is undertaken. In order to do so, I draw on the work of feminist post-structuralist thinkers to make sense of the relationships between language, gender, form, and materiality. The feminist thinkers I canvassed are concerned primarily with human life and representation through language. Their respective works (in the fields of philosophy, political economy, and psychoanalysis) suggest that the form and structure of writing can become disrupted—'hysteric'—when masculinist notions of the body (hermetic, self-reproducing, all-knowing, and the antithesis of feminine) fall apart. This is precisely the kind of writing that we see in the cases of *EC–Biotech* and *Nuclear Weapons*.

One of the ways in which I respond to this work is to take up their call for 'semanalysis', which seeks to 'reconcile what writing is *about* with what writing is *doing*'.[18] The term, coined by Julia Kristeva, is a portmanteau of 'psychoanalysis' and 'semiotics' and describes how bodily drives make their way into language.[19] Also known as '*écriture feminine*' or women's writing,[20] semanalysis includes a multitude of disruptive (poetic) forms that challenge texts, such as the ones examined in Chapters 2 to 5, which

[18] As noted by Jacques Derrida, 'More than One Language' in *A Derrida Reader: Between the Blinds* (Peggy Kamuf trans., 1991 edn) 242, 221.

[19] Kelly Oliver (ed.), *The Portable Kristeva* (2002) xvi. See also Julia Kristeva, 'L'engendrement de la formule' in *Semeiotike: recherches pour une sémanalyse* (1969). Semiotics, the 'science of signs' stems from the structural linguistics of Ferdinand de Saussure, developed in particular by Roland Barthes.

[20] Hélène Cixous coined this term in her essay, 'The Laugh of the Medusa' 1(4) *Signs* 1976, 875 (Keith Cohen and Paula Cohen trans.). Other notable proponents include Clarice Lispector, Luce Irigaray, Monique Wittig, and Julia Kristeva. Écriture feminine focuses on the creation of theoretical fictions that provide a speaking position (not necessarily limited to biology) that disrupts or departs from a dominant symbolic (masculinist) discourse.

reproduce a certain story about what human life is and how it can be secured in an international domain.[21]

Écriture feminine describes a *poiēsis* or way of revealing the world.[22] Throughout this book, but particularly in Chapter 6, I use poetic writing and semanalysis to illustrate the gendered tropes that saturate post-war public discourse. The poem 'Maria' gathers key metaphors of the sun, the voyage, and the body of woman, as they emerge again and again in literary and legal texts that deal with tensions between church and state, to highlight what is at stake in the *Nuclear Weapons* and *EC–Biotech* cases. Poetic writing goes some way towards identifying and disrupting a dominant international narrative about what human life is and how it is reproduced. Writing international law and international law judgments by paying attention to the form and tropes of language is one alternative way, I suggest, of responding to the crisis identified in this book. I should note here that alongside my critique of international law texts in this book, I try to both extend my analysis and also demonstrate the potential of poetic writing by occasionally juxtaposing straight prose with analysis in a more poetic form.

1.3 INTERNATIONAL LAW'S END OF VIRTUE AS A PROBLEM OF ETHICS

Not only does international law imagine itself as dispensing what is 'just' (based on moral authority) and revealing what is true

[21] 'Monophallic' is a term coined by Julia Kristeva, and is described in *The Sense and Non-Sense of Revolt: The Powers and Limits of Psychoanalysis* (Jeanine Herman trans., 2001 edn) [trans. of: *Sens et non-sens de la révolte: Pouvoirs et limites de la psychanalyse*, 1999] 73. Here is her own description of it:

> The theory of phallic monism implies not only that the subject of both sexes is unaware of the existence of a sexual organ other than the penis but also that, correlatively, the absence of the penis ... is considered a sort of ... punishment against the man or the woman: The punishment is inflicted on the man to punish him and on the woman at the outset, because she is not equipped with this 'signifier' at birth ... I will add that it is a fantasy.

[22] For a helpful elaboration of the relation between poetics and ontology, see Jennifer Anna Gosetti-Ferencei, *Heidegger, Hölderlin, and the Subject of Poetic Language: Toward a New Poetics of Dasein* (2004).

(based on its aesthetic powers), it also purports to determine what is good, based on an idea of virtue that is a 'love of Fatherland and its laws'.[23] It is a virtue, in fact, that is measured by our willingness to sacrifice our material bodies for the body of the state, and to submit the contingency and particularity of individual lives to the interests of the state. It is a virtue that is measured in terms of outcomes for a sovereign state or states that are figured as being universal: a super-human form that can travel through time and space. It is a virtue that is expressed in terms of a jurisprudence of necessity, rather than a jurisprudence of care.

If international law is imagined to be a guarantor of what is *good*, how should this be measured, if not in terms of necessity for state security or the survival of humankind? If it is to engender love, but not for a Fatherland, to what or to whom should it turn? When faced with questions concerning the right relation of technology to human life and the international domain, jurists are unable or unwilling to decide. The very acknowledgement of this limitation, however, opens up a possibility for international lawyers to rethink the presumptions and purposes of the discipline. What I propose, in Chapter 6 at the end of my analysis, is that while the collapse of meaning, value, and authority in late modern societies would seem inevitably to lead to suffering, in such suffering it may in fact be possible to find the 'remnants of freedom'.[24] I argue that if we understand the 'end' of virtue to mean the abandonment of the ends/means frame altogether, law's technical production can be imagined as a process of becoming—if not more or less human, then a process of becoming for another kind of life.

[23] Maximillian Robespierre, *Speech at the French National Convention* (1794).

[24] Beardsworth, n 11, 13.

2

RISK, TECHNOLOGY, AND THE STATE

'[T]he nuclear weapon is not so powerful that it can sail above the law.'[1]

Justice Weeramantry

This chapter introduces two well-known international law cases relating to technological risk, which show how jurists struggle with the limits of international law as a technology of knowledge and of reproduction. It discusses the findings in the two cases and argues that the jurists in both cases are haunted by the destructive risks of technological proliferation, which risk subsuming international law altogether, as indicated in the opening quote by Justice Weeramantry. Not only that, but for multilateral decision-making bodies such as the World Trade Organization's (WTO) Dispute Settlement Body (DSB) and the International Court of Justice (ICJ), the incalculability of risk compounds their lack of enforceable and binding authority over time and space. I argue that the text of the ICJ and the WTO's DSB opinions manifest a 'hysteric' voice, in their excessive length, torrential use of (scientific, moral) authority, and in their inability to decide as to the legality of the state's use of these technologies. What is extraordinary about these texts is that in the face of 'failure' to make enforceable pronouncements about the law, the jurists nonetheless hold onto the materiality of life at stake in their decisions. In this light, the opinions can be understood as *resistance* (as opposed to failures) to the existential task with which international law has been burdened—or at the very least, they can be understood as resistance through the act of reading them as such.

[1] Judge Weeramantry, *Legality of the Use by a State of Nuclear Weapons in Armed Conflict*, Advisory Opinion, ICJ Reports, 1996, para. 139. This was Weeramantry J's dissenting opinion in response to the World Health Organization's (WHO) original request for advice.

2.1 THE *NUCLEAR WEAPONS* ADVISORY OPINION

The first case we will discuss took place at the end of the twentieth century and examined the question of whether the use (or threat of use) of nuclear weapons was legal or illegal under international law. In his advisory opinion, the President of the ICJ, Mohammed Bedjaoui made a departure from the technical language of international law—while the following extract is long, it is worth reproducing here in order to give a sense of the extraordinary conclusion to the judgment:

> With nuclear weapons, humanity is living on a kind of suspended sentence. For half a century now these terrifying weapons of mass destruction have formed part of the human condition ... Since Hiroshima, on the morning of 6 August 1945, fear has gradually become man's first nature. His life on earth has taken on the aspect of what the Koran calls 'a long nocturnal journey', like a nightmare whose end he cannot yet foresee.[2]
>
> Much still remains to be done to exorcise this new terror hanging over man, reminiscent of the terror of his ancestors, who feared being struck by a thunderbolt from the leaden, storm-laden skies. But twentieth-century man's situation differs in many ways from that of his ancestors ... Although endowed with reason, man has never been so unreasonable; his destiny is uncertain; his conscience is confused; his vision is clouded and his ethical co-ordinates are being shed, like dead leaves from the tree of life.[3]
>
> [T]he Court does not find the threat or use of nuclear weapons to be either legal or illegal; from the uncertainties surrounding the law and the facts it does not infer any freedom to take a position. Nor does it suggest that such license could in any way whatever be deduced therefrom. The moral dilemma which confronted individual consciences finds many a reflection in this Opinion. But the Court could obviously not go beyond what the law says.[4]
>
> It could not say what the law does not say.[5]

Reason. Law. Speech. Destiny. Conscience. Life. The stakes of the case seemed high indeed: the survival of the state vis-à-vis

[2] Declaration of Judge Bedjaoui, President of the ICJ for the *Legality of the Threat or Use of Nuclear Weapons*, Advisory Opinion, ICJ Reports, 8 July 1996, 226, para. 2.
[3] Ibid., para. 3. [4] Ibid., para. 14. [5] Ibid., para. 9.

that of the species.[6] The text evinces the Court's monumental struggle to figure law's relation to risk. Nuclear technology is 'part of the human condition'; this condition is 'uncertain', and yet the Court, whose role is surely to ensure certainty, is unable 'to say what the law does not say'. The Court cannot invoke international law to protect humanity from the terror of technology, nor can it act as a global conscience, nor will it release humanity from its 'suspended sentence'. The tone of this opinion indicates that the Court found this task more difficult than its usual task of reconciling international law rules with realpolitik; indeed, this was an altogether different task, requiring a mediation of matters far beyond the ordinary purview of law or politics.

The Court's delivery of its opinion was the culmination of a campaign called the 'World Court Project' organized by the International Association of Lawyers Against Nuclear Arms and other groups in order to obtain a proclamation of the illegality of the threat or use of nuclear weapons. The project led to a request made by the WHO to the ICJ, to consider this very question.[7] Specifically, the WHO requested the ICJ to advise whether the use of nuclear weapons in armed conflict would be in breach of the WHO's obligations under international law, in light of the effects on health and the environment in the event of their detonation. The ICJ declined to give an opinion on the basis that it did not have jurisdiction over the matter since the question related to the legality of the use of nuclear weapons generally, as opposed to the WHO's activities (i.e. the effect of the use of nuclear weapons on health). The Court also argued that the question of the legality of the use of nuclear weapons

[6] 'The conclusions are for the members of the international community to draw, not for the Court, which, at present, is competent only to apply a system of international law which still hesitates between the sovereignty of states and the protection of human beings.' Pierre-Marie Dupuy, 'Between the Individual and the State: International Law at a Crossroads?' in Laurence Boisson de Chazournes and Philippe Sands (eds) *International Law, the International Court of Justice and Nuclear Weapons* (1999) 461.

[7] Request for Advisory Opinion made by the World Health Organisation, ICJ, 3 September 1993; *Legality of the Use by a State of Nuclear Weapons in Armed Conflict*, Advisory Opinion, ICJ Reports, 1996.

had to be asked by the UN rather than the WHO, because of the division of functions (the so-called 'speciality principle') within the UN system. One scholar, Michael Bothe, argues that this reasoning is 'formalistic' and 'logically flawed' since the question of whether or not the use of nuclear weapons is legal has ramifications for state responsibility and for the WHO's provision of medical advice.[8] Moreover, he notes that 'the Court was of the view, and this is arguable indeed, that the pith and substance of the question were the laws of war and not health'.[9] Bothe's concern with international law's proper relation to technology and to human life is echoed by all of the judges at the ICJ in their opinions, discussed below.

In any event, the UN General Assembly did formally request the ICJ to examine the legality of the threat or use of nuclear weapons in 1994. The Court responded that (a) under the Charter of the United Nations the General Assembly was indeed entitled to request an opinion, given that nuclear weapons relate to 'the threat or use of force in international relations, the disarmament process, and the progressive development of international law', and that (b) under the Charter and its Statute the question proposed by the General Assembly was indeed a legal (as opposed to political) one. Several of the dissenting opinions lay out the background to the request, and the importance of the question at hand. Judge Weeramantry explains how the case has been 'the subject of a wave of global interest unparalleled in the annals of this Court', with thirty-five states filing statements before the Court, and twenty-four of those making oral submissions. The Court received nearly two million signatures from various organizations and individuals around the world. In addition, there have been other shipments of signatures so voluminous that the Court could not physically receive them, estimated by the Court's archivist to total over three million signatures.[10]

[8] Michael Bothe, 'The WHO Request' in Laurence Boisson de Chazournes and Philippe Sands (eds), above n 6, 104.

[9] Ibid., 108.

[10] Dissenting Opinion of Judge Weeramantry, *Legality of the Threat or Use of Nuclear Weapons*, ICJ Reports, 8 July 1996, 438.

The significance of this case was not lost on the judges. Vice-President Schwebel noted that despite the purported deterrent effect of nuclear weapons, their threatened use has always remained at the foreground: '[n]ot only have the nuclear Powers ... with vast effort and expense, manufactured, maintained and deployed nuclear weapons. They have affirmed that they are legally entitled to use nuclear weapons in certain circumstances and to threaten their use ... by a posture of readiness to launch nuclear weapons 365 days a year, 24 hours of every day ...' Furthermore, 'This nuclear practice is not a practice of a lone and secondary persistent objector ... This is the practice of five of the world's major Powers, of the permanent members of the Security Council, significantly supported for almost 50 years by their allies and other States sheltering under their nuclear umbrellas.'[11] This is the tone of someone noting the Realpolitik of a weaponized world, where nuclear technology is central to maintaining current global power relations.

The Court handed down its Advisory Opinion on 8 July 1996, and stated unanimously that there is neither customary nor conventional international law that specifically authorizes the threat or use of nuclear weapons. They also stated unanimously that a threat or use of force by means of nuclear weapons should be compatible with the international law of armed conflict, and that there exists an obligation to pursue in good faith negotiations leading to nuclear disarmament. By seven votes to seven (by the President's casting vote), however, the Court stated that it could not conclude whether the threat or use of nuclear weapons would be lawful or unlawful in an extreme case of self-defence, where the very survival of a state was at risk. And despite the unanimity of the Court on key aspects of international law, there were nonetheless three judges (Guillaume, Ranjeva, and Fleischhauer) who appended separate opinions to the Court's Advisory Opinion, and six judges (Schwebel, Oda, Shahabuddeen, Weeramantry, Koroma, and Higgins) who appended dissenting opinions. It is the debates between the judges on meta-questions of international law (its relation to politics; the role of the Court; the relation

[11] Dissenting Opinion of Vice-President Schwebel, *Legality of the Threat or Use of Nuclear Weapons*, ICJ Reports, 8 July 1996, 311.

between states and international law; the relation between international law and technology; and responsibilities of international lawyers to human life) that is so illuminating for our analysis, and to which I now turn.

In their dissenting opinions, Judge Koroma outlines the effect of the nuclear weapons detonated in Japan at the end of the Second World War and Judge Weeramantry reminds the Court of the effect of nuclear weapons generally when they are used and of their fundamental ineffectiveness in preventing war. It is worth turning here to look at the language they employ in describing the technology and its use:

> According to the material before the Court, it is estimated that more than 40,000 nuclear warheads exist in the world today with a total destructive capacity around a million times greater than that of the bomb which devastated Hiroshima. A single nuclear bomb detonated over a large city is said to be capable of killing more than 1 million people. These weapons, if used massively, could result in the annihilation of the human race and the extinction of human civilization.[12]
>
> The Mayor of Nagasaki, in his testimony, described effects on his city ... 'The explosion of the atomic bomb generated an enormous fireball, 200 metres in radius, almost as though a small sun had appeared in the sky ... Four months after the atomic bombing, 74,000 people were dead and 75,000 had suffered injuries, that is, two-thirds of the city population had fallen victim to this calamity that came upon Nagasaki like a preview of the Apocalypse.' (CR95127, p. 38).[13] '... the bomb blasts in Hiroshima and Nagasaki produced temperatures of several million degrees centigrade and pressures of several hundred thousand atmospheres. In the bright fireball of the nuclear explosion, the temperature and pressure are said indeed to be the same as those at the centre of the sun'.[14] It ... is incorrect to speak of the nuclear weapon as having saved the world from wars, when well over 100 wars, resulting in 20 million deaths, have occurred since 1945.[15]

[12] Dissenting Opinion of Judge Koroma, *Legality of the Threat or Use of Nuclear Weapons*, ICJ Reports, 8 July 1996, 556.

[13] Ibid., 569. [14] Judge Weeramantry, above n. 10, 461.

[15] Judge Weeramantry, above n. 10, 551–2. Judge Weeramantry goes on to elaborate at 553:

> Some studies have shown that since the termination of World War II, there have been armed conflicts around the globe every year, with the possible exception of 1968, while more detailed estimates show that in the 2,340 weeks

Nuclear weapons:

(1) cause death and destruction;
(2) induce cancers, leukaemia, keloids and related afflictions;
(3) cause gastro-intestinal, cardiovascular and related afflictions;
(4) continue for decades after their use to induce the health-related problems mentioned above;
(5) damage the environmental rights of future generations;
(6) cause congenital deformities, mental retardation and genetic damage;
(7) carry the potential to cause a nuclear winter;
(8) contaminate and destroy the food chain;
(9) imperil the ecosystem;
(10) produce lethal levels of heat and blast;
(11) produce radiation and radioactive fallout;
(12) produce a disruptive electromagnetic pulse;
(13) produce social disintegration;
(14) imperil all civilization;
(15) threaten human survival;
(16) wreak cultural devastation;
(17) span a time range of thousands of years;
(18) threaten all life on the planet;
(19) irreversibly damage the rights of future generations;
(20) exterminate civilian populations;
(21) damage neighbouring States;
(22) produce psychological stress and fear syndromes as no other weapons do.[16]

The potential impact of the detonation of nuclear weapons, in other words, is more than political—it poses the risk of exploding politics altogether. Known to effect destruction that is potentially unlimited in time and space, the description above is one of a world that is teetering on the brink of annihilation. The spectre of the Apocalypse is invoked, with the detonation of a 'fireball' that exerts the same temperature and pressure as that found at the centre of the sun. The visual scope in this description expands outward and upward, from a horizontal plane to a vertical one. At the same time, this shift in visual scope reflects the shift in

between 1945 and 1990, the world enjoyed a grand total of only three that were truly war-free …

[16] Judge Weeramantry, above n. 10, 471.

the Court's jurisdiction, from one that makes decisions on *international* matters of law, to one that is called to make decisions on global, galactic, universal matters.

Indeed, this shift is reflected in Judge Shahabuddeen's description of the General Assembly's demand, of the court being a *world* court, as opposed to an international one: 'The General Assembly's question presents the Court, as a World Court, with a dilemma: to hold that States have a right to ... embark on a course of conduct which could result in ... the dissolution of all forms of life on the planet ... On the other hand, to deny ... that States have a sovereign right to do whatever is not prohibited under international law ...'[17]

I will go through the themes that emerge across the various opinions in a moment, but to highlight first the intractability of this question it is worth repeating that the panel of fourteen judges was split in half, with the President's (Judge Bedjaoui) casting vote concluding that the Court 'has reached a point in its reasoning beyond which it cannot proceed without running the risk of adopting a conclusion which would go beyond what seems to it to be legitimate'.[18] Bedjaoui states that the Court 'cannot lose sight of the fundamental right of every State to survival'[19] and that there is in neither customary nor conventional international law any comprehensive and universal prohibition on recourse to nuclear weapons as such.[20] The Court stated that it 'is led to observe that it *cannot* reach a definitive conclusion as to the legality or illegality of the use of nuclear weapons by a State in an extreme circumstance of self-defence, in which its very survival would be at stake'.[21] They did not make a decision. Or rather, the Court decided that it preferred not to decide.

This position was not without its critics. Judge Koroma said that the refusal to decide was a 'matter of profound regret', arguing that as a 'guarantor of legality' the Court should have declared the threat or use of nuclear weapons illegal.[22] Judge

[17] Dissenting Opinion of Judge Shahabuddeen, *Legality of the Threat or Use of Nuclear Weapons*, ICJ Reports, 8 July 1996, 169.

[18] Judge Bedjaoui, above n. 2, para. 18.

[19] Ibid., para. 96. [20] Ibid., para. 2B.

[21] Ibid., para. 97, 105 E; Declaration of Judge Bedjaoui, above n. 2, para. 6.

[22] Dissenting Opinion of Judge Koroma, above n. 12, 581.

Koroma's insistence that the Court is a 'guarantor of legality' is interesting in the context of the existential tumult with which the Court is faced. As a 'court of law', the ICJ is presented here as a protector of 'human beings'—not only of those living, but also those yet to come: in essence, the Court is a protector of the idea of the human, as well as the idea of 'nature' (which here is described in tautological terms). I will elaborate on this later in the chapter.

Of seven dissenting judges, three (including Justice Koroma) argued that there should be no exception (including the survival of a state) to the general principle that the use of nuclear weapons is illegal.[23] A fourth, Vice President Schwebel, remarks in his dissenting opinion that 'it cannot be accepted that the use of nuclear weapons on a scale which would—or could—result in the deaths of many millions in indiscriminate inferno and ... have pernicious effects in space and time ... could be lawful'.[24] 'This is an astounding conclusion', he says, for the Court to conclude 'on the supreme issue of the threat or use of force of our age that it has no opinion ... [and] have nothing to say.'[25]

After months of agonizing, the Court discovers there is no law. It has nothing to say about the legal relation between technology and human life. This condemnation—indeed the very nature of the split opinions—clearly indicate that this was a contentious question, leaving both the Court and the legal community divided as to the best response. And yet, the Court's 'ambivalence' can hardly be attributed to the Realpolitik of which Judge Schwebel accuses it. Rather, the language and form of the Advisory Opinion points to an existential crisis for the Court, and for international law. I suggest—and my argument is drawn out fully in Chapter 5—that the 'ambivalence' concerning Judge Schwebel is a radical *inability* to decide, manifested by a resistance against deciding.

[23] Namely, Judge Shahabuddeen of Guyana, Judge Weeramantry of Sri Lanka, and Judge Koroma of Sierra Leone.

[24] Dissenting Opinion of Judge Schwebel, above n. 11.

[25] Dissenting Opinion of Vice-President Schwebel, above n. 11, 311.

2.1.1 *The determination of proportionality*

There are several legal issues over which the judges disagreed, including: whether nuclear weapons used in self-defence could be in keeping with the principle of proportionality (2.1.1); if not, whether the use of nuclear weapons and annihilation of states would necessarily entail the collapse of international law, and whether international law owed a greater fidelity to the sovereign state or to humanity at large (2.1.2); and whether it was the task of the court or judges at all to determine this question (2.1.3).

On the first of these issues, the Court declared that the 'destructive power of nuclear weapons cannot be contained in either space or time. They have the potential to destroy all civilization and the entire ecosystem of the planet',[26] and yet—as Judge Bedjaoui notes—rather than quantifying such risks, states simply mark them as 'considerations to be borne in mind' as they believe 'they can exercise a nuclear response in self-defence in accordance with the requirements of proportionality'.[27] And indeed, the Court concurred with this view that it was for the state to decide whether or not the risks are proportionate to any situation calling for a nuclear response.

Asking whether there are any situations in which nuclear weapons might be used legally, Judge Higgins notes that the Court, in stating that the use of nuclear weapons is 'generally' contrary to rules of international law applicable in armed conflict, fails to explain whether this is 'a numerical allusion ... or ... a suggestion that the rules of humanitarian law cannot be met save for exceptions'.[28] Judge Higgins' discomfort with the term 'generally' points to the deliberate fuzziness obscuring the relationship between nuclear technology and international law: deliberate, and necessary, given the potential for one to annihilate the other. Judge Guillaume attempts to define the problem as one of an earthly scale, using the 1907 *Hague Convention* to argue that it is possible for the Court to determine the legality of the use of weapons in armed conflict:

26 Judge Bedjaoui, above n. 2, para. 35.
27 Ibid., para. 43.
28 Dissenting Opinion of Judge Higgins, *Legality of the Threat or Use of Nuclear Weapons*, ICJ Reports, 8 July 1996, 25.

> [C]ustomary law concerning the conduct of military operations derives mainly from the Annex to the Hague Convention IV respecting the Laws and Customs of War on Land of 18 October 1907 … States do not have unlimited freedom of choice in the weapons they use; they must never use weapons which are incapable of distinguishing between civilian and military targets; and they are prohibited to use weapons likely to cause unnecessary suffering to combatants … Article 51 of Additional Protocol I of 1977 to the Geneva Conventions … condemns attacks on military objectives which may be expected to cause 'excessive' incidental damage to the civilian population … in relation to 'the military advantage anticipated' … Hence nuclear weapons could not be regarded as illegal by the sole reason of the suffering which they are likely to cause. Such suffering must still be compared with the 'military advantage anticipated' or with the 'military objectives' pursued …[29]

Implicit in this statement (that collateral damage must not be excessive in relation to military objectives) is the assumption that it is in fact possible to calculate harm, or the risk of harm, at all. This assumption is contested by Judge Weeramantry in his dissenting opinion, where he highlights the totality and finality of destruction that a nuclear war would effect, saying that the 'self-extinction of our species is … an act that, without quite admitting it to ourselves, we plan in certain circumstances to commit'. This, of course, is something that we can do 'only if we don't quite know what we're doing …'.[30]

Although it is an act that states can plan to commit, the detonation of nuclear weapons is figured here as an act that nonetheless can only be carried out by accident, 'a kind of inadvertence', at a point at which we reach the limit of our human capacity to reason. Self-extinction cannot, in other words, ever be proportionate in relation to any kind of military objective. Judge Weeramantry continues: 'With nuclear war, the quality of measurability ceases. Total devastation admits of no scales of measurement.'[31] For Judge Weeramantry, therefore, like most of the other judges, the principle of proportionality was meaningless in the face of a technology as powerful as the nuclear weapon.

[29] Separate opinion of Judge Guillaume, *Legality of the Threat or Use of Nuclear Weapons*, ICJ Reports, 8 July 1996, para. 5.

[30] Dissenting Opinion of Judge Weeramantry, above n. 10, 504.

[31] Ibid., 515.

2.1.2 *Nuclear weapons vs international law*

With 'total devastation', continues Judge Weeramantry, comes the death of law itself, 'collaps[ing] upon its foundations ... with the greater entity of which they are a part':

> [A]ll the postulates of law presuppose that they contribute to and function within the premise of the continued existence of the community served by that law. Without the assumption of that continued existence, no rule of law and no legal system can have any claim to validity ... The legal system, which accommodates that rule, itself collapses upon its foundations, for legal systems are postulated upon the continued existence of society. Being part of society, they must themselves collapse with the greater entity of which they are a part. This assumption, lying at the very heart of the concept of law, often recedes from view in the midst of the nuclear discussion.[32]

Law, in other words, cannot exist without a community or society, and the idea of law is inextricably bound to the idea of humanity. Likewise, Judge Koroma argues that the right to exist is '*within* and not *outside* or *above* the law' (my emphasis): 'To suggest that it exists outside or above the law is to render it probable that force may be used unilaterally by a State when it by itself considers its survival to be at stake.'[33] While the right to self-defence (to exist) is fundamental to all states, argues Judge Koroma, this right is nonetheless subject to international law and cannot be deployed in a manner that threatens the existence of other states. Judge Koroma also argues, contrary to the majority opinion, that there is *opinio juris* on the illegality of the use of nuclear weapons:

> In its Opinion, the Court concludes that the succession of resolutions of the General Assembly on nuclear weapons 'still fall short of establishing the existence of an opinio juris on the illegality of the use of such weapons' (para. 71). In my view, they do not begin to do so. The seminal resolution, resolution 1653 (XVI) of 24 November 1961, declares that the use of nuclear weapons is 'a direct violation of the Charter of the United Nations' and 'is contrary to the rules of international law and to the laws of humanity', and that any State using nuclear weapons is to be considered 'as committing a crime against mankind and civilization'.[34]

[32] Ibid., 520.

[33] Dissenting Opinion of Judge Koroma, above n. 12, 560.

[34] Ibid., 581.

What is interesting about many of the judges' opinions in this case is their struggle with the intractability of the relationship between international law (which is created by states, unable to exist independently of that authorizing structure) and nuclear weapons (which are used by states to preserve their existence, while at the same time threatening the existence of the world). The judge's attempt to break open this bind by introducing a third element to the structure ('the laws of humanity', or 'mankind and civilisation' in Judge Koroma's opinion above) are examples. It is this third element from which international law derives its moral force, they claim, and to which it owes its fidelity. Quoting the 1955 *Russell-Einstein Manifesto*, Judge Shahabuddeen argues that we should 'remember [our] humanity, and forget the rest ... If you can do so, the way lies open to a new Paradise; if you cannot, there lies before you the risk of universal death'.[35]

The human race, human beings, humanity: alongside the material loss of life, it is the metaphysical quality of *humanness* that Judge Shahabuddeen sees at stake. Our humanness may find a 'new Paradise', or it may meet with 'universal death'. And it is the protection of this humanness that is the central responsibility of international law, similarly to Judge Koroma's invocation of 'humanity' as the central concept served by international law. This is mirrored again in Judge Weeramantry's comparison of the United Nations Charter, which 'opened a new vista of hope' to the atomic bomb, which 'opened new vistas of destruction'. The Charter, he argued, countered the latter with a valorization of 'the dignity and worth of the human person ... recognized as the cardinal unit of value in the global society of the future'.[36]

The 'cardinal unit of value', the 'human person', makes our idea of the 'global society of the future'—all of this language is determinedly metaphysical. And because of this language it is impossible, argues Judge Shahabuddeen, to impute a right of states to dismantle the metaphysical framework 'within which sovereignty itself exists': 'It is not that a State is prohibited from exercising a right which, but for the prohibition, it would have; a

[35] Dissenting Opinion of Judge Shahabuddeen, above n. 17, concluding remarks.

[36] Dissenting Opinion of Judge Weeramantry, above n. 10, 441.

State can have no such right to begin with.'[37] Judge Shahabuddeen makes clear that there can be no exception to a general prohibition on the use or threat of use of nuclear weapons, as states have no right to seek an exception to a rule that ensures their own existence (and the existence of the human). Not only would nuclear detonation by a state threaten its own existence, but by 'ending civilization and annihilating mankind' it would also deprive 'the sovereignty of all other States of meaning'.[38]

2.1.3 *The future of the world at the feet of the Court*

Most of the judges were thus in agreement that the use of nuclear weapons was incommensurable with the principle of proportionality. Furthermore, this incommensurability was so great that the possibility of nuclear detonation called into question the existence of international law itself. It was not, concurred most of the judges, sovereign states to which international law owed its ultimate fidelity, but to 'humanity' or the idea of humanness, and that it had to use as its moral compass.

Was it the task of the Court, then, to determine whether nuclear weapons were 'legal' or 'illegal'? It was on this point that opinion really diverged. In the following passage Judge Shahabuddeen places the 'future of the world' at the feet of the Court, which has to reconcile the need for a state to defend itself and the need for international law to ensure the survival of the human species:

> [T]he great unsettled issue on which the future of the world depends is how to reconcile the imperative need of a State to defend itself with the no less imperative need to ensure that, in doing so, it does not imperil the survival of the human species. Humanitarian law, it is said, must be read as being subject to an exception which allows a State to use nuclear weapons in self-defence when its survival is at stake, that is to say, even if such use would otherwise breach that law, and this for the reason that no system of law obliges those subject to it to commit suicide. The implication ... is that ... it is possible that the use of nuclear weapons could be lawful 'in an extreme circumstance of self-defence, in which the very survival of a State would be at stake', and hence even if humanitarian law would otherwise be violated ... The essence of the

[37] Dissenting Opinion of Judge Shahabuddeen, above n. 17, 171.

[38] Ibid., 175.

question is whether the exercise of the right of self-defence can be taken to the point of endangering the survival of mankind.[39]

No system of law, argues Judge Shahabuddeen, would oblige its subjects to commit suicide. The implication here is that there should therefore be a prohibition on any acts that lead to annihilation, and the Court should declare the use of nuclear weapons illegal in any circumstances whatsoever. A law that permitted states to exercise self-defence through detonation 'represents the very negation of the humanitarian concerns which underlie the structure of humanitarian law', states Judge Shahabuddeen, contradicting 'the fundamental principle of the dignity and worth of the human person on which all law depends'.[40]

For Judge Shahabuddeen, it was clearly within the Court's remit to protect the idea of the 'human person' by banishing anything that threatened it. Judge Shahabuddeen's vision of nuclear weapons as a threat to law and its creator (the human) is echoed by Judge Weeramantry, who lays out a conflict between nuclear weapons and international law. Stating that nuclear weapons are among the greatest threats to life and the right to life, Judge Weeramantry notes that this right to life 'is the foundation of the elaborate structure of human rights that has been painstakingly built by the world community in the post-war years'.[41] Judge Shahabuddeen's argument that international law cannot condone the suicide of its subjects is also echoed by Judge Fleischhauer, who in his Separate Opinion also sets international law and nuclear weapons 'in sharp opposition to each other':

The principles and rules of the humanitarian law … and the inherent right of self-defence … which are through the very existence of the nuclear weapon in sharp opposition to each other, are all principles and rules of law. None of these principles and rules is above the law, they are of equal rank in law and they can be altered by law. They are justiciable. Yet international law has so far not developed … a norm on how these principles can be reconciled in the face of the nuclear weapon. [T]here

39 Ibid., 426.

40 Dissenting Opinion of Judge Weeramantry, above n. 10, introductory remarks.

41 Ibid., 515, citing Gen. C 14123, reproduced in M. Nowak, *United Nations Covenant on Civil and Political Rights* (1983) 861.

is no rule giving prevalence of one over the other of these principles and rules ... no legal system is entitled to demand the self-abandonment, the suicide, of one of its subjects.[42]

As I have noted above, all of the opinions take on a religious tone, evoking Judeo–Christian, Islamic, and Hindu traditions that tend to condemn suicide (self-annihilation) on the basis that it is a sin, not because it destroys life per se but because to do so refuses the gift of salvation. The judgments thereby figure the Court as an entity that is in a position to offer salvation to its subjects—sovereign States. The texts also hint at nuclear weapons being (as per Judge Weeramantry) a 'new technics' brought into being by the 'spirit of mankind', which proceed 'irresistibly to destructions without limit ... as the spirit of mankind, which is taking possession of the forces of the universe, seems by its creations to be accelerating that devastating impetus'.[43]

Against this apocalyptic scene of total war, Judge Shahabuddeen reinserts international lawyers into the frame, depicting the judges of the International Court of Justice as a restraining force that shields humankind from death without salvation. And he reframes international law here as a law with 'roots reaching into the past of different civilisations'—a law that has endured 'throughout the ages' (rather than as a law that has been formalized only since the Second World War, if anything out of a legacy of colonialism).[44] Judge Weeramantry echoes this sentiment, describing 'the world system' as something produced by 'the millennia of civilization'.[45] The 'new technics' of nuclear weapons to which Judge Weeramantry refers can only be countered by an equally powerful invention: international law. The extent to which the Court can and should use its powers is contested among the judges, but one thing they are unanimous about is the extraordinary nature of the question with which they are faced. Judge Shahabuddeen, for example, notes that never before have '[c]ourts, whether international or national ... had to deal with the legal implications of actions which could annihilate

[42] Separate Opinion of Judge Fleischhauer, *Legality of the Threat or Use of Nuclear Weapons*, ICJ Reports, 8 July 1996, para. 5.

[43] Dissenting Opinion of Judge Weeramantry, above n. 10, 507.

[44] Ibid., introductory remarks.

[45] Ibid., 451.

mankind',[46] and Judge Schwebel points out that '[m]ore than any case in the history of the Court, this proceeding presents a titanic tension between State practice and legal principle ...'[47] (there is, I have argued above, a greater tension even than this).

The judges and the Court thus see themselves as important actors—as carriers of a trans-historical and cross-geographical law, who are called upon to determine the relation of this law to a new technology. In doing so, Judge Bedjaoui notes that the Court 'has constantly been mindful of its responsibilities as "the principal judicial organ of the United Nations" ',[48] and that its role is limited to stating the existing law, without creating law: 'It is clear that the Court cannot legislate, and in the circumstances of the present case, it is not called upon to do so ... it states the existing law and does not legislate.'[49] A strict prohibition against legal invention is thus foregrounded from the outset. To advise or to judge; to produce or to reproduce the law; the Court's very power to speak is endangered by the annihilating power of nuclear weapons. The question of legal speech is framed by the Court in terms of demand and response; a political demand of a judicial organ that may or may not refuse to speak law: 'An entirely different question is whether the Court' ruminates Judge Bedjaoui, 'will be able to give a complete answer to the question asked of it. However, that is a different matter from a refusal to answer at all'.[50]

The Court finally (and obtusely) declares that its 'real objective is clear: to *determine* the legality or illegality of the threat or use of nuclear weapons'.[51] This, it says, is a 'rescue operation for

[46] Dissenting Opinion of Judge Shahabuddeen, above n. 17, introductory remarks.

[47] Dissenting Opinion of Vice-President Schwebel, above n. 11, introductory remarks.

[48] Judge Bedjaoui, above n. 2, para. 15.

[49] Ibid., para. 18. Judge Guillaume seconds this in his Separate Opinion: 'I should like solemnly to reaffirm in conclusion that it is not the role of the judge to take the place of the legislator ... the Court must limit itself to recording the state of the law without being able to substitute its assessment for the will of sovereign States. It is the mark of the greatness of a judge to remain within his role in all humility, whatever religious, philosophical or moral debates he may conduct with himself' above n. 29, para. 14.

[50] Judge Bedjaoui, above n. 2, para. 19.

[51] Ibid., para. 20 (my emphasis).

humanity'[52] because 'progress in the technological sphere ... now makes possible the total and virtually instantaneous eradication of the human race'.[53] The idea of the Court being an entity conducting a 'rescue operation for humanity' is mirrored in Judge Koroma's dissenting Opinion, where he declares that the Advisory Opinion should have acted 'as a shield of humanity', supporting other international checks on war such as the regulation of arms, the prohibition of the use of force and the obligation to use peaceful means to settle international disputes.[54] This messianistic imagery is rendered complete by Judge Weeramantry's conclusion, which calls for international law to 'roll back the shadow of the mushroom cloud' to bring about the 'sunshine of a nuclear-free age'[55] and by Judge Shahabuddeen's invocation of nuclear detonation as having the 'radiance of a thousand suns':

> The Charter was signed on 26 June 1945. A less troubled world was its promise. But the clash of arms could still be heard. A new weapon was yet to come. It must first be tested. The date was 12 July 1945; the place Alamogordo. The countdown began. The moment came: 'The radiance of a thousand suns.' That was the line which came to the mind of the leader of the scientific team. He remembered also the end of the ancient verse: 'I am become death, The Shatterer of Worlds'.[56]

The judges stand at the threshold of universal death and paradise, a shield of humanity that in the face of an all-powerful technology cannot speak, but that *must* speak in order to bring about a coming community. The Court's refusal to come to a unanimous conclusion as to the legality of the threat or use of nuclear weapons can therefore be understood to be a failure to speak with authority for international law; a failure to guarantee human life. This failure—a productive one, I argue—enables us to identify a critical moment in international law where that monumental edifice falls apart, and where we can begin thinking about the relation between technology, human life, and the international domain.

52 Ibid., para. 6. 53 Ibid., para. 10.

54 Dissenting Opinion of Judge Koroma, above n. 12, 557.

55 Dissenting Opinion of Judge Weeramantry, above n. 10, concluding remarks.

56 Dissenting Opinion of Judge Shahabuddeen, above n. 17, introductory remarks.

2.2 LIBERATOR OILSEED RAPE (FOOD): THE WTO *EC–BIOTECH* CASE[57]

The ICJ's Advisory Opinion was followed ten years later by a similarly extraordinary international law case: this time at the WTO, heard by the DSB. Under enormous public scrutiny, the complaints were brought by the United States, Canada, and Argentina against the European Communities in 2003.[58] Given that the three complaints concerned largely the same issues, the DSB considered them together. An ad hoc panel of three men was established to assess whether the EC had prevented the importation of the United States' genetically modified organisms into Europe, in contravention of the *Sanitary and Phytosanitary Agreement* ('SPS Agreement', 'the Agreement').[59]

The *EC–Biotech* case was the latest in a relatively short string of national and international trade/environment jurisprudence. Like many disputes that involve some kind of 'weighing up' of trade expansion vs. environmental protection, it was the subject of intense public scrutiny and political pressure. What was unusual was the remarkably long time (almost three and a half years) it took to be decided: submissions to the Panel numbered 3,136 documents and the ruling, after being postponed six times,[60]

[57] The actual registered name of one GM product considered in this case was 'Liberator Oilseed Rape (Food)'.

[58] On 4 March 2004 the Director-General composed the Panel for *European Communities–Measures Affecting the Approval and Marketing of Biotech Products* (UN Doc WT/DS/291-3 2004) as follows: the Chairman was Mr Christian Häberli; Members included Mr Mohan Kumar; Mr Akio Shimizu. Argentina (in respect of the United States' and Canada's complaints), Australia, Brazil, Canada (in respect of the United States' and Argentina's complaints), Chile, China, Colombia, El Salvador, Honduras, Mexico, New Zealand, Norway, Paraguay, Peru, Chinese Taipei, Thailand, Uruguay, and the United States (in respect of Canada's and Argentina's complaints) reserved their rights to participate in the Panel proceedings as third parties: UN Doc WT/DS291/24; WT/DS292/18; WT/DS293/18 (2004).

[59] While the Panel's interim report found that the moratoria on biotech products had ended, its final report was changed to request the EC to bring the moratoria in line with the SPS Agreement 'if, and to the extent that those measures had not already ceased to exist'. *Sanitary and Phytosanitary Agreement* 1867 UNTS 493 (entered into force 1 January 1995).

[60] On 12 July 2004 the Chairman of the Panel informed the DSB that it would not be able to complete its work in six months. On 18 August 2004, the Chairman

itself extended to 1,200 pages.[61] As with the *Nuclear Weapons* case, the Panel was forced to encounter and address the proper relation between technology and human life when faced with the inherent unaccountability and unknowability of risk from the release of genetically modified organisms.

The claimants challenged three types of measures taken by the EC and its Member States: (1) an alleged moratorium by the EC on approvals of biotech products; (2) an alleged failure of the EC to consider specific applications for biotech products within a specified time frame; and (3) measures by some of the EC Member States including France, Germany, Italy, and Greece, relating to the import and/or marketing of specific biotech products. The claimants alleged that these latter measures were not based on scientific evidence as required by WTO rules. In 2006, the Panel concluded that a *de facto* moratorium on approvals was in effect in the EC between June 1999 and August 2003. It did not make determinations on the EC approval legislation itself, the EC Member States' right to take safeguard measures, or the safety or otherwise of GMOs.

As in the *Nuclear Weapons* case, the issues that arose in the *EC–Biotech* case involved questions of proportionality (in terms of whether or not the time the approval process took was in line with the time that it should have taken to assess the risks of importation); the role of international law in mediating risky behaviour by states, and whether it was the task of the Panel at all to determine the legality of certain (genetic) technologies and

of the Panel informed the DSB that that the Panel estimated that it would issue its final report to the parties by the end of March 2005. On 2 November 2004, the Chairman of the Panel informed the DSB that the Panel estimated that it would issue its final report to the parties by the end of June 2005. On 13 June 2005, the Panel informed the DSB that the Panel estimated that it would issue its final report to the parties by the end of October 2005. On 11 August 2005, the Panel estimated that it would issue its final report to the parties by the end of December 2005. On 21 December 2005, the Chairman of the Panel informed the DSB that the Panel required additional time to prepare and finalize its report. The Panel estimated that it would issue its final report to the parties by the end of March 2006. On 30 March 2006, the Chairman of the Panel informed the DSB that it would not be possible to issue its final reports to the parties at the end of March 2006.

[61] For a discussion on the unwieldiness of such a lengthy judgment, see Maria Lee, *EU Regulation of GMOs* (2008) 209–10.

certain safeguard measures. Similarly to the *Nuclear Weapons* case, the Panel, at the end of its tortuous deliberations, did not make a decision, insofar as they did not determine whether biotech products are safe or not, whether biotech products in general are 'like' their conventional counterparts, or whether the conclusions of EC scientific committees regarding the safety evaluation of specific biotech products were relevant. Their key recommendation was that the general de facto moratorium put in place by the EC be lifted, after it had in fact ceased to exist.

2.2.1 *To 'accept but not consider'*

In the course of its deliberations the Panel received unsolicited *amicus curiae* briefs from a large number of civil society interest groups, generally outlining the risks of introducing genetically modified organisms into the environment.[62] The United States stated unequivocally that 'the information provided in those briefs is of no assistance to the Panel',[63] and the Panel itself found that it 'has the ... authority either to accept and consider or to reject any information submitted ... In this case, we accepted the information ... However ... we did not find it necessary to take the ... briefs into account'.[64] The *amicus* briefs thus disappeared into a silent void—accepted, but not considered.

[62] By a group of university professors: Lawrence Busch (Michigan State University), Robin Grove-White (Lancaster University), Sheila Jasanoff (Harvard University), David Winickoff (Harvard University), and Brian Wynne (Lancaster University); from a group of non-governmental organizations represented by the Foundation for International Law and Development (FIELD); Gene Watch, Foundation for the International Environmental Law and Development (FIELD), Five Year Freeze, Royal Society for the Protection of Birds (RSPB) (UK), the Center for Food Safety (USA), Council of Canadians, Polaris Institute (Canada), Grupo de Reflexion Rural Argentina, Center for Human Rights and the Environment (CEDHA) (Argentina), Gene Campaign, Forum for Biotechnology and Food Security (India), Fundacion Sociedades Sustentables (Chile), Greenpeace International (The Netherlands), Californians for GE-Free Agriculture, International Forum on Globalisation; and from a group of non-governmental organizations represented by the Centre of International Environmental Law (CIEL); Friends of the Earth–United States (FOE–US), Defenders of Wildlife, the Institute for Agriculture and Trade Policy (IATP), and the Organic Consumers Association (OCA). (251 VII: 7.10).

[63] US second written assessment, 173.

[64] *Request by the European Communities to Seek Scientific or Technical Expert Advice* (251, VII: 7.11).

This swallowing of evidence by the Panel was repeated with respect to scientific evidence, gathered in abundance. The Complaining Parties expressed the view that they did not consider it necessary for the Panel to seek any scientific and technical advice.[65] Despite this objection, on 27 May 2004 the European Communities formally requested that the Panel seek the advice of at least two experts competent in at the least the following fields of expertise:

agrobiodiversity,
agronomy,
allergology,
animal husbandry,
animal pathology,
biochemistry,
biological diversity,
control and inspection methods,
crop husbandry,
DNA amplification,
ecology,
epidemiology,
entomology,
environmental impact monitoring methods,
environmental sciences,
food and feed safety,
gene expression,
gene sequencing,
genetics,
genetic modification detection methods,
genomic stability,
handling transport and packaging methods,
herbicide chemistry,
histopathology,
immunology,
medicine,
medical microbiology and antibiosis,
molecular biology,
nutrition,
ornithology,

[65] Ibid., 252, VII: 7.16.

phytopathology,
plant breeding,
plant development,
plant microbe interactions,
plant protection,
plant reproduction and plant biology,
population genetics,
risk assessment and risk analysis,
sampling methods,
soil chemistry and soil sciences,
soil microbiology therapeutics,
toxicology,
veterinary medicine, and
weed sciences.[66]

Evidence from this extraordinary range of biological sciences (accepted but eventually not considered by the Panel) was initially collected in order to ascertain the risks posed by GMOs, and to examine whether the measures taken by the EC were consistent with the science-related provisions of the SPS Agreement. This proliferation of technologies—a remarkable list of scientific disciplines—belies a sense that GMOs are unaccountable and uncontrollable in their reproductive power.

2.2.2 *Risk assessment and the SPS Agreement*

The SPS Agreement essentially sets down rules that expand on Article XX of the *General Agreement on Tariffs and Trade* (GATT).[67] These rules are mandatory for WTO members to observe, and since coming into force in 1995 the Agreement has been invoked in a series of high-profile disputes involving risk allocations pertaining to environmental and human health. A glance at the WTO's official website reveals that there is a '[p]roblem: "How

[66] Ibid., 253, VII: 7.20.

[67] Article XX lists general exceptions:

> Subject to the requirement that such measures are not applied in a manner which would constitute a means of arbitrary or unjustifiable discrimination between countries where the same conditions prevail, or a disguised restriction on international trade, nothing in this Agreement shall be construed to prevent the adoption or enforcement by any contracting party of measures: … (b) necessary to protect human, animal or plant life or health …

do you ensure that your country's consumers are being supplied with food that is safe to eat—'safe' by the standards you consider appropriate? And at the same time, how can you ensure that strict health and safety regulations are not being used as an excuse for protecting domestic producers?" '[68] The solution is produced in the form of the SPS Agreement, whose rules dictate that any trade-restrictive measures must be: (1) implemented 'only to the extent necessary'; (2) based on science; and (3) supported by adequate risk assessment.[69] The safety of (human, plant, and animal) life is the impetus for international regulation, and science is sacred in its technical capacity to produce evidence of it:

> In the assessment of risks, Members shall take into account available scientific evidence; relevant processes and production methods; relevant inspection, sampling and testing methods; prevalence of specific diseases or pests; existence of pest- or disease-free areas; relevant ecological and environmental conditions, and quarantine or other treatment.[70]

Science, furthermore, is held up as the key criterion for decision-making: 'Members of the WTO are obliged to ensure that any such measure is applied only to the extent necessary to protect human, animal or plant life or health, is based on scientific principles and is not maintained without scientific evidence',[71] and that measures can be applied without scientific evidence only where such evidence is insufficient. In such cases, members can adopt measures provisionally, but must 'seek to obtain additional information necessary' within 'a reasonable period of time'.[72]

Science enables objective risk assessment, ensuring the smooth exchange of goods and the safety of human, animal, and plant life and health. Under the SPS Agreement there is a system that establishes a proper time (measured by 'reason') maintained by

[68] From 'Understanding the WTO: The Agreements—Standards and Safety' http://www.wto.org/english/thewto_e/whatis_e/tif_e/agrm4_e.htm (accessed 10 May 2011).

[69] *Sanitary and Phytosanitary Agreement* 1867 UNTS 493 (entered into force 1 January 1995), article 2(2): 'Members shall ensure that any sanitary or phytosanitary measure is applied only to the extent necessary to protect human, animal or plant life or health, is based on scientific principles and is not maintained without sufficient scientific evidence …'

[70] Ibid., art. 5(2).

[71] Ibid., art. 2.

[72] Ibid., art. 5(7).

scientific evidence that guarantees safe, clean bodies with delineated boundaries. The Agreement relates to measures that need to be taken to protect animal or plant life or health within Member territories, and expounds 'hygienic practice' that prevents the 'entry, establishment or spread of disease within the territory of an importing Member ...'[73] This fear of corporeal transgression runs throughout the Agreement, reminding us of the possibility that the sovereign's territorial body is *not* in fact inviolate. The SPS Agreement's stated anxiety over levels of 'tolerances for contaminants' dictate that exporting Members must prove their own cleanliness, providing the necessary evidence 'in order to objectively demonstrate to the importing Member that such areas are, and are likely to remain, pest-or disease-free areas ...'[74]

Despite being provided with extensive evidence of the unpredictability of genetically modified organisms,[75] the Panel largely declined to examine the scientific submissions that it had itself solicited.[76] Indeed, the Panel did not examine whether biotech products in general are safe or not; whether the biotech products in dispute are 'like' their conventional counterparts; or the conclusions of the relevant EC scientific committees regarding the safety evaluation of specific biotech products.[77] Rather, the Panel frames its own 'important' task as being the arbiter of *reason*:

The Panel has been called upon to decide what the reasonable attitude of a prudent government should be faced with scientific complexity and uncertainty of a kind and on a scale unique and unprecedented in the

[73] Ibid., Annex A. [74] Ibid., art. 6(3).

[75] See the GM Science Review Panel, *First Report* (Executive Summary) (2003), where it was conceded that new consequences of GM plant breeding may be unexpected: 'even planned or anticipated expressions of traits may react unexpectedly in their new environment, potentially disrupting the delicate balance of their local ecosystems. The complex interactions involved in such ecosystems make it impossible to predict all of the possible health or environmental effects that any new gene may pose'. http://www.gmsciencedebate.org.uk (accessed 10 May 2011).

See generally, N. Ellstrand, 'Gene Flow and Introgression from Domesticated Plants into Their Wild Relatives' 30 (1999) *Annual Review of Ecology and Systematics* 539.

[76] *European Communities–Measures Affecting the Approval and Marketing of Biotech Products* WT/DS293/R, 29 September 2006 para. 8.3.

[77] Ibid.

history of trade in agricultural products. It is an important and delicate task and it will have consequences far beyond this case ...[78]

Finding that the general moratorium and the product-specific measures did not fall under the ambit of the SPS Agreement, the Panel rejected arguments about the scientific justification of the moratorium. The Panel held that although some of the Member States provided scientific studies to support the prohibition of the biotech products at issue, none provided an assessment of the risks to human health and/or the environment, thereby failing to meet obligations under the SPS Agreement. The part of the SPS Agreement that *was* considered by the Panel was the procedural obligation of members under Annex C, which requires members to complete their approval procedures 'without undue delay'. Specifically, the complaint referred to the failure of the EC to reconvene the Regulatory Committee for a vote on a draft measure, to the failure of the EC to submit draft measures to the European Council, and to delays by Member States.

2.2.3 Undue delays

In considering the term 'undue delay', *speed* becomes a primary consideration: 'when receiving an application, the competent body *promptly* examines ... the documentation ... with *any delay* being explained.' The visibility of this operation is important, as indicated by one heading, 'Transparency of Sanitary and Phytosanitary Regulations', which declares that 'Members shall ensure that all ... regulations ... are *published promptly*.'[79] Of these regulations, the Agreement states that '[t]he Secretariat shall *promptly circulate* copies of the notification'[80] and that 'procedures are undertaken and completed *without undue delay*'.[81]

In discussing what actually constitutes 'undue delay' the Panel states: 'what matters is whether there is a legitimate reason, or justification, for a given delay, not the length of a delay as such ...'[82] Furthermore, the Panel held, it was impossible to define the reasons which would render a delay undue,[83] and scientific

[78] Ibid., para. 4.525. [79] As above n. 69, Annex B (my emphasis).
[80] Ibid. [81] Ibid.
[82] *European Communities–Measures Affecting the Approval and Marketing of Biotech Products*, as above n. 76, para. 7.1489.
[83] Ibid., para. 7.1490.

uncertainty was not in itself a ground for delaying substantive approval decisions.[84] The Panel concluded that the EU's general and product-specific moratoria had led to 'undue delay' in approval procedures for biotech products because they had not proceeded with 'good faith'.[85] This 'good faith' to which they alluded presumably called for faith, not in science, but in the smooth and timely movement of goods from one Member State to another.

The Panel's obscure reasoning of 'undue delay' and 'good faith' resonates with their own undue delay in producing their findings, and the obscurity of the justification for those delays. Limitations to scientific knowledge are not in themselves a justification, and must be overcome by faith. For the jurists, this seems to entail faith neither in science, nor in the global economy, nor even in international law, but in the inevitability of technological invention itself as a driver of human life. The preoccupation with speed and delay in the *EC–Biotech* dispute mirrors the preoccupation with silence and speech in the *Nuclear Weapons* case. While the significance of this will be discussed later, I note here that their respective struggles with the theorization of time and technology indicate a common anxiety—bordering on the hysteric—about their capacity to guarantee humanness in the international domain.

The *EC–Biotech* case purports to provide a forum in which a discussion about levels of acceptable risk posed by genetically modified organisms to human health can take place. According to the EC and to the *amici curiae*, the dispute is one between producer and consumer countries, whereby producer countries both developed and developing are shifting risk onto consumer country populations for profit. Similarly, the *Nuclear Weapons Advisory Opinion* appears to be a contest between law and realpolitik: on its face, a debate about the allocation of technological risk to human life. What we see in the two cases, however, is that jurists' concerns lie not with specific assessments of risk or with some idea

[84] Ibid., para. 7.1519.

[85] Ibid., para. 7.1491. In terms of the existence of the moratorium, the Panel found that a general *de facto* or informal moratorium on approvals of biotech products was in effect at the time the Panel was established in 2003.

of equitable risk allocation, but rather, with a more fundamental inability to account for the past and for the future.

In trying to make sense of these disputes, therefore, it is more helpful to start by thinking of them not in terms of political power relations (a problem of state power) but in terms of an anxiety that international law has regarding the reproduction of humanness within an international domain (a problem of existence). While this will be discussed extensively in later chapters, it suffices to note here that the anxiety shown by the WTO Panel and by the ICJ's jurists is the result of the fear of a collapse of all values and an absolute loss of existential security in a secular world. While ruminating on the productive power of technology in an accelerating exchange (of risk and of obligations) between sovereign states, the jurists in *Nuclear Weapons* and *EC–Biotech* appear to be haunted by the destructive risks of its proliferation.

To further investigate the question of what relation technology has to human life and the international domain, the following chapter examines some writings of post-war thinkers to track how philosophical accounts of technology changed over the twentieth century, before turning in Chapters 4 and 5 to some formative public texts (political speeches and treaties) from the 1940s through to the 1980s to see whether the philosophers' conceptualizations of technology vis-à-vis human life are reflected in international discourse.

3

WHERE THE DANGER IS, GROWS THE SAVING POWER ALSO

3.1 THE QUESTION CONCERNING TECHNOLOGY

Nuclear power and genetic modification were twentieth-century inventions that held powers of destruction that could only hitherto be imagined. The invention of technologies that posed new risks and challenged existing regulatory regimes was not, however, confined to the twentieth century; indeed, the golden age of invention is often described as taking place through the previous century, ushering in technologies such as the steam engine, improved printing presses, the electric light bulb, the typewriter, the telephone, the sewing machine, the refrigerator, the machine gun, and the camera. These contributed to widespread industrialization in Western Europe, which rendered many forms of human and animal labour superfluous, causing large shifts in social, geographical, economic, and political organization. The adoption of such technologies threw open questions around the relation of the state to the church, of urban space to rural landscape, and of humans to nature, God, and machines.

This was the backdrop to the development of the military technologies (including nuclear power) of the First and Second World Wars in the first part of the twentieth century. It was also the backdrop to engagement by a series of twentieth-century thinkers (such as Sigmund Freud, Walter Benjamin, Carl Schmitt, Martin Heidegger, and Bernard Stiegler) on the relationship between technology and human life.[1] These engagements, I suggest, provide an interesting set of stories about technology, human life, and the international domain, which can be seen inflected in the

[1] In discussing the work of Carl Schmitt and Martin Heidegger I do not intend to endorse their involvement with the Nazi regime, but to read their writing after the Holocaust and the nuclear bombings of Japan as meditations, in part, on a post-apocalyptic world.

public language of international law jurists and commentators.[2] In particular, I argue in this chapter that they shed light on the theological tenor of the writings in *Nuclear Weapons* and *EC–Biotech*, showing how the jurists were bound by particular theologemes (theological forms of logic) in their discussions about human life and technology.

Why Freud, Benjamin, Schmitt, Heidegger, and Stiegler? Why not Marx, or Hegel, or Foucault, Agamben, or any other leading thinker of the twentieth century? And why not those scholars writing within the fields of science and technology studies, or law and technology studies? Certainly, there is much that could be said about the work of all of these thinkers in relation to the themes of this book, and in relation to the two cases discussed above. There is neither the space nor the time to do that here, although I hope that there will be scope for fruitful discussion about such scholars following on from my initial analysis conducted here. For now, I am interested in reflecting on my key themes through the prism of specific aspects of Freud, Benjamin, Schmitt, Heidegger, and Stiegler's work that touch upon (to use Heidegger's phrase) 'the question concerning technology' (see section 3.1).

To give brief examples, the Benjaminian story about technology is that it reduces difference to sameness, producing a uniform commodity that takes away the human capacity to make or experience the uniqueness of something (and hence the possibility of a divine emancipation). This story can be seen quite clearly in the *EC–Biotech* case, where the technology of genetic modification was a technology that commodified life itself, leaving jurists to struggle with a problem for which international law had no tools. The Heideggerian story about technology is one that requires the human to 'master' technology, as it poses both a destructive and emancipatory power. This story is a dominant one in the *Nuclear Weapons* case,

[2] In this, I follow on the work of Shaunnagh Dorsett and Shaun McVeigh:

> [F]ailure to pay attention to the difficulties of escaping from the metaphysics of law ensures only its repetition ... to think that it is possible simply to have done with questions of jurisdiction would be to forgo the possibility of questioning the concepts of limit and structure in law as well as the links between speech and law and voice and authority.

Shaunnagh Dorsett and Shaun McVeigh, 'Questions of Jurisdiction' in Shaun McVeigh (ed.), *Jurisprudence of Jurisdiction* (2007) 4.

with the jurists warning that regardless of states' insistence on the safeguarding power of the threat of nuclear weapons, their actual use would be entirely destructive, and therefore such a technology cannot be mastered. There is another version of this story that appears in *Nuclear Weapons*, too, whereby the actual detonation of nuclear weapons would be both destructive *and* emancipatory—this version attributes an ontological power to nuclear technology that throws the role of international law into turmoil.

In all of these accounts of technology, 'the human' is imagined in the masculine singular, and the production, protection, and realization of human life imagined in terms of earthly and divine existence. These philosophers (want to) forget, in other words, the meatliness of human existence, the violence of erasing the difference between sexes (and the distinctiveness of the feminine), and the possibility of talking about living in a-theological terms. The second part of this chapter (3.2) sets up a counter-narrative about who 'the human' is, and what the securability and reproducibility of human life should look like. I turn to present-day feminist thinkers (Julia Kristeva, Hélène Cixous, Luce Irigaray, Adriana Cavarero, Sara Beardsworth, and Anne Orford) for their critiques of the gendered metaphysics that underscores earlier accounts of what it is to be human and to live in political communities.[3] Here, I am interested in aspects of their work that show how this structural deficit shapes how jurists can understand the relationship between technology, humanness, and international law. I am also interested in how we can use their work to read the jurists' irregular writing and 'failure to decide' in *Nuclear Weapons* and *EC–Biotech* as a symptom and a resistance to international law's gendered metaphysics, and to expand the imaginative possibilities of what international law could become.[4]

[3] Irigaray's work, as Felman puts it, explains how 'women's oppression exists not only in the material, practical organization of economic, social, medical and political structures but ... in the subtle linguistic procedures and in the logical processes through which meaning itself is produced'. Shoshana Felman, *What Does a Woman Want? Reading and Sexual Difference* (1993) 25.

[4] This resistance, of course, could be what Shoshana Felman describes as 'an inadvertent textual transgression of its male assumptions and prescriptions'. See Felman, above n. 3, 6.

All of the thinkers noted above have been important to the development of critical legal theory.[5] Moreover, they are all indebted to the psychoanalytic work of Freud, who created not only what is 'arguably the most sophisticated and convincing account of subjectivity',[6] but also a lexicon that could articulate sociological problems of modernity, and metaphysical problems of ontology, in terms of subjective experiences of death and desire.[7] Accounts of political economy informed by psychoanalytic discourses are attentive to the difficulty of individuation and of representation,[8] and as such, is possibly an adequate means of thinking about the modern global Western politico-legal order—what Sara Beardsworth observes is 'a problem of which it forms a part'.[9] It seems pertinent, then, to

[5] For a helpful description of this trajectory, see Pheng Cheah, David Fraser, and Judith Grbich, 'Introduction: The Body of the Law' in Pheng Cheah, David Fraser, and Judith Grbich (eds), *Thinking Through the Body of the Law* (1996) xi, xii. The most prominent of these was the Critical Legal Studies movement in North America, which complicated the hegemonic ideal of liberal democracy and its discourse of human rights. From the 1980s onwards scholars based mainly in the English-speaking world (the UK, Europe, Canada, Australia, New Zealand, and South Africa) have examined international law using feminist and/or post-colonialist approaches, critiquing the dominance of the idea of white masculinity. These approaches think about law from the perspective of individual subjects who are sexed, gendered, raced, and live in a particular class, time, and place. While there has been this sustained jurisprudential critique of post-war international law structures and institutions, they have neither engaged with the question concerning technology nor with the question of 'the human'. For this reason, this body of work is not a focus of discussion in this book.

[6] Elizabeth Grosz, *Jacques Lacan: A Feminist Introduction* (1990) 3. Jacqueline Rose, in her book *States of Fantasy* (1998), argues for historical events and state relations to be informed by psychoanalysis.

[7] He did so through the interpretation of dreams based on an architectonics of mythic familial structures, the most famous of which is the Oedipal relation. Sigmund Freud, 'The Material and Sources of Dreams' in *The Interpretation of Dreams* (Ritchie Robertson (ed.)) (Joyce Crick trans., 2004 edn) [trans. of: *Die Traumdeutung*, 1900].

[8] See, for example, Gilles Deleuze and Félix Guattari, *Anti-Oedipus* (1977), which resists the myth of Oedipus as a narrative of origins. See also Jennifer Beard and Sundhya Pahuja, 'Divining the Source: Law's Foundation and the Question of Authority' 19 *Australian Feminist Law Journal* 2003, 1.

[9] Sara Beardsworth, *Julia Kristeva: Psychoanalysis and Modernity* (2004), 56.

begin our discussion here with Freud. In the interwar period in the face of military industrialization, he wrote:

> Men have gained control over the forces of nature to such an extent they would have no difficulty in exterminating one another to the last man. They know this, and hence comes a large part of their current unrest, their unhappiness and their mood of anxiety. And now it may be expected that the other of the two heavenly forces, eternal Eros, will put forth his strength so as to maintain himself alongside of his equally immortal adversary [Thanatos].[10]

Freud imagined technological modernity as something that subjects man, not to a dominant class or to the sovereign state as such, but to the two 'heavenly forces' of death and desire. These forces are pitched against one another in an eschatological relation and located in the material body rather than in an abstract institution. His is a psychosocial account of the relation between humans and technology that remains firmly with the individual subject's corporeal desires, even as it extrapolates these desires to a more abstracted or plural form ('men').

By contrast, Walter Benjamin developed an account of technology, not as something that plays out in the material body, but as a vehicle of mechanical reproduction. For him technology is a power that is counter-posed to the power of the human body, and which in some sense usurps that human power. In a world where the encroaching phenomena of mechanical reproduction made explicit the alienation of human labour by capital, Benjamin was concerned for human labour to retain its creative emancipatory power, and for that power not to be used by the state for its cannibalistic ends.[11] The function of technology in Benjamin's thought can be understood in terms of his broader concern, that the human (and humanity) be released from its material conditions by what he calls 'messianic time' (*Jetztzeit*): a divine time that instantly and absolutely shatters politics, destroying the historical horizon of capitalism, which is the time

[10] Sigmund Freud, *Civilisation and its Discontents* (1930) final paragraph [*Das Unbehagen in der Kultur* 1930].

[11] Walter Benjamin, 'The Work of Art in the Age of Mechanical Reproduction' in *Illuminations* (1999) 217. [trans. of: *Das Kunstwerk im Zeitalter seiner technischen Reproduzierbarkeit*, 1936].

of the modern state.[12] Benjamin's technology is thus imagined as a force within a Judaic eschatology, and it promises happiness, as much as it threatens doom.[13] This same tension appears in the *EC–Biotech* story, where genetic modification threatens to commodify the production of life itself, while at the same time promising the emancipation of humans from the vicissitudes of 'natural' reproduction, or promising to give control of the divine power of creation to man himself. The question faced by the jurists as to whether states have the right not to engage with this technology (the moratorium on the GMO approval process) is met with bewilderment.

For Benjamin's contemporary Carl Schmitt,[14] technology is 'rootless', threatening to 'dislocate the modern European state',[15] and together with the 'domination of "capital" ... can undermine ... existing political form and make it an empty façade'.[16] This leaves (he argued) the Roman Catholic Church to be the 'only agency [for] political thinking and political form' capable of representing both material and transcendent being.[17] A critic

[12] See generally, Walter Benjamin, *On the Concept of History/Theses on the Philosophy of History* [trans. of: *Über den Begriff der Geschichte*, 1940] in ibid. As with all of the thinkers canvassed in this chapter, there is a large industry that has grown around him, with extensive debates on the correct textual interpretation or application of each work. While I urge the reader to examine these at leisure, I do not reproduce any of them here, as the purpose of this section is merely to illustrate the general landscape that shapes international discourse on technology in the twentieth century.

[13] Howard Eiland and Michael Jennings (eds), *Walter Benjamin: Selected Writings* (1999) Volume II, 321.

[14] Born in the homeland of one international law myth, the *Treaty of Westphalia*, Schmitt was baptized Catholic by his mother and raised in a Protestant town. David Pan, 'Preface to the English Translation' in *Carl Schmitt's Hamlet or Hecuba: The Intrusion of Time into the Play* (David Pan and Jennifer Rust trans., 2009) [trans. of. *Hamlet oder Hekuba*] xxxviii. In *Hamlet or Hecuba*, Schmitt is preoccupied with the way in which Shakespeare's play represents the crisis of the Reformation.

[15] Carl Schmitt, *The Nomos of the Earth in the International Law of Jus Publicum Europaeum* (G.L. Ulmen trans., 2003 edn) 126–7 [trans. of: *Der Nomos der Erde*, 1950] 178.

[16] Carl Schmitt, *Roman Catholicism and Political Form* (G.L. Ulmen trans., 1996 edn) 25.

[17] Ibid.

of secular, liberal capitalist modernity, Schmitt argued that the modern theory of the state is based on secularized theological concepts, and endorsed politics in the form of an empire that structurally mirrors a Catholic eschatology.[18] Apparently following on from Benjamin's work on political community (although without heeding his warning against the aestheticization of politics),[19] Schmitt identifies the figure of the sovereign as a 'katechon': the one who withholds both the coming of the Antichrist *and* redemption.[20] By this, Schmitt clearly envisions the sovereign as the only (secular) force capable of withstanding the corrupting power of technology, which is identified closely with capitalism itself.

Without endorsing, of course, Schmitt's politics, it is helpful to refer here to his account of political theology as it is clearly replicated in some of the concerns by the jurists in the *Nuclear Weapons* case. Nuclear technology, the state, and the ICJ are variously presented as the katechon: the restraining force on the looming annihilation and redemption of humanity. Combined with Benjamin's insight that *any* force that mediates between humanity and its destiny can be described as a technology, this pushes us to see how nuclear weapons, states, and the ICJ, while radically different in form, can all be understood to be technologies.

3.1.1 *Martin Heidegger's technology: making the human by representing the world*

The work of Martin Heidegger runs parallel to these inquiries: while Schmitt is concerned with the centrality of theology to state and to empire, Heidegger is concerned with the relation of theology to living itself—with the problem he frames in terms

[18] Carl Schmitt, *Political Theology: Four Chapters on the Concept of Sovereignty* (George D. Schwab trans. and Tracy B. Strong contrib., 2006 edn) [trans. of: *Politische Theologie. Vier Kapitel zur Lehre von der Souveränität*, 1922, revised edn, 1934].

[19] Walter Benjamin, *The Origins of German Tragic Drama* (John Osborne trans., 1998 edn) [trans. of: *Ursprung des Deutschen Trauerspiels*, 1964].

[20] By 'katechon' Carl Schmitt refers to the concept from the Greek τὸ κατέχ ον, 'that what withholds', or ὁ κατέχων, 'the one who withholds': a theological concept that is often referred to within political philosophy.

of conceptualizing 'Being'.[21] For him, technology emerges here as a question that enables us to understand what it is to *be*, and to be free. In his essay 'The Question Concerning Technology' he begins:

> We ask the question concerning technology when we ask what it is. Everyone knows the two statements that answer our question. One says: Technology is a means to an end. The other says: Technology is a human activity. The two definitions of technology belong together ... The whole complex of these contrivances is technology. Technology itself is a contrivance, or, in Latin, an instrumentum.[22]

There is no such thing, in other words, as technology that is in itself 'technological',[23] but only a concept that describes human activity as an end in itself. Indeed, Heidegger includes not only machine technology and science in his definition of 'technology', but all human activity, including endeavour in domains such as art and religion. Furthermore, it is activity that takes place in response to a shift from a medieval period where salvation or perpetual security was guaranteed through a good relation with God, to a modern age where this security had to be created by Man himself, through representation:

> In the *ego cogito [ergo] sum* of Descartes, man found his self-certainty *within himself* ... Man could *represent* reality to himself ... as it *appeared* to him, as an *object* of thought. In so doing, he felt assured at once of his own existence and of the existence of the reality thus conceived.[24]

For Heidegger, technology is thus an activity or process whereby Man is able to make himself human, for himself, through representation of his world. This world, a 'dominion of man as self-conscious, representing subject'[25] is referred to by Heidegger as a 'world picture' that is riven by Christian doctrine:

[21] Martin Heidegger, 'Introduction' in *The Basic Problems of Phenomenology* (Albert Hofstadter trans., 1988) xviii.

[22] Martin Heidegger, 'The Question Concerning Technology' in *The Question Concerning Technology and Other Essays* (William Lovitt trans., 1977 edn) [trans. of: *Die Frage nach der Technik* 1954] 4.

[23] Heidegger states: 'The essence of technology is by no means anything technological.' Ibid.

[24] William Lovitt, 'Introduction' in above n. 22, xxv.

[25] Ibid., xxxii.

A … phenomenon of the modern age is the loss of the gods … On the one hand, the world picture is Christianized inasmuch as the cause of the world is posited as infinite, unconditional, absolute. On the other hand, Christendom transforms Christian doctrine into a world view (the Christian world view).[26]

It is when this world comes into being as a picture represented by man that 'humanism first arises'.[27] By this, Heidegger means an ontology whereby what we call 'human' becomes the condition of its own world; effectively, becoming a modern subject: 'Man becomes that being upon which all that is, is grounded as regards the manner of its Being and its truth. Man becomes the relational center of that which is as such.'[28] This belief 'arises out of the claim of man to a … self-supported, unshakable foundation of truth'[29] whereby man 'frees himself from obligation to Christian revelational truth and Church doctrine',[30] becoming bound instead by 'human reason and its law'.[31] To return to Heidegger's conceptualization of technology, it is through technology—a process of representing the world—that the modern human is created.

Like Schmitt, Heidegger thus proposes that thinking about living in secular modernity is always already captured by theological frames of reference. However, rather than describing technology as something that threatens human life, Heidegger argues that the truth or essence of such life (life without God) is revealed by technology.[32] By this, he means that technology has the power to reconstitute the human relation to the world *tout court*. This process of revelation, Heidegger proposes, constitutes a transcendental horizon that guarantees human existence; a temporal horizon projected by singular beings themselves, towards themselves.[33] Echoing Schmitt and Benjamin and referring to Friedrich Hölderlin's poetic phrase, 'but where the danger is,

[26] Martin Heidegger, 'The Age of the World Picture' in ibid. 28.

[27] Martin Heidegger, 'The Question Concerning Technology', above n. 22, 133.

[28] Ibid., 128. [29] Ibid., 148. [30] Ibid. [31] Ibid.

[32] He uses the term 'ontotheology' to describe this: *Identity and Difference* (Joan Stambaugh 2002 edn) [trans. of: *Identitat und Differenz* 1957]. See also Iain Thomson, *Heidegger on Ontotheology: Technology and the Politics of Education* (2005).

[33] Martin Heidegger, *Being and Time* (John Macquarie and Edward Robinson trans., 1978 edn) [trans. of: *Sein und Zeit* 1953; originally published 1927].

grows the saving power also', Heidegger argues that this projection has a katechonic relation to the human—in other words, as the essence of becoming human is revealed through this projection, the human faces the concomitant 'danger' and 'saving' (or freeing) power of technology.[34]

It appears that for Heidegger it is possible to strive for a 'free' relationship to technology, which is engendered through 'openness' of 'human existence to the essence of technology'.[35] While Heidegger's articulation of the potential destructive and saving power of technology echoes that of Benjamin, his understanding of technology is more clearly transhistorical, presenting it as a description of a necessary process of subjectivization (becoming human) through representation. Heidegger warns that if technology is merely seen in instrumental terms as something to be 'mastered', that technology will inevitably 'slip from human control'.[36] As with the work of Carl Schmitt, Heidegger's later work is haunted by its association with fascist politics. Without apologizing for that association I suggest that his post-war writing nonetheless opens up the possibility of thinking about technology, or 'technics', as Judge Weeramantry put it, as a leitmotif through which the very history of metaphysics can be understood.[37] His post-war work on technology does so by contesting the Aristotelian view that technics should be thought in terms of 'ends' and 'means', proposing that technical production is itself a *revelation* of human existence, or in other words, that it determines how we experience our existence in a world without God. This crucial shift in thinking about technology and about invention (vis-à-vis human life) clarifies both the

[34] Heidegger stresses that '[w]hat is dangerous is not technology ... The essence of technology, as a destining of revealing, is the danger', and juxtaposes this danger with the human who encounters technology 'in a state of "sober readiness" to be astounded before the coming of the dawn': Martin Heidegger, above n. 22, 28.

[35] Ibid., 3. [36] Ibid., 5.

[37] 'In texts ... after the "turning," the question [of technics] is articulated no longer in terms of the existential dimension of the analytic of Dasein but as the motif constitutive of the very possibility of the deconstruction of the history of metaphysics.' Bernard Stiegler, *Technics and Time, 1: The Fault of Epimetheus* (George Collins and Richard Beardsworth trans., 1998 edn) [trans of: *La technique et le temps, 1: La faute d'Épiméthée*, 1994] 6.

ideology behind the rhetoric of post-war technological production *and* the response of international lawyers to it, half a century later.

3.1.2 Bernard Stiegler's technology: the invention of humanness

The leitmotif of technological production is taken up some decades later by the French philosopher Bernard Stiegler.[38] Stiegler draws on Heidegger's account of time and technology to argue that we are only human insofar as we invent things that enable us to transcend our material existence. It is technology (he says) that undertakes the process of making the human, rather than the other way around. In describing what he means by 'technology', Stiegler explains that while the human as a 'bearer of tools' could be described as an individual who makes technical objects, the advent of 'modern technics' (a term he borrows from Heidegger to describe the epistemological capture of human life through invention) has unsettled that unilateral relation.[39] The human, argues Stiegler, 'is no longer a technical individual; the human becomes either the machine's servant or its assembler: the human's relation to the technical object proves to have profoundly changed'.[40]

[38] Stiegler's work is indebted to Jacques Derrida, who himself commented on questions of technology, human life, and the international domain: see for example Jacques Derrida, *Of Spirit: Heidegger and the Question* (Geoffrey Bennington and Rachel Bowlby trans., 1991 edn) [trans. of: *De l'esprit*, 1987]. For an analysis of Derrida's engagement with Martin Heidegger's question of technology, see Tom Paul Barker, *Disclosure and Inscription: Heidegger, Derrida and Technological Difference* (2003) (unpublished doctoral degree, University of Warwick, Department of Philosophy). Available at: http://wrap.warwick.ac.uk/2326/, and Arthur Bradley, *Originary Technicity: The Theory of Technology from Marx to Derrida* (2011). The discussions invoked in these works are outside the scope of this book, but nevertheless provide interesting perspectives on the theme of technology.

[39] Technics, he explains, 'becomes modern when metaphysics expresses and completes itself as the project of calculative reason with a view to the mastery and possession of nature, itself no longer understood as phusis'. Bernard Stiegler, above n. 37, 10. Stiegler's project is outlined in three books that comprise the series, including above n. 37; *Technics and Time, 2: Disorientation* (Stephen Barker trans., 2008 edn) [trans. of: *La Désorientation*, 1996], and *Technics and Time, 3: Cinematic Time and the Question of Malaise* (Stephen Barker trans., 2010 edn) [trans of: *Le Temps du Cinéma et la Question du mal-être*, 2001].

[40] Bernard Stiegler, above n. 37, 23.

While Heidegger tentatively retains the idea that there is some original humanness that can be revealed (as well as destroyed) by technology, Stiegler proposes that the idea of the human is itself entirely constitutive. The modern human, in other words, can no longer be assumed to be a rational body that bears some kind of originary power or knowledge, but rather, becomes a concept that exists only insofar as it is perpetuated by objects with which it has a relation. Stiegler goes on to describe how we might think about 'inorganic organized beings' as 'technical' objects that evoke a certain experience of time:

> [B]etween the inorganic beings of the physical sciences and the organised beings of biology, there does indeed exist a third genre of 'being' 'inorganic organized beings', or technical objects ... There is today a conjunction between the question of technics and the question of time, one made evident by the speed of technical evolution, by the ruptures in temporalization (eventization) that this evolution provokes, and by the processes of deterritorialization accompanying it ... organized inorganic beings are originarily ... constitutive (in the strict phenomenological sense) of temporality ...[41]

In short, the experience of becoming human is created through relations to external technological artefacts.[42] Stiegler understands the relation between time and human life to therefore be a *technical* one, whereby human temporality is distinguished from divine temporality by means of inventions that make knowable a universal human history and future.[43] Stiegler proposes that this process can be observed in writing describing it as 'a kind of clockwork, of objective memory ... [forming the] dehiscence of difference in its historical "as such" '.[44] It is interesting that Stiegler focuses on writing as a privileged form of human invention, in which we can see the very process of becoming human. Later, in Chapters 5 and 6 I will look at the forms that writing takes to make sense of *Nuclear Weapons* and *EC–Biotech*, and discuss whether there might be ways of writing using a poetic method or *poiēsis* to approach the question

[41] Ibid., 17. 'To think time in terms of time is to think it first in terms of the clock', ibid., 212.

[42] Ibid., 234. [43] Ibid., 27. [44] Ibid., 223.

concerning technology and human life in the international domain, differently.

Before some remarks on the implications of Stiegler's work for how we can think about international law, let me summarize our discussion to this point. The fifty years following the Second World War witnessed a focused philosophical inquiry by German (and French) philosophers on the relation between technology and human life. Writing after the age of invention that dominated the late nineteenth century and the gradual militarization of Germany, Freud, Benjamin, Schmitt, and Heidegger draw on Christian and Judaic theology to argue (variously) that technology is a saving or a destroying force. Freud treats technology as a threatening entity that subjects humans to the universal forces of death and desire. Benjamin draws this eschatological formulation in relation to the state, arguing that technology intervenes to 'shatter' the structures wrought by capitalist and fascist politics, thus threatening humanity but at the same time promising a divine redemption. Schmitt draws a similarly apocalyptic vision of the technological threat, proposing, however, that this threat is an expression of a corrupting capitalism, and should be held in check by a strong sovereign. Heidegger arguably remains with a more critical position, concluding that technology should be understood as a process of representing the world through human reason and law, and that this process of self-invention simultaneously poses the freedom and the destruction of an essential human*ness*.

Reading the work of these thinkers grappling with the relation between technology and human life in the face of unprecedented industrial and military production offers insight into their ideas as we see them expressed in public discourse. In particular, the eschatological formula that their set of stories invokes (humans as being made/revealed/saved by technology while also being inexorably annihilated by it) can be seen time and time again in public texts, from the Second World War to the present day. Before moving on to look at feminist counter-narratives to the stories above, I will briefly address the implication of Stiegler's argument about the relationship between technology and humanness, for international law.

3.1.3 International law as technology

Drawing on the work of philosophers through the twentieth century, Bernard Stiegler proposes that technology is the only way in which we can know ourselves to be human, inventing ourselves to be something more than mere corporeal beings. It is through this process of invention (argues Stiegler) that we create a human time or history that extends into the past and into the future, that is similar to, but distinct from, divine time.[45] His argument goes further than those of the other thinkers discussed, as it presumes that technological invention is a *condition* of becoming human and entering a human society, rather than simply something that has to be mastered. Moreover, technological invention in a modern world takes on a particular significance, as this form of knowing can stand in for the knowing of a God.

In these terms, then, we can think about international law as a specific kind of technological invention that is able to provide a measure of existential security, by performing and archiving a secular process of knowing (principles, codes, and forms). Legal decision-making and its orthography in the international domain thus becomes what Stiegler refers to as 'clockwork', that operates both as a clock (marking human time) and as time itself (a key referent for the experience of modern human*ness*).[46] It constitutes a time in a world where human*ness* is no longer determined solely by a divine authority. In this sense, international law is an ontological and epistemological invention par excellence, as it enables what Stiegler describes the 'pursuit of life by means other than life'.[47]

The jurists in *Nuclear Weapons* and *EC–Biotech* present international law as a special kind of technology: a katechonical one that promises humankind security, civility, and immunity from

[45] Ibid., 27.

[46] 'Ortho-' derives from the Greek 'orthos', which means 'correct', and 'orthographic' usually denotes the proper way of using a writing system. I use 'orthographic' to mean a culturally constructed frame based on written language, and that those saved items—incorruptible, perfectly transformed each time from information into rational language—stipulate what is correct for, and proper to, law.

[47] This is taken from Bernard Stiegler, who describes technology as 'the pursuit of life by means other than life ...' above n. 37, 17.

harm.[48] It is a technology, however, that begins to fall apart in the face of the radical unknowability and potentially annihilating risk of nuclear genetic technologies. I propose that this falling apart may be due precisely to the stories upon which it relies: stories about a humanness that only exists in a symbolic sense, on a metaphysical plane. They are stories and eschatologies that can only imagine destruction and salvation in terms of corporeal annihilation: of *escaping* the body. The following section offers a different set of stories about the human, which provide a critical counterpoint to the first.

3.2 THE QUESTION CONCERNING THE HUMAN

Feminist theories indicate, in other words, that the existential crisis symptomatic of international law cases dealing with questions of technology and risk has its basis not only in religious eschatology but also in the privileging of a masculine sex over others. Various lines of feminist critique suggest that the attempt to enact a human transcendence (religious or secular), premised on the idea of a single sex, erases the material conditions of reproduction. It sustains the delusion that it is possible to produce life *ex nihilo*: a life that is unconditional, virtuous, and immortal. In section 3.2.1 I elaborate the idea of unconditional life to reveal—through a reading of post-war feminist theory—how it is premised on familiar gendered tropes of reproduction. Central to this critique is the work of the French philosopher Luce Irigaray. Section 3.2.2 turns to the work of Adriana Cavarero, an Italian philosopher who extends the work of Irigaray to give a psychosocial account of the state. Her work describes how gendered tropes have long sustained theological and (in a parallel tradition) philosophical visions of a human life produced *ex nihilo* in, for example, the abstraction of a life-sustaining state. In each case,

[48] This particular set of promises framed the questions around which the *Melbourne Legal Theory Workshop* was organized: 'Reasons of State: Civility, Security, Immunity Life', convened by Anne Orford in 2009. Thanks go to my discussants at that workshop for their helpful comments. There is also some very interesting work that focuses on technology as a structuring framework for legal decision-making: see in particular Fleur Johns, *Non-Legality in International Law: Unruly Law* (2015).

she argues, this immaterial humanness permits the assumption of a solely masculine reproductive order. As Cavarero's work pertains mainly to the political economies of city-states, I draw out her and Irigaray's accounts of human life to see how they relate to the post-war international domain. Section 3.2.3 shows how the 'hysteric' register and form of writing in *Nuclear Weapons* and *EC–Biotech* can be reread through Hélène Cixous' work, which appropriates the term 'hysteria' from Freudian psychoanalysis. The chapter ends with a reflection on how hysterical writing—or more specifically, what Cixous calls '*écriture feminine*'—is a form of technology that can be used by international lawyers to attend to the material conditions of human life.

3.2.1 Luce Irigaray's human: the indivisible man

The substitution of a masculine divine authority for any kind of feminine subjectivity is the focus of Luce Irigaray's oeuvre.[49] Responding to canonical philosophers' stories of subjectivity, Irigaray (in her work *Speculum of the Other Woman*) deconstructs key concepts used to privilege the idea of 'masculine' over 'feminine', including mirrors; the cave; the sun; vision; light; and speech. Irigaray begins one of her analyses with Plato's cave allegory,[50] which is a story of men, prisoners who from childhood have been chained within a dark cave; their gaze fixed to a wall against which shadows of statues paraded by people behind them are cast by a fire. The prisoners play at naming the shadows, and believe that the echo of the statue-carrying people's speech is the voice of the shadows they see. The allegory proposes that if one prisoner is released and made to turn around, he would be momentarily blinded by the sun (and think the shadows real, the statues fake) until, after a gradual ascent through the passage from the cave to the ground above, he would see the sun and the world for what it

[49] Luce Irigaray's work as a whole, Felman notes, reminds us 'that women's oppression exists not only in the material, practical organization of economic, social, medical and political structures but also in the very foundations of logos reasoning, and articulation—in the subtle linguistic procedures and in the logical processes through which meaning itself is produced.' Shoshana Felman, *What Does a Woman Want? Reading and Sexual Difference* (1993) 25.

[50] Recounted by Socrates at the beginning of Book 7 (514a–520a) in Plato, *The Republic* (C.D.C. Reeve trans., 2004 edn).

is. Compelled to return and free his companions, he would find that back in the dark his unadjusted eyesight makes him appear temporarily blinded to his fellow prisoners, who will be difficult to convince to undertake the ascent. Plato's allegory, as recounted by Irigaray, describes 'the philosopher's progression from the material shadows of the cave to the bright world of ideas':[51]

> [T]he prison-house is the world of sight, the light of the fire is the sun, and you will not misapprehend me if you interpret the journey upwards to be the ascent of the soul into the intellectual world ... in the world of knowledge, the idea of good appears last of all, and is seen only with an effort; and, when seen, is also inferred to be the universal author of all things beautiful and right, parent of light and of the lord of light in this visible world, and the immediate source of reason and truth in the intellectual; and that this is the power upon which he who would act rationally, either in public or private life, must have his eye fixed.[52]

In this reading, the sun is 'the author of all things', 'parent of light', and the 'source of reason and truth'. The rational actor must 'have his eye fixed' to this heliotrope which, in a deft sleight of hand, is substituted for the origin and source of all things. Luce Irigaray excavates these strategies of substitution by retelling this story as Plato's *hystera* (womb), where men leave the body of the mother to 'identify with the law-giving father, with his proper names, his desires for making capital, in every sense of the word, desires that prefer the possession of territory [extending even to] language'.[53] The fantasy of the state (constructed by the bodies of men) is predicated upon possession through occupation of every space; a possession recognized and ratified by not-quite same mirror images of themselves. Irigaray describes this process thus:

> The place the man had once inhabited must be mimicked by turning it inside out and back to front and by gradually raising it up. By gradually verticalising and erecting it ... This is an effective way to prevent anything from remaining concealed, buried, shrouded, to stop it hiding, lurking ...[54] For Being's domination requires that whatever has been

[51] Anne Caldwell, 'Transforming Sacrifice: Irigaray and the Politics of Sexual Difference' 17(4) *Hypatia* 2002, 24.

[52] Luce Irigaray, 'Any Theory of the Subject' in *Speculum of the Other Woman* (Gillian G. Gill trans., 1985 edn) [trans. of: *Speculum de l'autre femme*, 1984] 140.

[53] Ibid., 36. [54] Luce Irigaray, 'Plato's Hystera' in ibid., 285.

defined … as 'more' (true, right, clear, reasonable, intelligible, paternal, masculine …) should progressively win out over its 'other' …its negative, its 'less' (fantastic, harmful, obscure, 'mad', sensible, maternal, feminine …). Finally the fiction reigns of a simple, indivisible, ideal origin.[55]

This fiction, says Irigaray, must never be recognized as such by men in the world of light. The passage to the place from which man has always already been expelled[56] must be forgotten[57] and the Father/Sun must remain at once an origin without beginning[58] and an infinitely expanding yet infinitely receding destination. The Father/Sun, moreover, 'holds nothing outside of itself … [it] conserves its own indefinitely identical identity',[59] 'immortalised in deathly copies'.[60] Irigaray puts it thus: 'man will be taken out of the cave and referred to an other origin—the origin of sameness—an other life, which both predate everything and are still to come …'[61] Irigaray's contemporary, psychoanalyst Julia Kristeva also describes the creation of symbolic masculinity as being predicated upon a rejection of corporeal origin, which she puts thus:

[W]e see that the social and symbolic pact … brothers rebelling against the father's authority in order to establish a socius—is a transversal link

[55] Ibid. Irigaray's work has previously been criticised as being essentialist (Judith Butler, for example, insists that the idea of a 'maternal feminine' presumes a 'female' subject when in fact all gender subjectivities are constructed): Judith Butler, *Gender Trouble* (1990). I argue that the so-called essentialism deployed by Irigaray in work such as *Speculum* can be read as a strategic disruption of the heteronormative subject. Irigaray, in her reading of Plato's cave, substitutes cave for womb in order to disclose the tropisms of both metaphorical devices.

[56] Luce Irigaray, above n. 52, 292: 'man will have to be expelled from this speculum, from this still specular cave, so that no possibility of a self-portrait may remain.'

[57] Ibid 310: 'It must, absolutely must, not be known how much the procreation of the 'son', of the logos, by the father, owes to inversion.' See also Anne Caldwell, above n. 51, 24. Caldwell describes Irigaray's work here thus:

> The forgetting of passage thus shapes the understanding of the conditions for symbolic mediation that have remained in effect since Plato and reappear in liberalism, deconstruction and psychoanalysis … By recovering the forgotten passage connecting the material and the intelligible, Irigaray shows that concepts and subjectivity emerge within a dynamic interaction between the material and the intelligible, neither of which can be reduced to the other.

[58] Luce Irigaray, above n. 52, 295. [59] Ibid., 298.

[60] Ibid., 355. [61] Ibid., 293.

that is constituted by the evacuation of the maternal: in order to establish the symbolic pact, one has to get rid of the domestic, corporal, maternal container.[62]

Kristeva thus proposes that the triadic relation offered by both (Judeo-Christian) theological and (Lacanian) psychoanalytic thought offers the possibility of becoming subjects only through a God/symbolic Father, which 'forgets its rootedness in affective [material] relations'.[63] Beginning with the question, 'Does the "mirror stage" emerge out of nowhere?'[64] Kristeva reformulates the Lacanian imaginary to identify the subject as being constituted, not by the optic illusion of recognition but by its separation from the maternal body. In other words, where Freud and Lacan designated the subject as recognizing itself at the appearance of a prohibiting Father, Kristeva proposes a 'ternary conception of primary narcissism, arguing that the dyadic relationship is modified not from without (the externality of the symbolic function or the appearance of the Father), but from within (the relation to the early mother)'.[65]

Sara Beardsworth identifies Kristeva's retrieval of transcendence as a radical response to the problem of secular modernity, calling it the discovery of the 'loss of loss'. She describes it thus: 'the struggle with the impact of the symbolic on the preverbal child turns around loss/emptiness. Kristeva's account ... presents foundations of the imaginary that precede the imaginary and its relation to the symbolic.'[66] In other words, Kristeva contests what she calls the 'monophallic'[67] framing of the nihilism problematic, and unfolds instead a corporeal event of archaic separation:

[T]he death drive restores to the subject the destabilizing materiality that is prior to the assumption of 'a total body form' (mirror imago), and

[62] Julia Kristeva, *The Sense and Non-Sense of Revolt: The Powers and Limits of Psychoanalysis* (Jeanine Herman, trans., 2001 edn) [trans. of: *Sens et non-sens de la révolte: Pouvoirs et limites de la psychanalyse*, 1999] 21.

[63] Richard Beardsworth, *Derrida and the Political* (1996) 15.

[64] Sarah Beardsworth, above n. 9, 22.

[65] Ibid., 65.

[66] Ibid., 62.

[67] Julia Kristeva, above n. 62, 73. Kristeva explains:

'phallic monism' [is] the notion that every human being unconsciously imagines every other human being to possess a penis. The theory of phallic monism supposes an ignorance of the vagina for both sexes ... the absence of the penis, or even castration, is considered a sort of 'eye for an eye' certainly to the emergence of a body as such (le corps propre). Kristeva situates the advent of death drive—the material inscription of the most archaic exposure to exteriority—within the bodily exchange between mother and child, making it a condition of the elementary separateness that has shown up in the narcissistic structure.[68]

This 'elementary separateness' is figured by Kristeva in terms of what she calls 'abjection'; a process situated between non-differentiation and the emergence of an imago separate from the maternal body.[69] Abjection turns 'the maternal container into a … "space" from which the subject to-be may separate … Abjection can therefore be understood, first, as a response to a presymbolic imperative to separate …'[70] We have seen Irigaray's metaphors (the sun, revealing, sameness, light) and Kristeva's process of abjection (states' struggle to establish themselves as separate-yet-connected[71]) in both post-war public language and the *Nuclear Weapons* case. We have seen, too, the mimetic structure of a secular international domain play out in those texts and in the *EC–Biotech* case. In public language, the sovereign state is presented as reflecting 'sameness in itself and for itself',[72] and the international political economy is maintained through the exchange of words (treaties, cases), guaranteed through the exchange of material resources (bodies and land).

Lacan himself noted that 'the myth that God is dead … perhaps … is simply a shelter against the threat of castration'.[73] What becomes most evident after reading Kristeva and Irigaray's critiques is that the primary metaphysical tension underscoring the post-war international domain is not between Church and State

punishment against the man on the woman … The question then becomes who is responsible for the punishment … It is the father, as you may have guessed … I will add that it is a fantasy …

[68] Sarah Beardsworth, above n. 9, 76.

[69] See Julia Kristeva, above n. 62.

[70] Sarah Beardsworth, above n. 9, 84.

[71] Julia Kristeva, *In the Beginning was Love: Psychoanalysis and Faith* (Leon Arthur Goldhammer trans., 1987 edn) [trans. of: *Au commencement etait l'amour*, 1985] 22–3.

[72] Luce Irigaray, above n. 52, 229.

[73] Jacques Lacan, *The Four Fundamental Concepts of Psychoanalysis: The Seminar of Jacques Lacan: Book XI* (Jacques-Alain Miller ed.) (Alan Sheridan trans., 1991 edn) [trans. of: *Le Seminaire de Jacques Lacan: Livre XI, Les quatres concepts fondamentaux de la psychoanalyse by Éditions du Seuil*, 1973], 27.

(as Carl Schmitt might have us believe) but between idioms of masculinity and femininity. Cavarero, Kristeva, and Irigaray's work, in other words, show us how the rhetorical shift from God to Man, Church to State, and a popular rhetoric of equality (sameness) and legitimacy (clean-and-proper bodies of men and their territories) is merely a substitution of a papal authority for a patriarchal one. Women's bodies are effectively sacrificed,[74] they argue, appearing within the symbolic order only as icon (virgin or queen) or as monstrous (abject) feminine.[75]

The existence of the state is consolidated through the operation of recognition between states, which functions to unify each subject with their (masculine) mirror image.[76] Given that modern international law presents itself as a secular system, there is no immediate transcendental (in psychoanalytic terms, no Father) able to constitute each state's subjectivity. Their relations to one another are homosocial, impelled by a desire to consolidate the fiction of a whole, white, 'clean-and proper' identity.[77] Feminist commentators argue that these ideas of hermetic wholeness are based on gendered tropes that recur throughout the history of Western philosophy and are reproduced in Freudian and Lacanian psychoanalysis. Anne Orford reads

[74] Luce Irigaray, above n. 52, 122–3:

> in appropriating the body of the other, he must lose access to his own … In exchange for the body he has to sacrifice (the polymorphous pleasures of the pre-oedipal period) he is granted access to the bodies of women whose bodies replace the place from whence he came (the maternal womb). Women's bodies are the socially guaranteed compensation for men's acquisition of phallic status, the repositories of men's own lost corporeality, and the guardians of men's mortality.

On this account, the female subject, insofar as she exists, must live a double life with an imperative to have the phallus while simultaneously being signified as being the phallus.

[75] On the concept of 'abjection', see Julia Kristeva, *Powers of Horror: An Essay on Abjection* (Leon S. Roudiez, trans., 1982 edn) [trans. of: *Pouvoirs de l'horreur*, 1980] 82.

[76] Recognition, according to Kojève, is only possible when enacted between *equals*, since man can only be satisfied by recognition from those whom he himself recognizes. On Kojèvian recognition see, for example, Alexandre Kojève, *Outline of a Phenomenology of Right* (2000) (BP Frost ed.) (BP Frost and R Howse trans.).

[77] See Eve Sedgwick's response to this term, coined by Girard in *Between Men: English Literature and Male Homosocial Desire* (1985).

this critique into international law and international relations, proposing that the 'economic nature of Christian sacrifice'[78] 'founded on the circulation of risk and reward between fathers ... and sons'[79] is based on a 'prior unacknowledged sacrifice of the feminine'[80] that 'haunts the institutions founded on [that] economy'.[81] The state as a political form is thus based on an idea of humanness that is itself predicated upon a prior metaphysical violence: the privileging of a masculine, over a feminine, political economy. This symbolic reproduction of humanness in the international domain perpetuates a delusion that it is possible to produce 'humanity' *ex nihilo*, without God or a material (i.e. maternal) body.

If the conceptual apparatus of international law depends on this founding violence Orford describes as a sacrifice of the feminine[82] remaining taboo, there is evidently a lot at stake whenever international law is faced with the risk of its disclosure. The 'weakness' of what Kristeva calls our 'discourses of separateness'[83] comes through in *Nuclear Weapons* and *EC–Biotech*, whereby jurists have struggled to guarantee humanness in the international domain. This is due in part to the designation of humanness as *masculine*, which necessitates a hermetic process of symbolic reproduction (through theories of statehood, international legal texts, judicial interpretation, international public discourse, and so on) that is constantly threatening to collapse. The following part describes this process in more detail.

[78] Anne Orford, 'Beyond Harmonization: Trade, Human Rights and the Economy of Sacrifice' 18(2) *Leiden Journal of International Law* 2005, 179, 197.

[79] Ibid., 198. [80] Ibid. [81] Ibid.

[82] Ibid., 198 and 212.

> The protagonists don't understand what is going on. No one knows any longer who is the deceiver and who the deceived. How are the parts being cast? ... Meanwhile, on that set-up stage of men's representation, we find a minimum of two men [who] uphold the process of mimesis from each side of a wall curtain in which their stratagems are lost in infinite regression.

Richard Beardsworth explains: 'There can be no identity without repetition; and yet, this very repetition puts into question the identity it procures.' Richard Beardsworth, above n. 63, 17.

[83] Julia Kristeva, above n. 75, 81.

3.2.2 *Adriana Cavarero's human: the prototype for a gendered state*

> It would ... be puzzling, even naïve, were we, as sophisticated modernists ... to explain our unease about internationalization as the loss of something called 'sovereignty'. It would be doubly strange, in fact, because *internationalization* has also, in a sense, been carried out in the name of sovereignty. However much we love to hate sovereignty, it reappears in our dreams and desires.[84]

Even as unconditional sovereignty—the exclusive right to govern territory—is consigned to the dustbin of history by internationalists and Kantian cosmopolitans who demand a supra-national world order, sovereignty remains a central unit of account in international law.[85] A cursory glance at the contemporary rhetoric of international law reveals a landscape of territories and populations over which desacralized governments wield supreme authority. The state is described in international law as a whole, inhabited body with stable and inviolate borders.[86] Jurisdictional force transforms this creature into a 'legal person' that 'has a degree of centralization of its organs not found elsewhere'.[87] The maintenance of effective and exclusive jurisdiction over its corporeal territory by 'administrative and legislative organs', is, declares the international law commentator Ian Brownlie, 'the best evidence of a stable political community'.[88] This exclusive control over land creates an absolute authority over a delimited territory. Sovereign power, the story goes, is not conditional on divine mandate.[89]

[84] David Kennedy, 'Receiving the International' 10(1) *Connecticut Journal of International Law* 1994, 1, 7.

[85] See, for example, Benjamin Straumann, 'The Peace of Westphalia (1648) as a Secular Constitution' *IILJ Working Paper* 2007/07. The turn to 'cosmopolitanism' in international law is discussed by Anne Orford in 'Cosmopolitanism and the Future of International Law', paper presented at the *3rd Melbourne Legal Theory Workshop on Limit, Exception, Emergency, Miracle*, Melbourne Law School, 22–24 November 2006.

[86] See, for example, article 1 of the *Montevideo Convention on Rights and Duties of States* (signed 26 December 1933).

[87] James Crawford, *Brownlie's Principles of International Law* (2012) 130.

[88] Ian Brownlie, *Principles of Public International Law* (2003) 70.

[89] Max Weber famously describes the secular state as a 'monopoly of the legitimate use of violence in the enforcement of its order'. *The Theory of Social and Economic Organization* (1964) 154.

This legal person—the sovereign state—who emerges out of nowhere, free from any material condition, is an invention: a figure of speech that describes a particular political arrangement by asserting that it exists because it satisfies certain universal criteria. Deanna Shemeck notes that in Thomas Hobbes' *Leviathan*, which intends an originary account of civilized political life, Hobbes 'turns repeatedly to the body in his figurations of the state ... [a body that is] a gigantic political automaton, an imitation by men of God's mechanical artistry'.[90] To borrow the philosopher Adriana Cavarero's term, we can describe Hobbes' use of this metaphor as 'organological'; that is; it borrows the human body as a model for its imaginary form.[91] This organology is exemplified by the picture-image of the Leviathan—a giant constituted of the bodies of ordinary men—that appears on the cover of Hobbes' 1651 book.[92] In late modernity this vision becomes suffused with the mechanical imagery of the mid-eighteenth-century and nineteenth-century physical and biological sciences.[93] The masculine state becomes the perfect machine: a formative invention that secures the existence of humanness in a world without God. Its working population animates this machine. Cavarero describes this early modern body politic as 'always an adult male body that has no history of birth':[94]

> ... perfect, harmonious, and vigorous ... At least two bodies seem to be involved here, or rather, at least two accepted meanings of the body appear to mingle within this context. The first, which the polis banishes from its armored walls, is a body with dreadfully female characteristics ...

[90] Deanna Shemek, 'Introduction' in Adriana Cavarero, *Stately Bodies: Literature, Philosophy and the Question of Gender* (Robert de Lucca and Deanna Schamek trans., 2002 edn) [trans. of: *Corpo in figure*, 1995] 7.

[91] I take the term 'organology' from Adriana Cavarero, *Stately Bodies*, ibid., 5, discussed in more detail below.

[92] For a contemporary description see, for example, Ian Brownlie, above n. 88, 106; and Ian Brownlie, above n. 88, 432; 617 for discussion of the various organs of state. These organs include the head of state, head of government and of executive departments, diplomatic representatives, the courts, and the army, among others.

[93] Pheng Cheah, David Fraser, and Judith Grbich (eds), *Thinking Through the Body of the Law* (1996) 141.

[94] Adriana Cavarero, above n. 90, 5.

The second, which politics welcomes in suitable metaphor, is a male body, largely static and bloodless, whose nature has been tamed to the commands of an overbearing reason that determines its functioning and structure.[95]

What Cavarero makes clear is that whereas the feminine body has the power to create something other than itself, to 'not simply repeat itself but [become] itself ... by becoming-other',[96] the 'universal' humanness secured by international law through this Hobbesian image of the sovereign state relies upon the perpetuation of a gender binary whereby 'masculine' attributes of rationality and a hermetic physicality are privileged over 'feminine' attributes of a permeable and fecund corporeality. I will extend her analysis briefly to explore how exactly the state as a metaphor for masculinity plays out in an international domain, beginning with their interpellation (calling into being) through the process of recognition.[97]

The identification of a territorial body as a state and the recognition of its inviolable sovereignty cannot take place, in a secular international domain, through the medium of a divine authority (God). Recognition relies, therefore, on the idea that by virtue of every state being equal (in an existential sense) to every other state, interpellation can be effected by one state for another. The ideals of equality and coexistence are central to international law accounts, from 1758 (where the Swiss philosopher and lawyer Emmerich de Vattel writes of the 'perfect equality of rights between independent nations')[98] to the present day (where Ian

[95] Ibid., x.

[96] Paul Patton, 'Nietzsche and the Body of the Philosopher' in *Cartographies* (Rosalyn Diprose and Robyn Ferrell eds) (1991) 43, 51.

[97] Louis Althusser coined the term 'interpellation' to describe the animation of subjectivity at the moment of being named or called to respond. I refer here to the practice of addressing constituents directly; word becoming law as it was spoken throughout the territory. Louis Althusser, *Ideology and Ideological State Apparatuses (Notes towards an Investigation)*, Monthly Review Press (Ben Brewster trans., 1971) [trans. of: *Idéologie et appareils idéologiques d'État (Notes pour une researche)*, 1970].

[98] Laying out an exposition of state constitution, commerce, the secularism of government, resource management, relations to other states, and rules of war and diplomacy, Vattel wrote that nature has established 'a perfect equality of rights between independent nations'. Emmerich De Vattel, *The Law of Nations*, Joseph

Brownlie says that 'the whole of the law could be expressed in terms of the coexistence of sovereignties'):

> The sovereignty and equality of states represent the basic constitutional doctrine of the law of nations, which governs a community consisting primarily of states having a uniform legal personality. If international law exists, then the dynamics of state sovereignty can be expressed in terms of law, and, as states are equal and have legal personality, sovereignty is in a major aspect a relation to other states ...[99]

This 'relation to other states' takes place through a system of mutual authentication. Sovereignty is 'recognized', constituted, either externally[100] or by meeting certain structural criteria outlined in the *Montevideo Convention*: '(a) a permanent population; (b) a defined territory; (c) government; and (d) capacity to enter into relations with the other States.'[101]

While there is some debate around which theory is the more useful in international law,[102] the question of where authority actually derives from, remains, since recognition is a gesture made by an entity which itself must be the recipient of that same gesture of recognition.[103] In thinking about this paradox it is helpful to turn to psychoanalysis, which as a discipline has been concerned

Chitty (ed.) (1858) [trans. of: *Droit des gens; ou, Principes de la loi naturelle appliqués à la conduite et aux affaires des nations et des souverains*, 1758] Book 2, Chapter 3, 36.

[99] Ian Brownlie, above n. 88, 287.

[100] In 'Jurisdiction without Territory: From the Holy Roman Empire to the Responsibility to Protect' 30(3) *Michigan Journal of International Law* 2009, 981, 991–2, Anne Orford describes it thus in her discussion (within the context of post-Westphalian jurisdiction):

> International lawyers such as Henry Wheaton were confronted with frequent changes in membership of the "Family of Nations" as a result of revolutions in Europe and the New World, and questions about the normative criteria of statehood began to appear ... States began to treat external recognition as an act that 'renders the sovereignty of a new State perfect and complete'.

[101] Article 1 of the *Montevideo Convention on Rights and Duties of States*, above n. 86.

[102] For further discussion of the debates surrounding the two theories ('constitutive' vs 'declaratory'), see: Hersch Lauterpacht, *Recognition in International Law* (1947); Hans Kelsen, *Principles of International Law* (2nd edn, 1967) 387–416; and James Crawford, *The Creation of States in International Law* (1979) 10–25.

[103] Ian Brownlie, above n. 88, 87–8.

with 'recognition' as a psychosocial event, in which they ask how a subject learns to self-authorize *as* a subject.[104] The observation by Sara Beardsworth that psychoanalysis 'is an adequate means of approach to a problem of which it forms a part'[105] and the fact that it remains 'arguably the most sophisticated and convincing account of subjectivity'[106] makes it a crucial set of references for this current investigation.[107] The main theorists with regard to the concept of 'recognition' have been Sigmund Freud and Jacques Lacan, whom I will here approach through the analysis of the feminist thinker Elizabeth Grosz.

Let us begin by looking at Freud's story of impossible desire, where he describes the subject's emergence into selfhood in terms of a struggle with an impossible desire to be unified with the mother:

> It is the fate of all of us, perhaps, to direct our first sexual impulse towards our mother and our first hatred and our first murderous wish against our father. Our dreams convince us that that is so. King Oedipus, who slew his father Laïus and married his mother Jocasta, merely shows us the fulfillment of our own childhood wishes. But, more fortunate than he, we have meanwhile succeeded, in so far as we have not become psychoneurotics, in detaching our sexual impulses from our mothers and in forgetting our jealousy of our fathers.[108]

[104] Psychoanalysis is a theory and practice that evolved in response to 'Western European' people's struggle with secular modernity: the same struggle within which international law is enmeshed and which can be understood as parallel discourses. Sigmund Freud, the grandfather of psychoanalysis, created a lexicon that could articulate sociological problems of modernity, and metaphysical problems of ontology, in terms of subjective experiences of death and desire. He did so through the interpretation of dreams based on an architectonics of mythic familial structures, the most famous of which is the Oedipal relation: Sigmund Freud, above n. 7.

[105] Sara Beardsworth, above n. 9, 56.

[106] Elizabeth Grosz, above n. 6, 3. Jacqueline Rose, in her book above *States of Fantasy* (1998), argues for historical events and state relations to be informed by psychoanalysis.

[107] Shaunnagh Dorsett and Shaun McVeigh, above n. 2.

[108] Sigmund Freud, above n. 7, 364. Freud remarks in a footnote (that he added in 1919): 'Later studies have shown that the "Oedipus complex" ... throws a light ... on the history of the human race and the evolution of religion and morality', 365.

Both an initial desire for the mother and jealousy or resentment of the father are repressed, claims Freud, due to a fear of castration by the father. Grosz explains that while Freud's subject 'nostalgically ... seek[s] out a past symbiotic completeness' with the mother, it simultaneously realizes the impossibility of reunification with her.[109] The imagined mother must then be incorporated (internalized and repressed) by the subject in order that it may deny the 'internal rupture and [conceive] of itself as the source of its own origin and unity'.[110] Grosz suggests that this imaginary relation, however, 'although structurally necessary, is ... ultimately stifling and unproductive'[111] and must be mediated by a 'third term': the father.[112]

Lacan elaborates on this process by which the subject learns to recognize itself as an entity independent of the mother by internalizing the authority of the father.[113] He describes it in terms of a 'mirror stage' whereby a child, looking in the mirror, sees a whole, unified, self reflected back, ratified by the gaze of the father who recognizes them as an object (of knowledge).[114] As Grosz puts it:

> [R]ecognition of absence is the pivotal moment around which the mirror stage revolves ... Only at this moment does it [the subject] become capable of distinguishing itself from the 'outside' world, and thus of locating itself in the world ... In other words, its recognition of itself as a (potential) totality is correlative with its recognition that the world as a whole is not its own.[115]

[109] Elizabeth Grosz, above n. 6, 39–40. [110] Ibid., 47.

[111] Ibid., 46. [112] Ibid., 50–1.

[113] In the 1960s Freud's project was extended by the psychoanalyst and philosopher Jacques Lacan, whose work focused on the constitution of the human subject through its entry into language. Many of the feminist works I engage for the purposes of making sense of international law have emerged specifically in resistance to Lacan's story of subjectivity, highlighting the gendered nature of the tropes perpetuated throughout Western metaphysical thought, of which Lacanian psychoanalysis is one account.

[114] By 'gaze' I use here Jacques Lacan's definition: 'The gaze I encounter ... is not a seen gaze, but a gaze imagined by me in the field of the Other.' Jacques Lacan, above n. 73 at 84.

[115] Elizabeth Grosz above n. 6, 35. From the early 1950s onwards Lacan considered the 'mirror stage' as having primarily structural value in describing what he calls the 'Imaginary' order, over its explicatory value in describing the development of the infant.

The subject's entry into a social world is therefore described as being predicated on a regulatory Father, with whose name and image the subject must identify (this is what Lacan refers to as the authoritative 'name-of-the-father').[116] Ultimately, then, this process of identification is not directed towards the maternal feminine but to a masculinity that subjects perceive as being their own animating force. The need for recognition is manifest as a desire for the masculine—for the same—or at least, for approval and recognition by the same.[117]

The focus that psychoanalytic stories have on male desire and masculine bodies has been criticized as 'phallocentric in its perspectives, methods, and assumptions'[118] by feminist thinkers who have tried to articulate what is missing from its accounts of subjectivity.[119] Common to these critiques is the sense that Freud and Lacan have buried an (original) object of desire: the maternal body. This desire—for the inhabitation of a space that is entirely secure—is distorted by a universe of fathers, brothers, and absent mothers, even to the extent of identifying masculinity as the transcendent characteristic of human life.[120] Reading these

[116] This description of specular identification also relies on the Kojèvian theme of recognition, which according to Alexandre Kojève is only possible when enacted between equals, since man can only be satisfied by recognition from those whom he himself recognizes. Maurizio Meloni, 'A Triangle of Thoughts: Girard, Freud, Lacan' *Journal of European Psychoanalysis* 2002, 29. On Kojèvian recognition see, for example, Alexandre Kojève, *Outline of a Phenomenology of Right* (Bryan-Paul Frost ed.) (Bryan-Paul Frost and Robert Howse trans., 2000 edn) [trans. of: *Equisse d'une phenomenologie du droit*, 1981].

[117] Elizabeth Grosz, above n. 6, 39–40. [118] Ibid., 3.

[119] Feminist psychoanalytic thinkers critiquing Sigmund Freud's work include Hélène Deutsch, *Psychoanalysis of the Sexual Functions of Women* (Paul Roazen trans., 1991 ed.) [trans. of: *Psychoanalyse der weiblichen Sexualfunktionen*, 1925] and Nancy Chodorow, *The Reproduction of Mothering: Psychoanalysis and the Sociology of Gender* (1978); *Feminism and Psychoanalytic Theory* (1989); and most recently *The Power of Feelings: Personal Meaning in Psychoanalysis, Gender, and Culture* (2001). Eve Sedgwick, in her book *Between Men: English Literature and Male Homosocial Desire* (1985) has also used the Girardian idea of mimesis, but has inverted it to demonstrate (through literary critique) the oppressive nature of what she terms 'homosocial' relations between men.

[120] I.e. representing the constitution of subjectivity as centring around the having or lacking of a phallus. The feminist response to psychoanalytic theories has been very varied. It is exemplified by the conflict between the Lacanian view (Juliet Mitchell and Jacqueline Rose (eds), *Feminine Sexuality. Jacques Lacan and the*

accounts of subjectivity it becomes clear that post-war public discourses of global fraternity reflect these dominant ideas about the gender of 'humankind' (masculine); how they become subjects (through recognition); and what they desire (mimetic identification with one another).[121] This idea of the state *as a metaphor* of a gendered body allows us to understand what a global 'fraternity' really means, and to understand how public discourse in the international domain fails—as in *Nuclear Weapons* and *EC–Biotech*—to guarantee the security of a material, corporeal human life. If we must invent our own humanness in an international domain—through international law, moreover—is it possible to produce

École Freudienne, 1982), which follows Freud's key tenets, and the object relations view (Nancy Chodorow), which critiqued Freud. Put simply:

> while the Lacanian view takes the phallus or father as [sic] starting point, the object relations view takes the mother. For the adherents of Freud, masculinity is presumed and femininity defined as its other; for the revisionists, maternal identification is primary and masculinity comes into being as not-mother.

Jessica Benjamin, *Shadow of the Other: Intersubjectivity and Gender in Psychoanalysis* (1998) xvi. It is my view that the object relations theory, in its revisionist attempt to establish a counter-hegemony through the simple inversion of a binary relation is less helpful than the post-Lacanian feminist position (exemplified by thinkers such as Jacqueline Rose, Julia Kristeva, Luce Irigaray, and Jacques Derrida) which critiques the very structure of the binary relation—see the following section for further discussion on this point.

[121] Grosz describes this desire for recognition as a kind of mimicry: 'Mimetic identifications and recognitions ... may explain processes of social inculcation and positioning.' Elizabeth Grosz, above n. 6, 39–40. For a detailed account of the historical shift from colonial tutelage towards a neo-colonial mode of relations (the 'recognition' of colonies as equal states) initiated in the interwar period, see Antony Anghie, 'Colonialism and the Birth of International Institutions: Sovereignty, Economy, and the Mandate System of the League of Nations' 34 *NYU Journal of International Law and Politics* 2001–2002, 513, and Antony Anghie, *Imperialism, Sovereignty and the Making of International Law* (2005). While I elaborate this in the following chapter, I should note here that this equality of fraternal sovereigns is shot through with Orientalist discourse, whereby homoerotic desire of the 'West' is directed at a feminized 'East': see, for example, John M. MacKenzie *Orientalism: History, Theory and the Arts* (1995) 25; Ueno Chizuko, 'In the Feminine Guise: A Trap of Reverse Orientalism' in Richard Calichman, *Contemporary Japanese Thought* (2005), and Hsu-Ming Teo, 'Orientalism and Mass Market Romance Novels in the Twentieth Century' in Debjani Ganguly and Ned Curthoys (eds), *Edward Said: The Legacy of a Public Intellectual* (2007) 242.

a different kind of writing that acknowledges a humanness with the attributes of more than one sex? The final part of this chapter turns to look at how the 'hysteric' writing of the *Nuclear Weapons* and *EC–Biotech* can be understood to open up this possibility for a different kind of international law writing, and a different order of political life.

3.2.3 *International law as* écriture feminine

At first glance, the writing of these judicial pronouncements might not appear to have much in common with the affliction diagnosed by Freud as the female symptom of repression *par excellence*: hysteria. The concept of hysteria (from the Greek word *hystera*, meaning womb) has alternately been accorded status as a (usually female) disease or illness, or as a medical category under which uncontrollable elements of difference and danger—the feminine being one such element—have been placed. In the early twentieth century, Freud described hysteria as 'the product of a psychical trauma which had been forgotten by the patient',[122] 'a series of perfectly rational thoughts ... [that] have been transformed into the symptom by means of condensation and formation of compromises'.[123] 'Condensation' was a term Freud used to describe a psychic process (such as dreaming) by means of which symbols (or words) come to take on disguised meanings, in order that repressed urges and memories can find a means of expression.

The appropriation of hysteria as a 'specifically feminine pathology that speaks to and against patriarchy'[124] dates from the late 1960s. The 'French feminists' canvassed above (Irigaray, Kristeva and, additionally, Hélène Cixous) have stressed that hysteria should be understood not as an illness, but as a garbled expression of resistance, through a language comprised of 'repetitive, spasmodic separations from the dominant discourse'.[125] The hysteric voice,

[122] Sigmund Freud, above n. 7, 14. [123] Ibid., 756.

[124] Elaine Showalter, in Gilman, King, Porter et al. (eds), *Hysteria Beyond Freud* (1993) ix, at http://publishing.cdlib.org/ucpressebooks/view?docId=ft0p3003d3&brand=ucpress, 286.

[125] 'The body entering the text disrupts the masculine economy of superimposed linearity and tyranny: the feminine is the "overflow of luminous torrents".' Hélène Cixous 'The Laugh of the Medusa' (I) *Signs* (1976) 876.

provoked by the 'loss of loss' itself, is manifest both as silence and as an excess of speech.[126] This manifestation is aesthetic: so much is acknowledged by Freud's collaborator Josef Breuer, who referred to his hysterical patients as 'the flowers of mankind, as sterile, no doubt, but as beautiful as double flowers'.[127] This image of woman-as-cultivated flower is redescribed by the feminist Olive Schreiner as a divestment of feminine sexuality, whereby the flower, 'having no more need to seed turns all its sexual organs into petals, and doubles, and doubles; it becomes entirely aesthetic'.[128]

Psychic trauma that manifests as an aesthetic proliferation: repetitive, impotent, self-referential—such a description resonates with the form and tone of the writings in *Nuclear Weapons* and *EC–Biotech* This resistance in each text to itself, 'its own ... inadvertent textual transgression of its male assumptions and prescriptions',[129] is a revolt of the powerless, as Schreiner alludes and as Shoshana Felman advocates. We can conclude, then, that the anxieties of the jurists in our two cases manifest, consciously or not, as writing that resists what they are called upon to do. The hysteric voice—here a mimicry or self-parody—can then be said to occur when international law is no longer able to reproduce itself. Hysteria emerges as a symptom when the jurists—standing in as a 'shield for humanity' have no unitary voice, no power to enforce the word, nor polis to stand in for the clean-and-proper body. The drive to revolt against their impossible office can only be discharged through aesthetic signification: silence—a refusal to decide, and a proliferation of words.[130]

[126] See Sarah Beardsworth, above n. 9.

[127] Joseph Breuer and Sigmund Freud, *Studies on Hysteria* (2004) (Nicola Luckhurst, trans.).

[128] Olive Schreiner, letter to Karl Pearson, in *The Letters of Olive Schreiner* (1988) (R Rive, ed.), 86.

[129] Shoshana Felman, *What Does a Woman Want? Reading and Sexual Difference* (1993) 6.

[130] Julia Kristeva, above n. 62, 56 explains:

> This, in sum, represents a profound integration of the Hegelian dialectic into Freudian thought. The libido detached from the object turns toward Narcissus and threatens him. What will act as a counterbalance and prevent Narcissus from being destroyed? It is a new object, which is not mommy or daddy, the breast or any other external erotic object, or the body itself, but an artificial, internal object that Narcissus is capable of producing: his own representations, speech, sounds, colors, and so forth.

A feminist analysis of *Nuclear Weapons* and *EC–Biotech* can thus identify international law's hysteric struggle with its existential paradox, and in doing so, itself enact a resistance to blackletter readings of these cases. In both instances the jurists would not reach substantive decisions. Both cases were delayed and opinions divided. Called upon to take responsibility for a decision they could not make, the judges' opinions, dissenting and separate, ran to hundreds and to thousands of pages. Irigaray, with Cixous and others, has taken on 'hysteric' writing (which Cixous describes as *écriture feminine* or 'women's writing') as a technique with which to counter dominant discourses. Could *écriture feminine*, or poetic, political writing that inverts masculine logic, be any kind of answer to the serious problems of legal authority, risk management, and the orderly functioning of the laws of war and trade? And what does it mean to propose a 'feminine' technics against a 'masculine' one? 'Feminism' in international law lingers between a rock and a hard place: the Anglo-American tradition would on the one hand rebuild an order based on a problematic conception of women's identity. And while the critical impetus of *écriture feminine* demands that there is no such thing as an absolute femininity, 'only a set of ontologically tenuous codes that normatively induct the female subject into the social practice of "being" woman',[131] the French feminists deconstruct the dominant social symbolic order by relying upon a reappropriated but nonetheless rarefied concept of the female body. Feminist projects in international law likewise have for the most part relied on making 'woman' the equivalent/same/identical of 'man', or reversed the ontological hierarchy of oppression to make 'man' the *bad*, and 'woman' the *good*. Such arguments are based on essentialist conceptions of 'man' and 'woman' which assume that people are born with either masculine or feminine attributes of their sex; that all desire is heterosexual (and unidirectional); that there are only two genders (equivalent to biological sex); and that violence (coded as sexual violence) is only enacted by one upon the other.

The creation of such stable and positive identities does enable the gathering of people into a singular identifiable political

[131] Ibid., 33, discussing the work of the early twentieth-century analyst Joan Riviere.

movement. However, it also makes it difficult to critique the ideological construction of the discourses around the terms ('man' and 'woman'), since to do so would undermine the very claims that are made in those names.[132] What we must note is that even as some feminists may call for emancipation, these are usually either calls for a 'good/better' paternal law, or for freedom from the material human body to identify with a transcendent form of life: a fantasy that is not so very different to that I have been calling 'humanness' and 'the fantasy of unconditional life'.

Is there then, as Luce Irigaray suggests, 'a revolutionary potential in hysteria', and a place for *écriture feminine* in international law?[133] There are two main opposing feminist views on hysteria: one that proposes it is the 'very stuff of revolutions',[134] and the other that is 'skeptical about the ultimate power of hysteria as a form of feminine subversion'.[135] I suggest a place for hysteria (and *écriture feminine*) which lies somewhere between the two. Rather than conflating the performance of hysteria with an affirmation of the female sex, it may be more useful to consider it a phenomenon that arises out of, and in reaction to, the struggle of jurists faced with an intractable and deadly set of stories about what it is to be human in the international domain. For them, in that case, and for those of us invested in thinking about international law, *écriture feminine* may indeed be the best response. Certainly, if international law is a technology whereby judgments have an educative and creative effect, it is worthwhile trying to find a form that would enable us to rethink the stories and political economies within which we are currently enmeshed.

I will return to this later in Chapter 5. For now, it is enough to note that across the twentieth century, the relationship between human life, technology, and the international domain has been of interest to key thinkers whose accounts of this relationship are heavily inflected in public discourse since the Second World War.

[132] Elizabeth Wright, *Lacan and Postfeminism* (2000) 3.

[133] Luce Irigaray, 'Any Theory of the "Subject"' in *Speculum of the Other Woman* (1985) (G.G. Gill, trans.) 47: 'It is because they want neither to see nor hear that movement that they so despise the hysteric.'

[134] Anne Stevenson, 'The Hysterical Women's Movement' *Times Literary Supplement* (9 September 1983) 961.

[135] Elaine Showalter, above n. 124, 332.

Feminist critiques of those accounts show that they rely on a gendered political economy that attributes a (privileged) masculinity to state bodies; this unitary conception of subjectivity, however, combined with theologies that guarantee the security of human life only through its imminent annihilation, brings with it an existential conundrum that is manifest in the *Nuclear Weapons* and *EC–Biotech cases*. The next chapter elaborates on what I mean when I say that gendered political economy and theological ideas are inflected in public discourse.

4

ATOMIC AGE

4.1 UNCONDITIONAL SURRENDER

> The founding of the United Nations, as we know, coincided with the profound upheavals that humanity experienced when reference to the meaning of transcendence and natural reason was abandoned ...[1]
>
> —Pope Benedict XVI, 2008

In a recent address to the United Nations General Assembly, the head of state of the Holy See invoked the loss of 'transcendence and natural reason' in relation to the founding of the United Nations after the Second World War.[2] Equating the 'profound upheavals of humanity' experienced during the war, together with the broader abandonment of a universal God, the Pope narrated a tale of crisis without salvation—a tale foregrounding the twentieth century and coming to a head in the twenty-first.

This tale is one of many accounts of the scission between Church and State that underpins the humanism found in international public discourse. For the Roman Catholic Church, in whose name the speech was delivered, the meaning of the term 'humanity' was indeed in crisis: not because of the Second World War, but because of the creation of another global order that made a competing claim to that term. This global order—held together by the new fraternal contracts of the twentieth century—uses state-centric discourses of perpetual peace, equality, recognition, justice, and unconditional sovereignty that are underwritten by the idea of an unconditional life: *human* life that can be reproduced without the Church's guarantee of existential security. Expressed by President Roosevelt and Prime Minister Churchill

[1] His Holiness Benedict XVI, 'Address to the United Nations General Assembly' (Speech delivered at the 62nd session of the United Nations General Assembly 95th plenary meeting, New York, 18 April 2008).

[2] Ibid.

as 'freedom from fear and freedom from want',[3] human life in this new international domain is declared no longer to be tied to any material or religious condition.

The idea of unconditional sovereignty, in other words, promises to guarantee unconditional human life. Moreover, unconditional sovereignty can only be declared *ex nihilo* (since this kind of political authority does not come from a transcendent God). It is not constituted in any particular moment or instrument, but rather (and paradoxically), an act of unconditional surrender. Such total surrender to a global economy, of course, creates a dynamic whereby recognition of sovereignty and membership of the United Nations is entirely *conditional*—upon the rejection of feminine divinity (in the case of post-war Japan), or the handing over of industrial resources (in the case of post-war Germany). As I explained in the Introduction to this book, the impossibility of this demand is foregrounded in the paradoxical logic of 'unconditional sovereignty' that founds international law's authority, and is illustrated by the performative 'fragmentation' (profanation) of the Japanese emperor's two bodies in his metamorphosis from a divine authority to a secular one.

The first part of this chapter examines the United States' call for Germany's unconditional surrender and the United Nations Charter, showing that the call for unconditional surrender is a call for *faith*—an invitation that mimics the Christian demand but is in fact a call to join a different kind of universal community, bound by international law. The second part of this chapter focuses on the United States' call for Japan's unconditional surrender, as a demand for it to abandon its divine, feminine sovereign authority and join the global capitalist order. 'A Lover's Discourse' tracks the transformation of the two states' rhetoric from that of enmity to a harmonious affirmation of economic fraternity in the names of Empire, Peace, and Justice. Both countries invoke a perpetual peace and the spectres of a genealogy presented in its perfection *a priori*—both call and answer are written in the language of Empire. To demonstrate this I have collaged a dialogue between Hirohito (the then Emperor of Japan) and

[3] Joint Statement by President Roosevelt and Prime Minister Churchill, 14 August 1941.

Truman (the then President of the United States), using extracts from their original speeches.

Also running through these texts of unconditional surrender are the stories of technology recounted by the thinkers discussed in the first part of Chapter 3. Technology, both in the form of nuclear power and in the form of a new international order, takes on a katechonic relation with the state and/or with human life. It is particularly interesting to look at the surrenders of Germany and Japan because of their interventions (Germany through the EC, and Japan as *amicus curiae*) in *EC–Biotech* and *Nuclear Weapons* fifty years later. It is also pertinent to look at these two countries in particular because they were both colonizers with their own visions of what human life would become in the international domain, and yet surrendered to that of the Allied Forces.

4.1.1 *The Atlantic Charter*

On 12 August 1941, two ships—the heavy cruiser *USS Augusta* and the battle cruiser *HMS Prince of Wales*—pulled up alongside one another, somewhere in the middle of the Atlantic Ocean. This moment marked one of the most significant (and secret) diplomatic meetings of the twentieth century. In this place between nations—the high seas—where the fantasy of a relation without body, territory, and conditions could best be realized, President Franklin D. Roosevelt and Prime Minister Winston Churchill sat and discussed the general strategy for their war against the Axis powers. They ended their meeting with an unsigned agreement known as the Atlantic Charter, which later formed the basis of the United Nations Charter. Most significantly, the short Charter (a policy document) outlined the specific obligations that would be repeated, again and again, in treaties and other fraternal contracts throughout the rest of the twentieth century. Nations 'will endeavour', for example, 'to further the enjoyment by all States, great or small, victor or vanquished, of access, *on equal terms*, to the trade and *to the raw materials of the world* which are needed for their economic prosperity'. Allies 'hope to see established … the means of dwelling in safety *within their own boundaries* which will afford assurance that all the men in all the lands may live out their lives in *freedom from fear and want*'. One of the final provisions of the Charter provides that peace 'should enable all men to traverse the high seas and oceans without hindrance'.[4]

The meeting concluded with a church service on the ship, at which Churchill and Roosevelt sang two hymns chosen by the former and one by the latter. The first, 'Onward, Christian Soldiers' was nominated by Churchill to commemorate a cause for which 'a trumpet sounded from on high' to 'save the world from measureless degradation'.[5] The lyrics recall a sacrifice of soldiers 'marching as to war, with the cross of Jesus' at which 'Satan's host doth flee'. It evokes the body of the Leviathan: 'we are not divided, all one body are we, one in hope and doctrine, one in charity' and ends with a declaration of eternal Christian faith: 'Long as earth endureth, men the faith will hold; Kingdoms, nations, empires, In destruction rolled.' The second hymn, 'Oh God, Our Help in Ages Past' originally published in 1719, evokes again the theme of sacrifice for the divine: 'Thy Word commands our flesh to dust, return, ye sons of men' and the mortality of human life: 'Time, like an ever rolling stream, bears all its sons away; They fly, forgotten, as a dream dies at the opening day.' The themes of patriarchy, militarism, mortality, and the eternal guarantee of divine faith is continued in the hymn chosen by Roosevelt, 'Eternal Father, Strong to Save': 'Eternal Father, strong to save, Whose arm hath bound the restless wave, O Trinity of love and power! Our brethren shield in danger's hour.'

These gestures towards a Christian God took place before the signing of the Atlantic Charter. It is important to maintain sensitivity to the forms in which authority is expressed because they belie a historical subtext or, as described by Shaunnagh Dorsett and Shaun McVeigh, because doing so 'returns the process of jurisdiction both to a structure (or metaphysics) of law and to a history of the institutions that carry the meaning of legal life'.[6] As such, the form in which this utopic vision was laid out is significant. In particular, it reflects charter colony documents

[4] *The Atlantic Charter*, 14 August 1941.

[5] As explained by Winston Churchill in a later radio broadcast: Ace Collins, *Songs Behind the Hymns that Inspire America* (2003) 153–4.

[6] Shaunnagh Dorsett and Shaun McVeigh, 'Questions of Jurisdiction' in *Jurisprudence of Jurisdiction* (Shaun McVeigh ed.) (2007) 4.

which have traditionally been used for the granting of proprietary rights by a sovereign authority, granting permission to start colonies abroad. Despite its egalitarian gesture towards 'all States, great or small, victor or vanquished' the Atlantic Charter retains this colonial flavour in that the so-called 'trade' of raw materials has historically occurred through the exploitation of weaker ('barbaric') communities by more powerful ('civilized') ones. Although the Charter marks the end of 'old' colonialism,[7] the legal form in which it arrives subverts its purported aim to divulge a neo-colonial impulse: the unrestricted access to goods and labour in another name. Implicit in the language of the Charter is an assumption that the status of 'all States' entitled to enjoy access to raw materials remains restricted to those who are party to a civilized brotherhood, the core of which comprises the Western Allied nations.

The promise of freedom and of what I call 'unconditional life' is encapsulated by the desire for 'dwelling in safety within their own boundaries' and 'travers[ing] the high seas and oceans without hindrance'.[8] This desire for impermeable territorial–corporeal boundaries, combined with an opposing desire for fluid movement between and beyond them finds its ultimate expression in the paradoxical declaration that 'all the men in all the lands' may live in 'freedom from fear and want'.[9] The juxtaposition of 'freedom' (deriving from the old English which means 'friend, to love' and describing the state of being unbonded) with the absolute and abstract terms 'fear' and 'want' hint of something that is here unarticulated. The greatest fear is *fear of non-existence*—death, annihilation, or the disappearance of the subject of human history—and the greatest want (or need) is *desire itself*. Fear of the loss of human subjectivity and desire for desire itself are both unable to be calculated or guaranteed: indeed, it is impossible to give an account of them and, thus, to give effect to any repudiation of them.

[7] The so-called decolonization process was institutionalized after the First World War under Article 22 of the *Covenant of the League of Nations* (as agreed on 28 June 1919).

[8] *Treaty of Versailles*, signed 28 June 1919.

[9] His Holiness Benedict XVI, above n. 1.

Outside of international law and international relations, the concept of the divine works to guarantee both death and desire, standing in for, as His Holiness Pope Benedict XVI describes half a century later, 'the absolute and the essence of freedom'.[10] The Pope also noted that '[r]efusal to recognize ... the religious dimension ... would fragment the unity of the person'.[11] The Pope's observation that a secular law leads to the fragmentation of the human/legal subject's unity is evidenced in the speeches of those vanquished in the war (discussed later in this chapter). I argue that this fragmentation, a threat latent in the modern subject and described by Beardsworth as the 'nihilism problematic',[12] leads to the creation of the fantasy of a whole, impenetrable (unconditional), progressive body, which itself is based upon the binary opposition of masculine and feminine.

David Kennedy describes how 'internationalization has always been announced as both the triumph of a *particular* vision of sovereignty, a *particular* conception of international government and law, and as sovereignty's last death rattle'.[13] This view of internationalization as a political process that entails the simultaneous consolidation and destruction of state sovereignty can be traced through definitive events of the twentieth century, and in particular, through the political economies of exchange and consumption which enabled that process. On the one hand, the concept of state sovereignty was seen as the foundation of international law during the inter-war period, upon which a practice of codification and legal method could be placed.[14] On the other, the sovereign state was threatened with non-differentiation by the universalizing impetus. This tension within the project of internationalization (which will be further elaborated shortly) was mediated by two major systems of exchange in the world: communism and capitalism. While in one sense ideologically opposed (the capitalist body guaranteed through *currency* stamped with the

[10] Ibid. [11] Ibid.

[12] See generally, Sara Beardsworth, *Julia Kristeva: Psychoanalysis and Modernity* (2004) and the discussion in the second half of Chapter 3.

[13] David Kennedy, 'Receiving the International' 10(1) *Connecticut Journal of International Law* 1994, 1.

[14] Ibid., 8.

sovereign's head and the communist body imagined as an economic entity that is not premised upon a single sovereign), they were nonetheless underwritten by a single practice: the 'free' exchange and consumption of goods and labour.

4.1.2 Demand for unconditional surrender: a new world

A year and a half after the Atlantic Charter meeting, on 14 January 1943 Roosevelt and Churchill met again at a conference (codenamed 'Symbol') convened in Casablanca, Morocco for all of the Allied powers. The results of the conference were declared by Roosevelt on American radio on 12 February, confirming that 'from the people and the people alone flows the authority of government'.[15] Most significantly, the Allies proclaimed: 'the only terms on which we shall deal with an Axis government ... are the terms proclaimed at Casablanca: Unconditional Surrender.'[16] Roosevelt's address offered to the public not sovereign jurisdiction guaranteed through the sovereign subject's contract with God, but a universal jurisdiction authorized by the people and guaranteed through their tenuous recognition of other states' (masculine) subjectivity. The address simultaneously introduces the term 'unconditional' to the global context, prefiguring its subsequent appearance in international law texts throughout the twentieth century.[17]

It is no coincidence that the concept of unconditionality is afforded so much precedence in this text that seeks to undertake the impossible: the universalization of a jurisdiction that is *not* guaranteed by a transcendental figure in common. The ultimate unconditional relation is that of the subject's relation to the transcendental (in other words, to an authority outside of itself which guarantees its existence). This relation is, paradoxically, a relation that is also entirely *with* condition: that of faith, to which everything (including subjectivity itself) must be surrendered. The Allies' demand for unconditional surrender, therefore, is a

[15] Franklin D. Roosevelt, 'Casablanca Conference Radio Address' (Speech delivered 12 February 1943) *The Public Papers of F.D. Roosevelt* (1969) 12, 71.

[16] Ibid.

[17] The term 'unconditional surrender' was famously first used in the American Civil War.

demand for the Axis powers to enter into an international (secularized) community with *absolute faith*. This is brought out in the Casablanca Conference's presumption of jurisdiction, first in their statement that they 'mean no harm to the common people of the Axis nations. But … do mean to impose punishment and retribution in full upon their guilty, barbaric leaders …'[18] Here, the barbarism of the Axis nations has already condemned them to guilt, even before the creation of the Nuremberg and Tokyo War Crimes Trials. Roosevelt concluded his radio address on the Conference by saying that 'it is the unalterable purpose of the United Nations to restore to conquered peoples their sacred rights'.[19] This final move consolidates the universal jurisdiction of the (victors') United Nations, inscribing the new subjects of law with an (unconditional) gift of 'sacred' rights.

Prior to the surrenders of Japan and Germany, an inaugural United Nations Conference was held in San Francisco in April 1945. A now-famous speech was delivered by President Truman at its opening session, and an examination of this text reveals how it played a crucial part in the transfer of law's authority from a Christian one to a new universal one. Truman begins by declaring that '[t]he world has experienced a revival of an old faith in the everlasting moral force of justice'.[20] Presenting an 'old faith' (in God) alongside an abiding 'force of justice', President Truman sets the stage for a subtle substitution of one for the other. 'Words are not enough,' he declares. 'We must build a new world.'[21] The exchange of 'words and rewards with God',[22] so to speak, does not suffice as a guarantee of relations between states. Large sections of the speech are given over to discussing the 'supreme sacrifice' of those who died during the war, proposing that they died 'to insure justice'. Truman transforms the war dead from a national loss into a sacrifice—not for God, but for its secular avatar,

[18] Franklin Roosevelt, above n. 15. [19] Ibid.

[20] Harry Truman, 'Address to the Opening Session of the United Nations Conference on International Organisation' (Speech delivered to the *Opening Session of the United Nations Conference on International Organisation* at San Francisco, 25 April 1945).

[21] Ibid.

[22] Anne Orford, 'Beyond Harmonization: Trade, Human Rights and the Economy of Sacrifice' 18 *Leiden Journal of International Law* 2005, 179–213.

justice. He continues, saying that people 'must work … to guarantee justice—for all'.[23] Truman's evocation of *work* here is interesting, and is echoed a few lines later when he calls the members of the Conference 'architects of the better world, [who by their] *labors* … we shall know if suffering humanity is to achieve a just and lasting peace … worthy of [the dead's] … sacrifice'.[24] Five years before the speech, in the heat of the war and shortly before his own death, the thinker Walter Benjamin wrote on the nature of labour:

> The old Protestant ethics of work was resurrected among German workers in secularized form … the confusion [of Marx's proposal] spread, and soon thereafter Josef Dietzgen proclaimed: 'The saviour of modern times is called work.'[25] … Social Democracy thought fit to assign to the working class the role of the redeemer of future generations, in this way cutting the sinews of its greatest strength. This training made the working class forget both its hatred and its spirit of sacrifice, for both are nourished by the image of enslaved ancestors rather than that of liberated grandchildren.[26]

Benjamin here refers (somewhat prophetically) to the pro-war German Socialist party's misappropriation of Marx's call for workers to take back the conditions of production. His critique can also be applied to Truman's secular appeal to the Protestant work ethic. Truman's demand could be understood, under this critique, as the mitigation of any possible revolt by both legislators and the subjects of international law-to-be. Returning to Truman's speech, it is clear that 'perpetual peace', as well as 'justice', is called upon here to stand in for the missing unconditional guarantor (God). Truman proclaims:

> With ever-increasing brutality and destruction, modern warfare, if unchecked, would ultimately crush all civilization. We still have a choice between the alternatives: The continuation of international chaos, or the establishment of a world organization for the enforcement of peace.[27]

[23] Harry Truman, above n. 20. [24] Ibid.

[25] Walter Benjamin, 'On the Concept of History' (or, 'Theses on the Philosophy of History') in Walter Benjamin, *Illuminations: Essays and Reflections* (Peter Demetz ed.) (1986) [trans. of: *Zur Kritik der Gewalt*, 1921] XI.

[26] Ibid., XII. [27] Harry Truman, above n. 20.

Brutality is 'ever increasing', its logical end point the end of civilization. The 'choice' presented to the members of the Conference mirrors that which was presented to the Axis powers in the demand for unconditional surrender: annihilation, or peace. The form that this peace must take is not a treaty 'in the old sense of that term'. Evoking the Treaties of Versailles and Westphalia, Truman insists that it is not the members' assignment 'to settle specific questions of territories, boundaries, citizenship, and reparations',[28] but rather, to 'write the fundamental charter ... [to make peace] not only possible but certain'.[29] The President thus draws a visible line between the 'old' relations between sovereign states which are recognized as being conditional, marked by territories and boundaries, and the 'new' relations which are grounded by a single charter—under a single jurisdiction—purportedly unconditional and unbounded, 'founded upon justice for peace'. Truman continues: 'Justice remains the greatest power on earth. To that tremendous power alone will we submit.'[30] This phrase encapsulates the problem of the loss of God (both generally as a symptom of modernity and specifically in terms of the lack of a common transcendental figure in the place between nations) and its solution: *justice* is created in its place.

At the climax of the speech, Truman declares that with '[d]ivine guidance, friendly cooperation, and hard work we shall find an adequate answer to the problem history has put before us'.[31] This tripartite solution to a problem couched as being one of 'history' is particularly revealing of the speech's operations. It is ambiguous here as to whether the 'problem' is that of the violent military struggle between sovereign powers (and violence generally), or that of a lack of a common transcendental guarantor of peace (a problem of modernity and of globalization). The framing of such problems as arising out of socio-economic *fate* (problems that 'history has put before us') has been critiqued by Walter Benjamin as a misappropriation of Marx's work, whereby a historicism promoting the 'concept of the historical progress ... through a homogenous, empty time [towards] an infinite perfectibility of mankind'[32] stands in for a historical materialism engaged

[28] Ibid. [29] Ibid. [30] Ibid. [31] Ibid.

[32] Walter Benjamin, above n. 20, XIII.

with *jetztzeit* ('now time'), capable of recognizing a real state of emergency.

With 'Divine guidance, friendly cooperation, and hard work', Truman identifies the 'answer' to history's provocations. He gestures to the old order of divine authority, even beseeching 'Almighty God to guide us in building a permanent monument to those who gave their lives'[33] and proposes (yet again) *work* as both the expiatory and redeeming practice. It *is* possible, Truman suggests, to exist in an international domain where enemies recognize one another as friends. Later in the speech Truman again emphasizes this last: 'Man has learned long ago that it is impossible to live unto himself. This same basic principle applies today to nations ... We dare not become isolated in peace.'[34] The dissolution of the friend/enemy distinction is a driving project of President Truman's, an attempt to eliminate the possibility of war.[35] His speech ends with the evocation of two tropes:

> Differences between men, and between nations, will always remain. In fact, if held within reasonable limits, such disagreements are actually wholesome. All progress begins with differences of opinion and moves onward as the differences are adjusted through reason ...[36]

The first trope is that of the reasonable subject/man/nation, echoed in 2008 by His Holiness Pope Benedict XVI who described 'natural reason shared by all nations ... and an international order whose task it was to regulate relations between peoples'.[37] The fear of non-differentiation (due to the loss of an external, transcendental guarantor) coalesces here with a fear of being out of history, or in other words, losing a subjective experience of time as linear, continuous, and seamless. Such a fear accompanies the abandonment of God in the place between nations. In order to shore up the modern secular subjectivity as one constructed by socio-economic factors and Enlightenment reason (both determinable), Truman utilizes a second trope: progress. Here, he presents a theatre of separately defined, secular sovereign bodies able

[33] Truman, above n. 20. [34] Ibid.

[35] Jacques Derrida, *The Politics of Friendship* (George Collins trans., 1997 edn) [trans. of: *Politiques de l'amitié*, 1994].

[36] Truman, above n. 20. [37] His Holiness Benedict XVI, above n. 1.

to recognize each other as historical subjects, travelling together towards a magical place where *difference itself*, as opposed to *subjectivity*, becomes synthesized.

4.1.3 The United Nations Charter

A few months after President Truman's address, Germany, followed by Japan, surrendered to the Allied Forces. Europe, together with the rest of the world, exhaled as the second devastating war of the twentieth century drew to a close. Nearly 300 years had passed since the signing of the Westphalia Treaties; the vision of a global fraternity was a step closer to realization. The vision outlined in the Atlantic Charter and developed in Truman's speech to the UN Conference was given form in another Charter, this one fleshing out the figure of the United Nations body as a solid entity with organs.

The preamble of the UN Charter begins with a declaration that the 'people of the United Nations' are '*determined*' to 'reaffirm faith' in the 'equal rights of men and women and of nations large and small'. This reaffirmation of faith, not in God but in equality and in rights, is repeated throughout the UN Charter: 'The Purposes of the United Nations are: To develop friendly relations among nations based on respect for the principle of equal rights ... to strengthen universal peace.'[38] The tropes of friendship and equality are used again and again to bolster the idea of a universal and perpetual peace, itself (according to a circular logic) 'based on the principle of the sovereign equality of all its Members'.[39] The tension between the fantasy of unconditional sovereignty (which is predicated on some kind of territorial–corporeal integrity) and the reality of secular relations based upon conditional recognition of each (equal) other's sovereignty is laid bare in the UN Charter. While 'sovereign equality' (quoted above) and 'territorial integrity'[40] are vaunted, the UN Charter seeks nonetheless 'to establish *conditions* under which justice and respect ... can be maintained'.[41] Membership in the United Nations is also restricted

[38] *Charter of the United Nations* (signed on 26 June 1945) 1 UNTS XVI, Article 1(2).

[39] Ibid., Article 2(1).

[40] Ibid., Article 2(4).

[41] Ibid., Preamble.

to those states 'which accept the obligations contained in the present Charter'.[42] The entirely conditional nature of membership—of entering the universalizing jurisdiction of the UN body—as well as the mandate of the body itself to create conditions, lies in stark contrast to the founding story of unconditionality also espoused by the UN Charter. The preamble of the Charter contains distinctly Christian overtones: 'live … with one another as good neighbours'.[43] It continues:

> Members of the United Nations which have or assume responsibilities for the administration of territories whose peoples have not yet attained a full measure of self-government recognize the principle that the interests of the inhabitants of these territories are paramount, and accept as a sacred trust the obligation to promote to the utmost, within the system of international peace and security established by the present Charter, the well-being of the inhabitants of these territories … [44]

This provision, relating to 'non-self-governing territories' (colonies and former colonies), takes on as 'sacred trust' the 'obligation' to promote the well-being of their subjects, in the name of international peace. The shift from Truman's speech to the UN Charter is a subtle but definite one. 'Peace' (like 'justice') emerges as the transcendental guarantee, and the *image of the collective nations* made possible by the fraternal contract becomes the figure who may both name and receive sacrifice. By renaming their jurisdiction over the 'inhabitants' and 'peoples' of colonial outposts as 'sacred trust', the members of the UN call upon them as subjects of the new faith and thereby extend their jurisdiction. This founds a particular kind of jurisdiction, one predicated on state sovereignty and an international authority that looks like a trusteeship, from God.

The United Nations members propose to ensure 'fundamental freedoms for all'[45] by becoming 'a centre for harmonizing the actions of nations in the attainment of these common ends'.[46] 'Equal rights' become 'fundamental freedoms' and the story of origin is complete. Man is born again, free from fear and from desire.

[42] Ibid., Article 4(1). [43] Ibid., Preamble.

[44] Ibid., Chapter XI, 'Declaration Regarding Non-Self Governing Territories', Article 73.

[45] Ibid., Chapter VIII, 'Organs', Article 62. [46] Ibid., Article 1(4).

The UN Charter proposes 'the UN body harmonize the actions of nations ... Fundamental freedoms are to be guaranteed by the International Court of Justice', the 'principal judicial organ of the United Nations'.[47] The creation of the figure of a full body with organs enables a visceral jurisdiction (the speaking of law), which becomes transcendental, universal, and all-encompassing. States must officially recognize the jurisdiction of the court before disputes can be heard. Nonetheless, the UN Charter declares that '[a]ll Members of the United Nations are *ipso facto* parties to the Statute of the International Court of Justice'.[48] The original and universal jurisdiction of the new body is extended, too, to states that are not members of the UN, 'on conditions to be determined in each case by the General Assembly upon the recommendation of the Security Council'.[49] The fantasy of unconditionality is thus both consolidated and broken in this Charter, with the promise of a free, original sovereign subjectivity (through recognition between states, guaranteed by the figure of the UN and the name of peace) sutured to conditions at every turn. Significantly, the Charter does not end with a plea to God (as Truman's speech does), but rather, with a declaration that it is 'in faith' that 'the representatives of the Governments of the United Nations have signed the present Charter'.[50]

4.2 A LOVERS' DISCOURSE

In 1852, an American envoy called Commodore Perry sailed into Japan after several unsuccessful visits by US representatives to negotiate trading agreements. He visited again in 1854 with coal-fired war ships, forcing Japan to sign a 'Treaty of Amity and Commerce'.[51] The pretext of commerce lay hand in hand with

[47] Ibid., Chapter XI, 'Declaration Regarding Non-Self Governing Territories', Article 92.

[48] Ibid., Article 93(1).

[49] *Charter of the United Nations* (signed on 26 June 1945) 1 UNTS XVI, Article 93(2).

[50] Ibid., Conclusion.

[51] *Treaty of Amity and Commerce*, 1854. Japan had maintained amicable trade relations with Portugal since the sixteenth century and this was the first time that the country had experienced such direct military threat by a foreign power.

what the US saw as being also the civilizing mission of 'carrying the gospel of God to the heathen'.[52] This encounter ended Japan's seclusion from the rest of the world and began a gradual militarization of the nation, leading to its brutal expansion of empire throughout East Asia and South-East Asia from 1867 to 1945.[53] On 15 August 1945, nearly 100 years after Commodore Perry's visit and towards the end of the Second World War, a second encounter between the two states took place: this time involving the use of nuclear weapons, and this time, ending in Japan's unconditional surrender.

I argue here that the Allied Forces' call and Japanese response to surrender signifies a symbolic performance of secularization and fraternal salvation. This expression of phallic monism relies upon a promise of unconditional recognition, which itself takes place through a forgetting of the last vestiges of feminine transcendental authority. Despite the historically different racial and religious relations of the Axis powers vis-à-vis the Allied powers, the rhetoric surrounding their defeat and their subsequent salvation into the world order is remarkably similar. Both were imperial powers forced to surrender unconditionally, and both were subject—through the Nuremberg and Tokyo trials—to the jurisdiction of the new universal order into which they were brought. Following on from the trials and the injections of capital and credit into the countries by the United States, both became 'tigers' of the international economy—tigers that were nonetheless toothless, demilitarized as a condition of the post-war settlement.

4.2.1 Germany's surrender

On 8 May 1945 the German military surrendered to the 'Supreme Commander, Allied Expeditionary Force and High Command

[52] As described in the painting by James G. Evans, 'The US Japan Fleet. Com. Perry Carrying the "Gospel of God" to the Heathen', oil on canvas (1853), which depicts a wave-battered fleet carrying full sails that catch the light of the morning sky.

[53] The drive to access raw materials and new markets led to the push for what was termed a 'Greater East-Asian Co-Prosperity Sphere', a concept created by the Japanese government and military in order to create a bloc of Asian nations led by the Japanese: William de Bary, *Sources of East Asian Tradition: The Modern Period* (2008) 622.

of the Red Army all forces on land, at sea, and in the air ... under German control'.[54] It is worth noting that (similarly to the Japanese instrument of surrender) the German instrument of surrender was drawn up in English, Russian, and German, but specifically states that '[t]he English and Russian are the only authentic texts'.[55] Legal instruments of the Middle Ages, and indeed, even the Treaties of Westphalia, were drawn up in more than one language and all were declared authentic. The modern practice of claiming a distinction between authentic and inauthentic text is a neo-colonial one, and points to a deeper anxiety relating to the founding authority of their secular jurisdiction.

On the same day that the instrument of surrender was signed, Grand Admiral Karl Doenitz, President of the German Reich (his promotion following Adolf Hitler's suicide) broadcast a radio address to the 'German men and women':

> When ... the Fuehrer had appointed me his successor, I said that my foremost task was to save the lives of the German people. In order to achieve this goal, I ordered the German High Command ... to sign the unconditional surrender for all fronts ... The unity of state and party does not exist any more ... All of us have to face a difficult path. We have to walk it with dignity, courage and discipline which those demand of us who sacrificed their all for us ... Without this unity we shall not be able to overcome the misery of the times to come ... On this thorny path, which we all will have to tread ...[56]

Doenitz begins this brief address by conjuring an image of himself as the saviour of the 'German people', with whom he will tread a 'thorny path' of misery. Thus inscribing the act of unconditional surrender with the trope of Christian sacrifice, Karl Doenitz offers up the fragmented body of 'state and party', symbolized by his own, as the sacrifice for German lives, alongside the war dead. The German surrender story is re-inscribed here

[54] *Instrument of Surrender of all German Forces to the Supreme Commander of the Allied Expeditionary Force, General Dwight D. Eisenhower, and to the Supreme High Command of the Red Army*, Berlin, 8 May 1945.

[55] Ibid.

[56] Grand Admiral Karl Doenitz, President of the German Reich, 'Radio Address to the German People on the Unconditional Surrender of Germany' (Speech delivered at Flensburg, 8 May 1945).

from defeat to unconditional sacrifice and thereby maintains in perpetuity the promise of salvation. Immediately following Doenitz's address, President Truman also broadcast a radio address in the United States:

> This is a solemn but a glorious hour ... We can repay the debt which we owe to our God, to our dead, and to our children only by work ... We must work to bind up the wounds of a suffering world—to build an abiding peace, a peace rooted in justice and in law. We can build such a peace only by hard, toilsome, painstaking work ...
>
> The Allied armies, through sacrifice and devotion and with God's help, have wrung from Germany a final and unconditional surrender. The western world has been freed of the evil forces which ... have imprisoned the bodies and broken the lives of millions upon millions of free-born men. They have violated their churches, destroyed their homes, corrupted their children, and murdered their loved ones.
>
> I, Harry S. Truman, President of the United States of America, do hereby appoint Sunday, May 13, 1945, to be a day of prayer. I call upon the people of the United States, whatever their faith, to unite in offering joyful thanks to God for the victory we have won and to pray that He will ... guide us into the way of peace.[57]

Mirroring his speech at the opening of the UN conference on international organization, the address reiterates the new story of sacrifice, debt, work, and peace. What is interesting here is the sleight of hand whereby the nation's debt (as well as the debt of the 'millions of free-born men') to the war dead is described as a sacrifice for 'justice/peace/law'. For this, God himself helped defeat the 'evil powers', which created a debt which can only be repaid through work—through the creation and trade of surplus. This debt is an infinite one (as the relation of state to both the transcendental and the dead is experienced as infinite) and requires an infinite increase in both production and reproduction in order to guarantee (the promise of) unconditional life. Unrestricted trade (of goods and services between men) therefore creates the conditions whereby the divine debt can be continuously repaid; where both debt and exchange are enabled to increase infinitely.

Some months after Germany's surrender, a conference was held between the three heads of government: the USSR, the US,

[57] Ibid.

and the UK. The 'Berlin Conference', as it was called, was held between 17 July and 2 August and resulted in a document known as the *Potsdam Proclamation*. The proclamation outlined the principles under which Germany was to be governed by the occupiers: namely, the 'complete disarmament and demilitarization of Germany and the elimination or control of all German industry that could be used for military production'.[58] This included controlling 'all economic and financial international transactions including exports and imports, with the aim of preventing Germany from developing a war potential'.[59] The demilitarization and deindustrialization of Germany went hand in hand with a system of mass re-education '[t]o convince the German people that their own ruthless warfare ... [has] destroyed the German economy and made chaos and suffering inevitable'[60] and 'to make possible the successful development of democratic ideas'.[61] This total crushing of Germany, both ideologically and economically, was to be undertaken in view of the 'eventual reconstruction of German political life on a democratic basis and for eventual peaceful cooperation in international life'.[62] Ironically, the systemic reorganization of Germany (including the reorganization of the juridical system) and re-education of its citizens was to be carried out in the name of 'democracy, of justice under law, and of equal rights for all citizens without distinction of race, nationality or religion'.[63]

The changes outlined in the *Potsdam Proclamation* were carried out almost immediately, until nearly one year later when the balance of world power began to shift. The perceived threat of communism throughout Europe and in key East Asian states led to a radical rethinking of the US relation with Europe, and specifically, the principles under which occupied Germany was governed. On 6 September 1946, the new Secretary of State J.F. Byrnes unveiled a restatement of policy on Germany in Stuttgart. The Marshall Plan, as it became known, began with an acknowledgement: 'We have learned, whether we like it or not, that we live in one world, from which world we cannot isolate

[58] *Potsdam Proclamation*, 'Political Principles', 3(i).
[59] Ibid., 3(d). [60] Ibid., 3(d) (ii). [61] Ibid., 7.
[62] Ibid., 3(iv). [63] Ibid., 8.

ourselves.'[64] Byrnes continues: 'We have learned that ... our peace and well-being cannot be purchased at the price of peace or the well-being of any other country.'[65] The second stumbling block is revealed; 'peace' is conditional upon being universally available. 'The principal purposes of the military occupation,'[66] proclaims the Secretary of State, 'were and are to demilitarize and de-Nazify Germany but not raise artificial barriers to the efforts of the German people to resume their peacetime economic life ...'[67] Here, the Potsdam story is retold using a new phrase, the 'peacetime economy' which Byrnes assures the world 'will give [the German people] the opportunity to show themselves worthy of the respect and friendship of peace-loving nations, and in time, to take an honorable place among members of the United Nations'.[68] Through participation in the world economy, Germans could make themselves 'worthy' of friendship, following which the necessary honour of membership will be bestowed. Byrnes ends with a succinct reiteration of the central themes: 'The American people want to help the German people to win their way back to an honorable place among the free and peace-loving nations of the world.'[69] This speech offering the gift of friendship and entry into the economy, addressed directly to the German people, neatly summarizes the problem of secular modernity and the international law response. An even starker example of this is the Japanese surrender, which additionally reveals the fraternal structure (and consequent subjugation of its binary opposite, the concept of the feminine) upon which 'peace' and 'justice' are based.

In June 1947 the then US Secretary of State George Marshall gave an address to the graduating class at Harvard University:

> The truth of the matter is that Europe's requirements for the next three or four years of foreign food and other essential products ... are so much greater than her present ability to pay ... Aside from the demoralizing effect on the world at large and the desperation of the people concerned, the consequences to the economy of the United States should be apparent to all. It is logical that the United States should do whatever it is able to do to assist in the return of normal economic health in the world,

[64] United States Secretary of State J.F. Byrnes, 'Restatement of Policy on Germany' (Speech delivered at Stuttgart, 6 September 1946).
[65] Ibid. [66] Ibid. [67] Ibid. [68] Ibid. [69] Ibid.

without which there can be no political stability and no assured peace. Our policy is directed not against any country or doctrine but against hunger, poverty, desperation, and chaos. Its purpose should be the revival of a working economy in the world so as to permit the emergence of political and social conditions in which free institutions can exist ...[70]

In the face of a Europe devastated by war, Marshall's gesture does more than notify the country's future political and economic leaders that aid will be given to overseas recipients. Rather, it ties 'political stability' to 'economic health', whereby United States' policy will create conditions in which 'free institutions can exist' to 'revive a working economy' and rid the world of 'desperation' and 'chaos'. The promise of perpetual peace is firmly bound to the fantasy of free (self-authorizing) institutions that at the same time are able to maintain their fraternal contract through a 'healthy' fluid economy of goods.

4.2.2 Japan's surrender

We see a similar story in relation to Japan. In 1941, after the Casablanca Conference and before the creation of the United Nations, the United States was attacked on home soil by the Japanese. The then President of the US proclaimed that the attacks marked 'the climax of a decade of international immorality'.[71] His radio address proceeded as follows:

I have prepared the full record of our past relations with Japan, and it will be submitted to the Congress. It begins with the visit of Commodore Perry to Japan 88 years ago. It ends with the visit of two Japanese emissaries to the Secretary of State last Sunday, an hour after Japanese forces had loosed their bombs and machine guns against our flag, our forces, and our citizens.[72]

The President evoked an obligation 'to our dead' as well as a 'sacred obligation to their children and our children'[73] not to

[70] Secretary of State George Marshall gave this address to the graduating class of Harvard University on 5 June 1947. Standing on the steps of Memorial Church in Harvard Yard, he outlined the US government's preparedness to contribute to European recovery after the Second World War.

[71] Franklin D. Roosevelt, 'Radio Address' (Broadcast from the Whitehouse delivered 9 December 1941).

[72] Ibid. [73] Ibid.

forget the attack, a moment which offered the nation a founding violence upon which to expand its jurisdiction (albeit in secular form) outside its territorial borders.

The demand for surrender was drafted by the Allied powers pursuant to an agreement made at Potsdam following the unconditional surrender of Nazi Germany and issued on the 26 July. The US call for unconditional surrender begins with the threat of almighty force ('the threshold of annihilation' and 'complete destruction of the Japanese armed forces') and salvation ('the path of reason'); 'a new order of peace, security and justice', and demands the 'revival and strengthening of democratic tendencies among the Japanese people' and the establishment of 'fundamental human rights'. It ends with the promise that 'eventual Japanese participation in world trade relations shall be permitted' once Japan emerges as 'peaceful and productive' people. It also promises that when they have a 'responsible government' that is the 'freely expressed will of the people', it will be 'permitted' into the international Allied fraternity. Japan, as evidenced in these texts, was the quintessential patient of what Upendra Baxi identifies as 'Operation Infinite Justice/ Enduring Freedom'.[74] The ultimatum was rejected by Japan on 29 July; on 6 and 9 August the United States dropped atomic bombs on Hiroshima and Nagasaki, respectively. On 15 August, Japan capitulated.

It was the Emperor himself who decided to break precedent and speak, for the first time in history, directly to his subjects. He completed the text of the declaration of surrender close to midnight and recorded it on a Japanese phonograph the next day. There were two attempts by Japanese military leaders to prevent the recording from being broadcast—once at the Emperor's palace (the recording was smuggled out in a laundry basket), and again at the radio station. The coups were both unsuccessful, and the recording was aired. John Dower notes that '[d]espite its chaotic genesis, the rescript emerged as a polished ideological gem'.[75] Here is the one of

[74] Upendra Baxi, 'Operation Enduring Freedom' in Anghie Antony, Chimni Bhupinder, and Mickelson Karin et al. (eds), *The Third World and International Order: Law, Politics and Globalization* (2003) 41.

[75] John Dower, *Embracing Defeat: Japan in the Wake of WWII* (2000) 35.

several versions of the speech, called the *Gyokuon Hoso*, (literally, 'Jewel Voice Broadcast'):

My subjects, I have ordered the Imperial Government
To inform the Joint Governments of the United States, Great Britain, China and the Soviet Union
That our Empire is willing to accept the provisions of their Joint Declaration
In addition, the enemy has recently used a most cruel explosive,
The frequent killing of innocents and the effect of destitution it entails
Are incalculable
The thought of our Imperial subjects dying in the battlefields
Pains my heart and body to the point of fragmentation
I am willing to endure the unendurable,
Tolerate the intolerable,
For peace to last thousands of generations
We must rally the nation
And continue from generation to generation
To entrench the imperishability of this sacred state[76]

The sovereign's speech was the diction of law, a juris-diction.[77] As such the Emperor, by recording and broadcasting his voice throughout Japan, re-transcribed the *Empire* Japan as the *Nation* Japan. In a single act, the Emperor simultaneously performed an unconditional surrender and re-marked his territory by restating sovereign jurisdiction on and in Western terms—by speaking directly to the people. Promising a future of perpetual peace, the Emperor's speech signified not only a transformation of Japan from Empire into Nation, but presented it as a rebirth.

Delivered in archaic aristocratic Japanese over crackly airwaves, the speech was not immediately understood by the public, although subsequently, particular phrases became 'locked in popular consciousness'.[78] The Emperor proposes that by accepting the

[76] Imperial Rescript on the Termination of the War (*Daitōa-sensō-shūketsu-no-shōsho*).

[77] Costas Douzinas, 'Speaking Law: On Bare Theological and Cosmopolitan Sovereignty' in Anne Orford (ed.), *International Law and its Others* (2006) 41: 'Jurisdiction speaks the law: it is juris diction, the diction of law, law's speech and word.'

[78] Dower, above n. 75, 4.

'terms of surrender', there would be a perpetual peace. He offers himself up as the sacrifice for this peace, exclaiming that his body is torn to the 'point of fragmentation'. In doing so the Emperor does not absolve himself of war responsibility, but rather, proclaims an absolute and unconditional responsibility—quote, for 'the whole of humanity'. 'Endure the unendurable', he says; 'tolerate the intolerable'—it appears as if this is the aporetic moment of law par excellence; what Jacques Derrida calls an unconditionality of the ethical act at its purest.[79] This act—which perhaps we could characterize as an act of hospitality (to use Derrida's term) is offered by the Emperor by mortgaging of part of his body (the Emperor's voice) for the whole (the Nation's body).[80] The Emperor's capacity to act as a 'host' (for the victorious occupying forces; for Western, secular, democratic, neoliberal ideology) thus relies on his concomitant existence as hostage (interestingly, an etymologically related term),[81] hence exposing the speaker's body to the risk of fragmentation.[82] In real terms, the Emperor had to

[79] Jacques Derrida, 'The University without Condition' in *Without Alibi* (Peggy Kamuf trans., 2002 edn) [trans. of: *Etats d'âme de psychanalyse*, 2000] 202–37, as referenced in Costas Douzinas, 'Speaking Law: On Bare Theological and Cosmopolitan Sovereignty' in Orford (ed.), *International Law and its Others*, above n. 78, 37). In thinking about unconditionality, I turn to unconditional hospitality and unconditional forgiveness, two terms that arise again and again in discussions within critical legal theory, and each addressed by Derrida. The Emperor's oath to account for, endure and tolerate the 'incalculable', 'unendurable', and 'intolerable' hints at the unimodular structure of sovereignty.

[80] Douzinas, above n. 77, 43: 'The confusion, the rolling together through the rhetorical figure of metalepsis ([where] the part stands in for the whole) is implicit in the nature of all jurisdiction and not only in constitution-making after revolutionary upheavals.'

[81] (1) 'Person who receives guests' *c.*1290, from O.Fr. hoste 'guest, host' (12.c); (2) 'Animal or plant having a parasite' *c.*1857; (3) 'Guest, enemy' from O.E. gaest, giest; (4) 'Multitude' from M.L. hostis 'army, war-like expedition'; (5) 'Body of Christ, consecrated bread' *c.*1303, from L. hostia 'sacrifice'. Interestingly, the word 'hostage' derives from the Latin obsidanus, 'condition of being held as security': Ernest Weekley, *An Etymological Dictionary of Modern English* 1 (1967) 729. This rich etymological heritage shows that security has always taken the form of a corporeal guarantee, and that the sacrificial being is inextricably tied together with the very life that it guarantees: enemy is guest, is host, receiver, and received.

[82] Fragmentation between host and hostage; between voice and body; between sacred and the profane.

sacrifice his sacred body in order to preserve his material (human) one, and he had to submit both to the service of the new Nation.

Calling upon an ancestral past and promising a future of perpetual peace, the Emperor's speech invoked the re-birth of a nation always-already formed[83] and attempted to establish a secular sovereign jurisdiction over Japan, before and beyond that of the victors. It was at this moment, 'sentimental royalists would soon put it, [that people actually heard] the sovereign's true voice ... It was "as if the sun had at long last emerged from behind the dark clouds" '.[84] One way of understanding this act of speech, then, is to think of it as a resistance against the call for unconditional surrender. In this reading, the Emperor performs a sleight of hand and re-marks his territory by restating sovereign jurisdiction on Western terms.[85]

There is, however, more to this story. The Emperor's move remakes his territory and re-establishes power (albeit on Western terms), without losing at any point his position as the privileged signifier. Whilst mimicking a language of unconditional hospitality ('to bear the unbearable', 'to tolerate the intolerable'), the Emperor obscures a dual operation: first, that the unconditional hospitality he offers is pegged to the always already hosting or hostage bodies of his subjects and the victims of Japanese colonization, and second, that the image of the new nation he promises—the Emperor's new body—is conditional upon entry into the fantasy of the fraternal relation.

[83] Douzinas, above n. 77, 40: 'There is no community without jurisdiction, since it comes together in the speaking of the law. We can call this the minimal expression of community, the zero degree of sovereignty or bare sovereignty.' See also Michael Hardt and Antonio Negri, *Empire* (2000) at 101:

> Identity is thus conceived not as the resolution of social and historical differences but as the product of a primordial unity. The nation is a complete figure of sovereignty prior to historical development, or better, there is no historical development that is not already prefigured in the origin. In other words, the nation sustains the concept of sovereignty by claiming to precede it.

The nation, in other words, is the bourgeoise's solution to the democratic deficit of sovereignty.

[84] Dower, above n. 75, 37.

[85] Not only in capitulating to the terms of unconditional surrender, but by speaking, as in the Roman law tradition, directly to the people.

By 'fraternal relation' I refer to the story of the modern international order, which is imagined as a story of nation-states comprising relations between men: of fathers, of sons, and of brothers.[86] This is a story that I have discussed at some length in the previous chapter. The United States' offer to spare Japan from annihilation was made only on the condition of Japan's subsequent integration in fraternal exchange called the international economy. The desire of sovereigns for a whole, white, clean-and-proper body, a priori, is manifest in these particular texts as the positioning of the US and Japan as what in today's vocabulary is called 'developed' as compared to 'developing'-countries who are written as nonetheless traversing a trajectory towards the same-yet-infinitely-retreating object of desire.[87]

Shortly following the surrender on 7 September 1945 the Emperor presented himself at the occupation force headquarters, saying: 'I come to you, General Macarthur, to offer myself to the judgment of the powers you represent as the one to bear sole responsibility for every political and military decision made.'[88] 'A tremendous impression swept me', wrote General Macarthur later in his journal. 'This courageous assumption of a responsibility implicit with death, a responsibility clearly belied by facts of which I was fully aware, moved me to the very marrow of my bones.'[89] Faced with Hirohito's Abrahamic gesture of unconditional hospitality (to sacrifice his body to save his skin) the Christian General granted a double salvation: he spared the body

[86] See, for example, David Kennedy, above n. 13, 16.

[87] There is an extensive literature in international law and development, as well as in post-colonial studies, on the dynamic and power relations between 'developed' and 'developing' countries. I have referred in an earlier footnote to the work of Antony Anghie (on the colonial history of international law) and the work of Edward Said (on the hierarchies of Orientalist ideology). Luce Irigaray describes this beautifully in terms of gendered metaphysics, in *Speculum of the Other Woman* (Gillian G. Gill trans., 1985 edn) [trans. of: *Speculum de l'autre femme*, 1984] 293: '[man] will only be able to move close to the infinite or away from it in asymptomatic fashion, by more or less good, true, enlightened visions, by more or less harmonious numerical relationships, by more or less appropriate language.' She also describes this state of being as a 'search for more and more copies of the same' (291).

[88] Kyōko Inoue, *MacArthur's Japanese Constitution: a Linguistic and Cultural Study of its Making* (1991) 162.

[89] Ibid.

of the Emperor in exchange for his faith. A few months later in January 1946, Hirohito, at the direction of the head of the occupying forces General Macarthur, renounced his divine ancestry in another radio transmission to the people. In this pronouncement Hirohito states:

> The ties between us and our people have always stood upon mutual trust and affection ... They are not predicated on the false conception that the Emperor is divine ... [Appealing to] 'the desires of the people' [he declares that] 'a bright future will undoubtedly be ours, not only for our country, but for the whole humanity'.[90]

Here, 'the people' are named the objects of war; however, peace is not described as having been brought about by their sacrifice. Rather than recognizing the people as victims to be venerated, the Emperor has already substituted his own 'fragmented body' in the initial broadcast. In the second broadcast, he sacrifices his feminine divinity—the goddess Amaterasu, who functions as the origin myth of Japan up until this moment. Furthermore, future violence is mitigated and a 'bright future' ensured by creating a harmonious brotherhood. The secularization of the sovereign's body and democratization of the state initiated in this speech is predicated upon 'mutual affection' within the fraternal relation that then stands in for 'the whole humanity'.

Consequently, the reply to the demands amounts to a confession,[91] with an exchange of the part (the word) for the whole (a secular body).[92] What begins as a religious conflict between the two states is transformed into an exchange of desire for mutual fraternal recognition of their respective possessions and

[90] Imperial Rescript on National Revitalisation (*Nentō, Kokuun Shinkō no Shōsho*) (1946).

[91] See Jennifer Beard, *The Political Economy of Desire: International Law, Development and the Nation State* (2007) 27–52 where the author undertakes a detailed discussion of the 'mimetic traces' of the practices of religious confession on western discourses of development (of colonized nations).

[92] Hardt and Negri, above n. 83, 94–5:

> The transformation of the absolutist and patrimonial model consisted in a gradual process that replaced the theological foundations of territorial patrimony with a new foundation that was equally transcendent. The spiritual identity of the nation rather than the divine body of the king now posed the territory and population as an ideal abstraction.

occupations of land. Sacrifice of the divine office, both by the US and by Japan, enables the rearticulation of authority over the subjects of both states by the Emperor-turned head of state.

This resurrection of sovereignty through the act of Imperial speech, the re-appropriation of the language of nation and empire, and the repositioning of Japan from the role of 'occupier' to 'occupied', signifies the beginning of Japan's re-writing of post-war history, 'where issues of war responsibility have more often than not deflected and bypassed the questions of Japanese colonialism'.[93] This was possible, as another commentator notes, because 'Japanese nationalism itself could accommodate US imperial nationalism, or even be an organ thereof'.[94] The 'purification and sanitisation of the social body',[95] performed through Hirohito's exchange of divine body and office for entry into the white fraternity simultaneously enabled the preservation of the discourse of 'nation' within Japan and the creation of a new discourse of the state.

This same moment is similarly related by the Russian director Alexander Sokurov in his 2004 film *Solnze* (The Sun), where one scene depicts the character of the Japanese Emperor standing in the garden of the Imperial Palace after Japan's unconditional surrender. Posing for US wartime photographers, Hirohito begins to mimic the American mime Charlie Chaplin, seemingly subverting

There is one interpretation of this pronouncement which argues that renunciation of divinity was not the purpose of the rescript, but rather, that the Emperor wished to emphasize the existence of Japan's democratic nature prior to the occupation (during the Meiji era): See Dower, above n. 75, 314. This argument, however, merely supports my proposition that the renunciation as such was not undertaken with the purpose of absolving the Emperor of power, but rather, to rearticulate and redefine the foundation of sovereign authority.

[93] Ching Leo, 'Give Me Japan and Nothing Else!: Postcoloniality, Identity, and the Traces of Colonialism' in Tomiko Yoda and Harry Harootunion (eds), *Japan after Japan: Social and Cultural Life from the Recessionary 1990s to the Present* (2006) 147–8.

[94] 'Even today, Japanese nationalists are incapable of confronting the complicity between their nationalism and US hegemony ... they would never be able to engage in serious negotiation with people in East and Southeast Asia who were directly victimized by ... Japanese imperial nationalism.' Sakai Naoki, '"You Asians": On the Historical Role of the West and Asia Binary' in Tomiko Yoda and Harry Harootunion, ibid. 186–7.

[95] Todorov Tzvetan, 'In Search of Lost Crime' *The New Republic* (2001) 29 January, 30.

their orientalizing gaze. It may be helpful at this point to refer to Homi Bhabha's discussion of colonial imitation:

> It is ... this area between mimicry and mockery, where the reforming, civilising mission is threatened by the displacing gaze of its disciplinary double ... Mimicry does not merely destroy narcissistic authority through the repetitious slippage of difference and desire. It is the process of the fixation of the colonial as a form of cross-classificatory, discriminatory knowledge within an interdictory discourse ... The ambivalence of colonial authority repeatedly turns from mimicry—a difference that is almost nothing but not quite—to menace—a difference that is almost total but not quite.[96]

For Bhabha, inherent in the mimicry of the colonizer is a potential for the 'displacing gaze': a potential to unsettle, if not emancipate, the mimic. In Sokurov's scopic exchange, however, parody becomes pastiche,[97] and the director's keen observation produces later scenes of fraternal intimacy between Emperor Hirohito and General Macarthur, which reveal the emptiness of that earlier exchange, devoid of the satirical impulse.

The substitution of the 'fragmented body' of the sovereign as the symbolic sacrifice obscures the structural sacrifice of a relation to the maternal feminine, as both states 'now work towards love of mankind'. The United States' demand for the Emperor's surrender of divine authority can be interpreted as being a demand for surrender of the maternal divinity and maternal origin—a surrender of the Emperor's claimed ancestor, the sun goddess Amaterasu. The prophecy of 'a bright future' will indeed be revealed as the Emperor ascends out of the ashes to bask in the s(p)ecular image of a body a priori, complete, in time and space. This is a masculine body. What we see here is the reincarnation of the divine

[96] Homi Bhabha, 'Of Mimicry and Man: The Ambivalence of Colonial Discourse' in *The Location of Culture* (1994) 85–92.

[97] Fredric Jameson terms 'pastiche' a blank parody:

> Pastiche is, like parody, the imitation of a peculiar or unique, idiosyncratic style, the wearing of a linguistic mask, speech in a dead language. But it is a neutral practice of such mimicry, without any of parody's ulterior motives, amputated of the satiric impulse, devoid of laughter ...

Fredric Jameson, *Postmodernism, or, the Cultural Logic of Late Capitalism* (1991) 16–17.

corporeal guarantor as secular phallic avatar within the mimetic discursive economy, precluding any recognition of the origin(al) sacrifice. Through phōne (sound, voice), the avatar's jurisdiction enables the remaking of territory in his (mirror) image: Hirohito ascends from his cavernous bunker after renouncing his maternal divinity—to speak as the Father of a new nation.[98]

Following the United States' 'occupation' of Japan, the Emperor was not brought to trial, but rather, was made to renounce his divine origins. He was transformed from a sovereign head of state into a symbolic one: from a divine sovereign into a so-called secular one. Since 1945 there has been much debate amongst lawyers, historians, and Japanologists as to why the Emperor was not prosecuted for war crimes. The question of Emperor Hirohito's war responsibility is one that has been shielded from public inquiry, for the most part, since the Second World War. Recently, however, this has changed, with scholars and politicians aligning themselves with either one or another view on Hirohito's accountability. The dominant school of thought proposes that the Supreme Commander General Douglas MacArthur 'saved' Hirohito to preserve public order within newly occupied Japan.[99] According to MacArthur's memoirs, the Emperor took full responsibility for the consequences of the war, and when the Australian representative to the United Nations War Crimes Commission indicated that he would introduce a motion to prosecute Hirohito, the Commander sent a telegram to Eisenhower saying that the Emperor was the symbol of Japanese unity, and that, if he were prosecuted, the nation would disintegrate.[100]

The issue, however, extends beyond a simple debate as to whether Hirohito had knowledge of the army's activities,

[98] This is not, of course, to suggest that Japan was in any way 'feminine' or 'feminist' in orientation—indeed, it was hyper-masculine in its military effort. However, Japan nonetheless did subscribe to the idea of a maternal origin (of the land; of its culture) which was publicly renounced in order for the Emperor to emerge as a male figure *without origin*; existing in a symbolic domain only insofar as he was recognized as part of a new global fraternity.

[99] See, for example, Dower, above n. 75 and Herbert P. Bix, *Hirohito and the Making of Modern Japan* (2001).

[100] Rudolf V.A. Janssens, *What Future for Japan?* (1995) 394–5.

and whether he was or should be responsible for war crimes. I argue that despite their demand for unconditional surrender and subsequent claim of debellatio, the Allied forces chose to retain the Emperor (albeit as a symbol rather than as an official sovereign head of state)[101] because they needed Japan to enter the emerging fraternity of states as a secular entity; an equal among brothers capable of recognizing its others and of being sutured into the new international economic system. The analysis undertaken here adds to existing analyses of the changing geopolitics of the time by developing a psychosocial reading of the surrender. It does so by focusing on the expression, by sovereigns and their representatives, of their own and their nations' physiology.

What appears merely to be a reprieve from (or missed opportunity for) prosecution, in fact signifies a critical moment in the history of international law. The founding of an emerging order is enacted in a spectacular form as the Emperor's two bodies (material and symbolic, temporal and atemporal) are saved in the name of perpetual peace, subsumed into the so-called secular fraternity. Within a (feminist) psychoanalytic idiom, moreover, it is possible to read the Emperor's fragmenting body as a symptom of anxiety that resists such easy commerce in this moment of colonial and patriarchal complicity. If we reformulate Freud's account of anxiety as arising from separation from the mother, and Lacan's definition of anxiety as arising from a lack of that separation (i.e. the inability to differentiate between one's own bodily boundaries and those of the mother), then we arrive at a subject torn between loss and the threat of non-differentiation.

4.2.3 Freedom from fear and freedom from want

Such tension is characteristic of international law, which fails to establish a discourse of separateness (for a particular-yet-connected experience of being). Freedom from fear, and freedom from want: the new international law promises human

[101] This in fact mirrored the Emperor's traditional role, where s/he would act as a symbolic head of state, not directly involved in politics and the day-to-day running of the country.

life without condition. International law grounds our humanity by using the sovereign state as its guarantee for our transubstantiation from material (beings indistinguishable from animal) to metaphysical (beings endowed with a humanness that transcends the individual creature). If international law is understood to be the technology of modern human life *par excellence*, what we see in the texts of the German and Japanese surrenders is a problem that lies at the heart of this invention—a problem of reproduction, whereby international law competes with other technologies to guarantee the production of humanness. Furthermore, we can see that it suffers from potentially conflicting loyalties, to the state and to the individual. The following poem is a collage of text from Truman's call for, and the Emperor's answer to, unconditional surrender. It seeks to make evident the convergence in ideology between the two enemies:

Incalculable
The killing of innocents
Of this sacred state
A statement of terms
There are no alternatives
We brook no delay
Most cruel explosive
Pains my body
To the point of fragmentation
Unconditional
The time has come for Japan
The path of reason
Peoples of the world
In fraternal contention
New order of peace
Tolerate the intolerable
For peace
To last thousands of generations
On a world conquest
The Empire of Japan
The United States[102]

[102] This poem is a collage of original text from the call and answer to unconditional surrender.

5

UNCONDITIONAL LIFE

International law came into its own in 1941, with Franklin D. Roosevelt's call for 'freedom from want' (referring to 'economic understandings which will secure to every nation a healthy peacetime life for its inhabitants—everywhere in the world') and 'freedom from fear' (referring to 'world-wide reduction of armaments to such a point ... that no nation will be in a position to commit an act of physical aggression against any neighbor').[1] These two of Roosevelt's famous 'four freedoms' (the other two were 'freedom of speech' and 'freedom of worship') were to ground the United Nations, at least according to the US Secretary of State at the time, at the San Francisco conference where the new global organization was founded in June 1945:

> The battle of peace has to be fought on two fronts. The first is the security front where victory spells freedom from fear. The second is the economic and social front where victory means freedom from want. Only victory on both fronts can assure the world of an enduring peace.[2]

These twinned freedoms of international law—freedom from want and from fear—were compelling because they gave some credence to the idea that I call an 'unconditional human life', whereby death and desire could be controlled through the institution of a global economic and military compact.

The first part of this chapter, 'Further, Faster, Deeper, and Cheaper' looks at some examples of how public language emerging out of the Cold War builds on this idea of unconditional life. These texts are largely concerned with the organization of a new global economy, and appear to rely on a rhetorical calculation and acceleration of *time* to distinguish secular humanness from

[1] Franklin D. Roosevelt, 'State of the Union Address to the Congress' (Speech delivered to the United States Congress, Washington, 6 January 1941).

[2] Cited in the UN Development Programme's 'Human Development Report 1994: New Dimensions of Human Security' (1994). The words are attributed to Edward R. Stettinius Jr., who subsequently became the first US ambassador to the United Nations.

the divine realm, which is *timeless*. My analysis shows how because the logical conclusion of an accelerated technology is the endangerment of biological human life, language in the international domain encounters an impasse, or what can be described as a 'crisis of modern nihilism'. The second part of this chapter, 'An Economy of Human Time: *Nuclear Weapons* and *EC–Biotech* Revisited' returns to our initial cases to discuss how this crisis manifests, examining the inability of the Court and the Panel to choose between the mutually constitutive bodies of the sovereign state and the biological human, and between international law and other technologies. I argue that this inability to choose is essentially a problem of production: international lawyers are responsible for guaranteeing the reproduction of humanness using international law as a technology, but are unable to do so within the eschatological constraints of post-war public discourse identified in the previous two chapters.

5.1 FURTHER, FASTER, DEEPER, AND CHEAPER

On the back of the Second World War, the Soviet Union and the United States launched a military and economic rivalry that would see the proliferation of new weapons systems and the commencement of proxy wars in third countries. This rivalry came to be known as the Cold War, during which the codex of international law expanded dramatically. The vanquished and domesticated nations of Germany and Japan were now subsumed within the 'civilized family of states', and the dream of an expansive international domain united in commerce was pursued with vigour by the Allied nations.[3]

The fall of the Berlin Wall punctuated the end of the Cold War and with it, the dissipation of a tension that had defined state relations for much of the century. While the risk of total violence (in war) and contamination (through trade) was contained in a discourse of unconditional fraternity up until the peace treaties following the Second World War, the end of the Cold War dissolved the enemy threat which Western political rhetoric had been

[3] For a mainstream account of the Cold War, see David Painter, *The Cold War: An International History* (1999).

reliant upon to give definition to its own territorial boundaries.[4] The most immediate response to the end of the Cold War was a declaration of a victorious 'revolution' for Western liberal democracy and the opening up of other state bodies—other economies.

5.1.1 *A democratic evolution ... and free market miracles*

In a 1988 address on foreign policy the United States President Ronald Reagan announced:

> This democratic revolution has been accompanied by a change in economic thinking comparable to the Newtonian revolution in physics, and that is no accident. Free-market economies have worked miracles in several nations of East Asia. A U.N. General Assembly special session on Africa has called for more market-oriented structural reform in that region ... even in China and the Soviet *Union* the theoretical underpinnings of Socialist economics are being reexamined ...[5]

Tying the scientific revolution to divine miracle and then to 'economic thinking', Reagan's speech invokes what Anne Orford calls the God/Market.[6] Since the Cold War period in particular, this new transcendental entity—the market—has been called upon to set up new relations between states based on the consolidation of territorial bodies and the smooth movement of goods between them. In this world, '[n]ormal trade is open ... diversified, developed ... Everything else, subsidies, dumping, cartels, dependence, instability, state trading, underdevelopment, undue vulnerability to imports ... is abnormal.'[7] The public discourse around this expansion is exemplified in the writings of *New York Times* columnist Thomas Friedman, who draws a parallel between metabolic and technological movement:

> [T]he inexorable integration of markets, nation-states, and technologies to a degree never witnessed before—in a way that is enabling *individuals*,

[4] In Carl Schmitt, *The Nomos of the Earth in the International Law of Jus Publicum Europaeum* (G.L. Ulmen trans., 2003 edn.) 126–7 [trans. of: *Der Nomos der Erde*, 1950] and Jacques Derrida, *The Politics of Friendship* (George Collins trans., 1997 edn.) [trans. of: *Politiques de l'amitié*, 1994].

[5] Ronald Reagan, 'Address on Foreign Policy' (Speech delivered at Cabell Hall, University of Virginia, Charlottesville, 16 December 1988).

[6] Anne Orford, 'Beyond Harmonization: Trade, Human Rights and the Economy of Sacrifice' 18 *Leiden Journal of International Law* 2005, 179–213.

[7] Ibid., 10.

corporations and nation-states to reach around the world farther, faster, deeper and cheaper than ever before ... the spread of free-market capitalism to virtually every country in the world.[8]

'Individuals, corporations and nation-states' are figured here as bodies that *move, extend*, and *penetrate*—one presumes—other bodies. The parallel that Friedman draws between corporeal and technological movement demonstrates the pervasiveness of this kind of discourse, where production and profit is premised on the conquest of time and space: further, faster, deeper, and cheaper. The French theorist Paul Virilio also describes the merging of political entities in terms of a metabolic and technological movement:

I believe we're heading towards universality. The universe-city; the universal city. The fact that today we have ... NATO, *SEATO*, the Warsaw Pact, etc.—to my mind, all of this has been outmoded by a kind of universal State, a State in its pure form which is the result of Pure War ... Capitalist and Communist ideologies are themselves being superseded by this vision of the world.[9]

He describes the dissolution of political blocs in the face of a vision of the world based on a universal, harmonized, non-differentiated space. In effect, the conquest of this space is determined by *speed*, a central notion for Virilio, whose work focuses on the degree to which physical territory is organized according to military and strategic imperatives. For Virilio, 'history progresses at the speed of its weapons systems'.[10] This notion that the speed of weapons deployment determines human history can surely be extended to argue that the speed of technology more generally has become, in late modernity, an important measure of human self-invention. Speed is an important measure of humanness, not least because it represents control over time itself,

[8] Thomas Friedman, *The Lexus and the Olive Tree* (1999) 7–8. This echoes another best-selling author, Francis Fukuyama's, more extravagant claim laid out in his book, *The End of History and the Last Man* (1992) to an evolutionarily inevitable triumph of political and economic liberalism.

[9] Paul Virilio and Sylvère Lotringer, *Pure War* (Mark Polizzotti trans., 2008) [trans. of: *La guerre pur*, 1983] 61.

[10] Paul Virilio, *Speed and Politics: An Essay on Dromology* (M. Polizzotti trans., 1986) [trans. of: *Vitesse et Politique: Essai de Dromologie*, 1977] 90.

by making it calculable in unitary terms and available for processing at ever-increasing rates.

Virilio's account of speed and its importance as a measure of technology that determines human life in the international domain is convincing, insofar as we can see how international law seeks to facilitate an infinitely increasing exchange of people and goods both in terms of time and volume. Similarly, David Kennedy cites one view of the international domain where 'technology and a naturally shrinking globe are creating a global economic area as a matter of fact, while the international political projects of regulation remain wedded to the false boundaries of state sovereignty'.[11] This takes Friedman's desire for speed to the next level, belying a fear/fantasy of the disappearance of state boundaries, so much so that the globe itself, 'naturally shrinking as a matter of fact', might disappear altogether.

This speed—at which men, without boundaries, will leave the material world altogether—has become a defining paradigm of international law following its so-called decolonization project of the post-war period. World unity, declares Virilio, 'is no longer a spatial unity'.[12] It is, rather, a unity defined by the rate at which humankind, 'inexorably interconnected' (inevitably in hierarchical networks and at different speeds) can move around the globe. The decline of territorial conquest in the name of unification during the post-war period necessitated a shift in the construction of material subjectivity for the sovereign state. Sovereignty had to be figured now, not only in terms of access to other bodies, but in terms of a metabolic *speed* of access.

5.1.2 *From animal organism to prosthetic god*

In a world where the efficacy of organizations and their ambit of control relies on the micromanagement of time, it is arguable that the key unit of measure of sovereign authority has shifted from marking distance primarily in spatial terms (extending power and knowledge over physical territory) to marking distance in temporal terms (extending power and knowledge

[11] David Kennedy, 'Receiving the International' 10(1) *Connecticut Journal of International Law* 1994, 117.

[12] Virilio and Lotringer, above n. 9, 127.

through speed of access and exploitation). Sovereign power is measured in terms of the seconds it takes for their military weapons to hit their target; financial power is determined primarily by the *speed* of transaction, rather than by the distance goods must be carried. The rate of this supplementation (time over space) seems to be in inverse relation to the ever-shrinking amount of conquerable land on earth, and it is tied inextricably to the growing dominance of computers and the Internet (as a discourse and as a framing logic).

The modern state, constituted by international law, is the focal point of these accelerating economies of war and trade. Through electronic capture (of rules, forms, legislation, and judgments) the state creates an orthographic memory: an archive at once invisible, at once able to be recollected. The promulgation of law takes place, no longer by means of sovereign speech or by notices pinned onto trees, but by written texts, and through the Internet. Legal precedent is no longer domiciled in dusty transcripts in library corners, but is now moving into digital reserve on databases, fluid in time and place.[13] This legal history and memory of the modern state is no longer only in one language, handwritten or typed onto paper, and filed at the court. Judgments are usually electronically produced, sometimes streamed live, and may be accessed from around the world. The rate of legal transplantation and transposition between states is increasing. As computer technologies too proliferate, the calculation of population statistics, the live capture of legal and illegal residents, metadata storage and analysis, the accuracy of military hardware, the production of judgments, and the rate of communication between states all become means to arriving at a utopic timelessness. Processing speed—in other words, an acceleration

[13] This is borne out by Stiegler, who describes this shift from the material to electronic transmission of information as follows: 'The difference between traditional societies and modern societies is characterized by the fact that, in the former, communicative action forms the basis of social authority (whether it be mythical, religious, or metaphysico-political), whereas in the latter, legitimation is dominated by technical and scientific rationality, which progressively spreads across all areas of life.' Bernard Stiegler, *Technics and Time, 1: The Fault of Epimetheus* (George Collins and Richard Beardsworth trans., 1998 edn) [trans. of: *La technique et le temps, 1: La faute d'Épiméthée*, 1994] 11.

of time—has in this way become an important end for sovereign power, with international lawyers the timekeepers of this chronological imaginary.[14]

This is important to our discussion of risk, since the political authority of sovereign states as the primary guarantors of human life is premised on their ability to make risk (the probability of loss over time) knowable and insurable. As Kessler argues, 'recent interest in risk ... points to an acceleration of time which transcends the confines of the vocabulary of norms [signifying] the emergence of a different rationality within the legal system ...'.[15] The acceleration of time, in other words, and particularly in the legal domain, is evidence of state desire to control (further, faster) both past and future. In this infinitely increasing economy, the paradox of speed emerges: in order for humans to *know* the future, technological risks must be accelerated to their limit, but in accelerating processes whereby risks may be expressed, human life itself is placed in danger. Such a process is described by Paul Virilio as 'liberation speed' that has 'attributes of the divine':[16] a speed that humankind will transcend its material conditions of existence altogether.

This paradox—thus framed by Virilio as an *eschatological* dilemma—is prefigured in the work of the philosophers discussed in Chapter 3. Freud expressed this paradox as an internal physiological struggle between death and desire (*Thanatos* and *Eros*) that emerges out of man's technological prowess and ability to 'exterminate one another to the last man'.[17] For Freud, man's creative and destructive power of invention is a phenomenon of a tension inherent in both the individual body and in human culture. This

[14] The term 'chronological imaginary' is used by Virilio and Lotringer, above n. 9, 81. In many important ways, of course, international lawyers are excluded from the production of this new world: they may not be consulted in various instances. Nonetheless, international lawyers are responsible for the creation and application of legal tests, processes, and concepts that have a material impact on the world.

[15] Oliver Kessler, 'Is Risk Changing the Politics of Legal Argumentation?' 21 *Leiden Journal of International Law* 2008, 863, 867.

[16] Virilio, above n. 10, 230.

[17] Sigmund Freud, *Civilisation and its Discontents* (1930) final paragraph [trans. of: *Das Unbehagen in der Kultur*, 1930].

tension, furthermore, arises out of a 'fairy tale wish' to transform from a 'feeble animal organism' into a 'prosthetic God':

> These things that, by his science and technology, man has brought about on this earth, on which he first appeared as a feeble animal *organism* and on which each individual of his species must once more make its entry as a helpless suckling—these things do not only sound like a fairy tale, they are an actual fulfilment of every—or of almost every—fairy tale wish ... Man has, as it were, become a kind of prosthetic God ...[18]

This idea of technology-as-secular-prosthesis is picked up in later decades by Jacques Derrida, and by Bernard Stiegler who identifies that at the core of this kind of thinking on technology is an essential *lack* that defines the human. While Benjamin, Schmitt, and Heidegger retain an opposition between 'technology' and of the 'human', Steigler dispenses with any distinction between the two, arguing that they are in fact co-emergent: we are only human insofar as we invent ourselves into existence, through supplementary prosthesis such as speech and writing.[19]

5.1.3 Ever-accelerating sovereign economies

The observation that technology evidences a creative capacity that defines our humanness is compelling, and yet incomplete. Man could indeed be defined by a powerlessness or lack that can be temporarily filled by prosthetic inventions, extending his power in the world. The goal that drives this activity, however—that of becoming God—is captured by a logic that we see played out in *Nuclear Weapons* and *EC–Biotech*, best described by thinkers writing in the face and aftermath of nuclear war. Walter Benjamin frames it in terms of a Judaic eschatology whereby the acceleration of technological risk leads to a 'messianic time' (the 'time of now', or *Jetztzeit*),[20] which instantly and absolutely shatters politics (or in other words, human life as it is sustained and guaranteed by the state). For Carl Schmitt, technology threatens to

[18] Ibid.

[19] See also Jacques Derrida, *Monolingualism of the Other or The Prosthesis of Origin* (Patrick Mensah trans., 1998) [trans. Of: *Le Monolinguisme de l'autre* 1996].

[20] See generally, Walter Benjamin, 'On the Concept of History, or, Theses on the Philosophy of History' in *Illuminations* (Hannah Arendt, ed.) (Harry Zohn trans., 1969 edn) [trans. of: *Uber den Begriff der Geschichte* 1940].

'dislocate the modern European state',[21] and is held back only by the figure of the sovereign that functions as, in a term he borrows from *Revelations*, a 'katechontic' restraint, both heralding and preventing the arrival of the Apocalypse and of Redemption.[22] For Martin Heidegger technology is a condition of knowledge, and it is in technological expression that the 'truth' of Being is encountered.[23] This encounter is not without its danger, which haunts the human as it seeks salvation.[24]

Ever-accelerating sovereign economies driven by technology were therefore understood by these pre- and post-war thinkers to prefigure something we could call, following Heidegger, an 'onto-theological' problem. In other words, they imagined human life (in terms of existential experience, psyche, culture, or politics) to be bound by a pre-existing structure whereby earthly life was created and protected by a transcendental authority. In the absence of such authority, the sovereign state (with its international laws, territorial boundaries, and liquid currency) becomes the primary security for a human life that was at once singular (material) and united (in an immanent humanness). What emerges from a reading of these thinkers is that within an eschatological structure the 'sovereign state', 'humanness', and 'technology' come into conflict with one another in the paradox of speed. Economies must accelerate using technology (armaments with further reach that can be controlled remotely; plants and animals that are bred artificially; and so on) in order to ensure the relevance or dominance of the state; at the same time, the logical conclusion of that technology (nuclear war; genetic pollution) endangers the sovereign state and human life itself.

Towards the end of the twentieth century the rhetoric of two freedoms (the 'freedom from want' and 'freedom from fear') was revived in the United Nations Development Program's 1994 *Human Development Report*, which cited them as 'the two major

[21] Carl Schmitt, above n. 4, 178. [22] Ibid., 59–60.

[23] See generally, Martin Heidegger, *Being and Time* (John Macquarrie and Edward Robinson trans., 1978 edn) [trans. of: *Sein und Zeit*, 1953; originally published 1927].

[24] Martin Heidegger, *The Question Concerning Technology and Other Essays* (William Lovitt trans., 1977 edn) [trans. of: *Die Frage nach der Technik*, 1954].

components of human security'. This desire for freedom from want and from fear, channelled into the creation of an international order based on territorial delineation and increasingly rapid economic integration, meets with a problem. The problem is that such a structure of international order is haunted by the eschatology set out and critiqued inter alia by the post-war thinkers discussed in Chapter 3, whereby the international law that has been called to respond to it has been trapped in the same logic.

5.2 AN ECONOMY OF HUMAN TIME: *NUCLEAR WEAPONS* AND *EC—BIOTECH* REVISITED

5.2.1 Speed and silence in the Nuclear Weapons *case*

Turning now to the cases introduced in Chapter 2, we can start to unravel their recurring themes. In *Nuclear Weapons* we can see how the sanctity of the sovereign state encounters a rival claim in the form of individual humans, to guarantee humanness. The state, in other words, is held up as the exemplary legal form that guarantees the metaphysical existence of the biological human, yet in their 'rescue operation for humanity'[25] the Court is torn between privileging the idea that humanness is represented primarily by the state,[26] and the idea that it is represented in individual bodies.

In their reasoning, the ICJ declares that the UN Charter 'neither expressly prohibits, nor permits, the use of any specific weapon, including nuclear weapons'[27] explicitly invoking a *non liquet*, the possibility of a gap or indeterminacy in (purportedly an otherwise gapless) international law. The Court goes on to say: 'State practice shows that the illegality of the use of certain

[25] Judge Bedjaoui, *Legality of the Use by a State of Nuclear Weapons in Armed Conflict*, Advisory Opinion, ICJ Reports, 1996.

[26] 'State survival, as a term of art, had never been used ...before the Advisory Opinion [and is] a concept invented by the Court.' Judge Koroma, *Legality of the Use by a State of Nuclear Weapons in Armed Conflict*, Advisory Opinion, ICJ Reports, 1996. See also Marcelo Kohen, 'The Notion of "State Survival" in International Law' in Laurence Boisson de Chazournes and Philippe Sands (eds), *International Law, the International Court of Justice and Nuclear Weapons* (1999) 294.

[27] *Legality of the Threat or Use of Nuclear Weapons*, Advisory Opinion, ICJ Reports 1996, para. 39.

weapons as such does not result from an absence of authorization but, on the contrary, is formulated in terms of prohibition.'[28] Even as it laments the potential annihilation of the entire planet, the Court maintains that such an eventuality would be merely a 'consideration' in any calculation of proportionality if nuclear weapons were to be deployed in the name of state survival.

The inconclusiveness of the prohibition against the use of nuclear weapons betrays, first, a need to save above all the universalizing order of human*ness* guaranteed by the sovereign state, and second, ambivalence in the face of a technology that, by its power of instant annihilation, symbolizes both absolute destruction *and* salvation.[29] As Virilio and Lotringer observe, '[a]bsolute unity is what [nuclear] deterrence aims toward. Deterrence has begun to realize this Pure State ... there is a tendency towards unity, but an exterminating unity ...'.[30] Within an eschatological structure, the potentially unifying power of nuclear weapons ('sheltering' countries from harm through their ability to instantly annihilate enemies) has a simultaneous destructive potential: to proliferate and to annihilate.

In this agonizing case it becomes clear how the technological risks created by human invention are neither known, nor knowable.[31] The vast unknown, uncontrollable, and unpredictable world of technological risk makes evident the ontological delineation (or 'enframing')[32] of human life, discussed earlier as

28 Ibid., para. 52.

29 '[T]he consecrated offering cannot be restored to the real order. This principle opens the way to passionate release; it liberates violence while marking off the domain in which violence reigns absolutely.' Georges Bataille, *The Accursed Share: The History of Eroticism and Sovereignty* vol. I (Robert Hurley trans., 1993 edn) [trans. of: *La Parte maudite*, 1949] 58.

30 Virilio and Lotringer, above n. 9, 177.

31 As Barbara Adam and Joost Van Loon explain, 'risks are necessarily constructed. However, they are not constructed on the basis of voluntary imagination ... risks are being revealed in their construction.' Barbara Adam and Joost Van Loon, 'Introduction' in Barbara Adam and Joost Van Loon (eds), *The Risk Society and Beyond: Critical Issues for Social Theory* (2000) 2.

32 This is Heidegger's term, which he describes in 'The Question Concerning Technology' as: 'that way of revealing which holds sway in the essence of modern technology and which is itself nothing technological.' Above n. 24, 20. By this, he refers to the power of modern technology to transform human relationships to nature, effectively reconstituting their world. It is this ontological power of

an eschatological bind. In turn, this provokes the impossibility of human decision-making to arise 'in a radical way'.[33] As Beck notes: 'in the face of ... catastrophic potential ... decisions are increasingly disabled. Hence, as the need for decidability increases, so does the pertinence of undecidability.'[34] This is precisely what we see in *Nuclear Weapons*, where the Court effectively finds that the question is undecidable.

In *Nuclear Weapons* we also see how the acceleration of time in the form of liberation speed—instantaneity and ubiquity—are described by Virilio as 'attributes of the divine'.[35] Sylvère Lotringer asks, 'Has Man revived the question of God through nuclear accident?'.[36] The theorist Paul Virilio responds: 'the species is now recognizing the possibility of its own death. Nuclear holocaust reintroduces the question of God—no longer on the scale of an individual or of a chosen race, but of a species.'[37] Time—a key thematic in the process of exchange between sovereign subjects—can only be figured within the text in terms of a liberation speed: the point at which the material body or place of origin disappears altogether. In its extreme form, therefore, technological risk finds its ultimate expression in the nuclear weapon, the detonation of which (at the speed of light) promises both absolute knowledge and the potential annihilation of both state and species.

These military thinkers are particularly concerned, as were the post-war philosophers discussed in the first part of Chapter 3, with the theological implications of our engagement with technology. This concern is carried over to the observations of international lawyer scholars, who remark that the issues considered by the Court were 'enormously contentious', touching 'the proper role of the International Court ... the normative value and effect of the rules', and 'transcend[ing] the specificity of the legal issues raised by the two requests before it'.[38] As well as

technology that Heidegger insists can be dangerous to humans, rather than any technological object in itself.

[33] Ulrich Beck, 'Risk Society Revisited: Theory, Politics and Research Programmes' in Barbara Adam and Joost Van Loon, above n. 31, 217.

[34] Adam and Van Loon, above n. 31, 'Introduction', 13.

[35] Virilio, above n. 10, 230. [36] Ibid., 143. [37] Ibid., 51.

[38] Boisson de Chazournes and Sands, 'Introduction' above n. 26, paras 2–3.

noting that 'the proceedings and the Advisory Opinions reflect a still powerful tension ... between a "state-oriented" approach and a more "humanist" approach',[39] one collection of scholarly responses to the *Nuclear Weapons* case includes a chapter by Martti Koskenniemi which claims to 'defend the Court's silence' and criticizes 'modern law's totalizing ambition'.[40] Koskenniemi frames the issue as one of faith: a demand by international law, of lawyers, for faith in the 'theology of the law—the idea of its universality, completeness and rationality',[41] calling instead for a faith, not in international law's or lawyers' ability to 'reason' but in a personal (and professional) ability to foreground human suffering. This echoes Judge Shahabuddeen's reference to the *Russell-Einstein Manifesto*, which urges decision-makers to '[r]emember your humanity, and forget the rest. If you can do so, the way lies open to a new Paradise ...'[42] Koskenniemi's position is interesting, since it is indeed critical of international law's claim to universality and to total knowledge. His resurrection, however, of an innate humanism that refuses the technological machine of international law has an enduring Heideggerian flavour: for Koskenniemi, the 'silence of the law' (the Court's non-decision) *is* the 'voice of justice' that reveals a human soul in the depths of the international lawyer.

In the same collection of scholarly responses, David Kennedy observes that the *Nuclear Weapons* case 'takes us to the heart of modernist darkness, at once horror and friend, act and symbol, norm and violation. This is the modernism of no exit and existential crisis: a problem set at mid-century for which we cannot yet glimpse an answer.'[43] Kennedy's posture could be helpful in moving away from a theological register, to one cast in the

[39] Boisson de Chazournes and Sands, 'Introduction' in Virilio, above n. 10, 15.

[40] Martti Koskenniemi, 'The Silence of Law/The Voice of Justice' in Boisson de Chazournes and Sands, above n. 26, 489.

[41] Boisson de Chazournes and Sands, 489. For a discussion of this piece in the context of the relationship between suffering and the logic of state power, see Anne Orford, 'The Passions of Protection: Sovereign Authority and Humanitarian War' in Didier Fassin and Mariella Pandolfi (eds), *Contemporary States of Emergency: The Politics of Military and Humanitarian Interventions* (2010) 230.

[42] Dissenting Opinion of Judge Shahabuddeen, *Legality of the Threat or Use of Nuclear Weapons*, ICJ Reports, 8 July 1996, concluding remarks.

[43] Ibid., 468.

philosophical language of nihilism. Here is a *total* collapse of values, to which there is no answer, or at least, not from within the stories told by Heidegger and Stiegler, and reiterated in various international law texts. This 'darkness' and 'existential crisis' indicates a problem that stems not only from a lack of faith in international law or a struggle against technology, but also from a deeper anxiety.

5.2.2 *Time and reproduction in the* EC–Biotech *case*

In examining what that anxiety is, let us turn to *EC–Biotech*. Similarly to *Nuclear Weapons*, we see a rival claim between uninterrupted international trade (for human security) and the sanctity of territorial inviolability (for human security). The health of the global economy is triangulated with the health of states and the health of individual human beings. This is the site of a simultaneous fear of annihilation through a corporeal pollution by genetically modified organisms, and anxiety about the state as a legal form that must be kept pure, clean, and whole. Genetic and nuclear technologies threaten human reproduction in the material sense—in terms of the survival of *Homo sapiens*—as well as in the metaphysical sense, questioning what it is to be human, outside of nature and the divine order. We see a futile categorization of the risks posed by genetically modified organisms, pointing to an epistemological crisis. Time is a key thematic in this case as well, not because of the speed of technological deployment but because of the necessity for speed in the global economy (evidenced by the WTO's designation of any delay to import approvals 'undue').

Reproduction is an important idiom in the case, because similarly to the ICJ's concerns of nuclear proliferation, there is an anxiety running through both the *amici curiae* submissions and the Panel's findings of genetic proliferation: the risk that technology will escape human control, revealing a different and dangerous world. An example of this is the *amicus curiae* brief submitted by the US-based Center for International Environmental Law, Friends of the Earth, the Defenders of Wildlife Institute for Agriculture and Trade Policy, and the Organic Consumers Association. In their brief, the NGOs warn against uncontrolled genetic transfers to non-genetically modified organisms:

Transgenes are ... parts of complex 'genetic constructs' or 'transformation vectors' that incorporate numerous other DNA segments from various organisms and of various function. These regulatory DNA segments include promoters, enhancers, origins of replication and termination sequences. Promoters, which are often of viral origin, instruct the host cell to generate the desired protein from the transgene. Constitutive promoters, such as the 35S cauliflower mosaic virus promoter sequence, drive production of the foreign protein in every tissue of the plant, creating numerous opportunities for the novel protein to cause potentially hazardous unintended effects through disruption of various cellular processes. Another hazard of promoters is their potential to inadvertently cause overproduction of native proteins, or to activate dormant (i.e. cryptic) genes, also thereby disrupting cellular metabolism.[44]

Here, DNA segments include 'origins of replication and termination sequences', can be 'viral' and can create 'potentially hazardous unintended effects', including the 'overproduction of native proteins' or the activation of 'dormant genes'. In other words, this technology can annihilate life as we know it. They also warn against 'contamination' of conventional seed and food crops, stressing the importance of 'purity':

Transgenic trait contamination occurs not only in conventional food and feed crops, but increasingly in conventional and organic seed crops as well. The contamination of conventional seed varieties with transgenic traits is particularly disturbing as seed crops are subject to extraordinary gene confinement protocols to maintain the purity of the particular variety. If even seed crops are becoming contaminated with transgenic traits, it becomes highly questionable whether co-existence schemes for genetically modified, conventional and organic crops are in fact feasible.[45]

In the background to these concerns of purity and pollution is the fear that genetic technology has an intrinsic drive to universalize

[44] *Amicus curiae* brief submitted by the Center for International Environmental Law (CIEL); Friends of the Earth–United States (FOE–US); Defenders of Wildlife Institute for Agriculture and Trade Policy (IATP), and the Organic Consumers Association–United States (OCA–USA), for the European Communities—Measures Affecting the Approval and Marketing of Biotech Products (WT/DS/291, 292, and 293) on 1 June 2004, para. 20.

[45] Ibid., para. 28.

particular strains, and to erase difference. There is also a concern that this technology has the power to create life *without* the oversight of either humans or God. In each of the *Nuclear Weapons* and *EC–Biotech* cases, the impossibility of human decision-making arises 'in a radical way'[46] with jurists unwilling to judge questions of technological risk. The WTO Panel emerged at the end of its deliberations with an unenforceable recommendation for the EC to bring its moratorium on GMOs in line with relevant WTO obligations, a moratorium that had effectively expired two years previously. In the face of incalculable risk and the limits of scientific knowledge, both the WTO Panel and the ICJ struggle to arrive at a legal decision. In their attempts to construct a symbolic identity predicated on speed, the ICJ and the Panel's writings become formless—kinedramatic events unbounded in time and space.[47]

5.2.3 *Fibre-optic desire to liberation speed*

It is through technological acceleration that the human may strive towards its completion, by transcending the space–time continuum altogether to become detached from the material earth: immortal, timeless.[48] The knowledge, revelation, and guarantee of human life then only becomes a possibility through international law's promise to know and to end time itself: a promise that is a fibre-optic desire towards a 'liberation speed'—this is the speed at which man escapes the labour economy: the first and last reminder of his mortality.[49] The imagined telos of international (desacralized and transcendental) law is thus the will to become a new technology: a body without anxiety or desire; free from want and free from fear.

[46] Ulrich Beck, 'Risk Society Revisited: Theory, Politics and Research Programmes' in Adam and Van Loon, above n. 31, 217.

[47] Term coined by Paul Virilio, *The Art of the Motor* (Julie Rose trans., 1995 edn) [trans. of: *L'art du moteur*, 1993] 23.

[48] Maurice Blanchot, *L'Entretien infini* (1969) 396.

[49] According to Sumerian mythology, humans were created by the gods to labour, create surplus wealth for them, and die as mortals: S.H. Hooke, *Middle Eastern Mythology* (1963) 29; 45 (on known Babylonian mythology, which accords with earlier Sumerian mythology that humans were created for the service of the gods, and also reveals that celestial order through the eternal rotation of planets and seasons was made before the creation of humans).

International lawyers can thus be described, on one hand, as marking a human time through the ordering of place, body, and image. On the other hand, it stages the modern state: a form through which the human will transcend the space–time continuum altogether to become astral, timeless. These two functions (keeping time and making it disappear) are in conflict, and—as I have also described using in terms of eschatology in Chapter 3—constitute a core tension of international law that we see in the *EC–Biotech* and *Nuclear Weapons* cases. The *EC–Biotech* findings were delayed and were lengthy to the point of absurdity. The *Nuclear Weapons* opinions are disparate and littered with apocalyptic visions. I suggest that the jurists called upon to decide these cases struggled not to become complicit in an institutionalized creation of risk, while wanting nonetheless to invent, to produce, and to reproduce humanness through technology. The inability of international lawyers to reproduce the legal form and to make decisions on time belies a realization that this kind of legal speculation is an impossible task. It is symptomatic of Kennedy's crisis; a juridical noticing of international law's existential conundrum—and a manifestation of what I have described as a 'hysteric voice' in Chapter 3.[50]

The metaphysics upon which international law currently relies presumes that ordering the state into perfect form will enact a human transcendence, which in turn will erase the material conditions of reproduction and enable man to produce a life *ex nihilo*: a life that is unconditional and immortal. Here we reach the limits of Freud's theory of desire; Stiegler's theory of the human; Virilio's theory of speed; and Benjamin, Heidegger, and Schmitt's theories of modern eschatology. We reach the limit of international law scholars' and practitioners' theories that reach for innate qualities of humanness, which would enable them to imbue international law with the same. What these theories do not explicitly acknowledge is that they are predicated on faith in

[50] Alexia Herwig, 'Wither Science in WTO Dispute Settlement?' 21 *Leiden Journal of International Law* 2008, 823–33 remarks: 'Perhaps it realised that examining the risk of GMOs seriously would have brought to light significant uncertainties and unclear standards of rational decision-making and, with them, would have diminished the law's role in controlling decisions.'

the idea of the human as a form of life that is determined not only biologically but also metaphysically. This human, furthermore, is imagined to be of a single sex: masculine. I have indicated this in the introduction to this book, explained it in Chapter 3, and demonstrated it in my analysis of various post-war texts in Chapter 4. The following and final chapter reflects on this foregoing analysis, framing it in terms of the philosophical frames introduced at the beginning of the book (metaphysics, aesthetics, and ethics). It offers an alternative paradigm through which we can begin thinking about the work of international law, and its role in adjudicating questions of trade, war, and the environment today.

6

THE HUMAN'S BODIES

6.1 INTERNATIONAL LAW FUTURES

This chapter returns to the framework set out in Chapter 1 to think about the implications of the analysis in the foregoing chapters. This chapter begins by looking at how we can think otherwise about international law in terms of metaphysics, aesthetics, and ethics (6.1). If international law indeed manifests crises because it is required to perform an impossible task (to dictate what is right, and what is good, and to reveal the truth) on the basis that it is an expression of transcendent human authority, then it may be time to change our conception of what international law is, and what it can do. The second part explores how changing the ways in which we write can work as both an analytic and expressive technique in legal scholarship (6.2). The chapter ends by reimagining the role of international law to help us better respond to problems of trade, war, and the environment that jurists encounter today (6.3).

To reiterate the opening question of this book: what does it mean to be human in today's globalized world? Twentieth-century public discourse on technology, the human, and the international domain, imagines technology (including the technology of international law) as being a condition of modern life. It does this insofar as the idea of a secular human world is supported by a capacity to control the existential boundaries of that world with nuclear weapons, genetic technologies, and a political formation called the state—in this sense, international law plays a central role in defining the metaphysical structure of our existence today. The question of how to *live* with this privileged role ascribed to international law, and to its technology, is a more difficult one. The public language of international law entrenches the idea that securing human life in an international domain is a masculine preserve. It also presents 'humanness' as a way of transcending the material constraints of becoming and living in a finite world. As my analysis in previous chapters has shown, the production of human life on these terms is problematic.

The *Nuclear Weapons* and *EC–Biotech* cases will not be the last international law cases to provoke a widespread sense of betrayal or failure in the international community. The authority of the ICJ and of the WTO dispute settlement mechanism was clouded over as they agonized over the existential risks of technology (*Nuclear Weapons*) and buried themselves in thousands of pages of legal and scientific detail (*EC–Biotech*). Both responses were certainly reactions to uncertainty about the role of jurists as the keepers of international law: Could they speak? Should they speak? When the existence of international law as an overriding authority (of humans, rather than God) was contingent upon a gendered trope running through narratives of sovereignty and free trade, should they do anything to undermine those narratives? These uncertainties were underscored by a growing awareness that the authority of international law *as a technology* was being called into question more generally, not only as a post-war settlement that favoured certain countries, but also as a global adjudicatory forum that no longer reflects our changing geopolitical landscape.

Amidst all this, there is an anxiety about the implications of a 'failing' international law for what it means to be human in today's world: so much of the discourse in the media, schools, and development programmes uncritically adopt the language of a 'global humanity' that is first promulgated in international agreements. This idea of a global humanity is compelling, of course, because it promises us that we are more than simply material beings—more than animal; we also have a body—or are part of a body—that is transcendent and immortal. The jurists of *EC–Biotech* and *Nuclear Weapons* struggled with their decisions because this—the very idea of humanness—was at stake.

The international law with which the jurists were grappling—a legacy of our post-war settlement—is also eschatological (reflecting our theological heritage), which means that the 'global humanity' is imagined to be moving towards the end of time. My analysis has shown that technology in its various forms—international law, nuclear weapons, and biotechnology, among others—is imagined to have a destructive and redemptive role in relation to this 'global humanity'. For international lawyers, this paradigm is a deeply troubling one as it forces them to step into the place of the Church, becoming an authority that reduces human lives to their destructibility, or redemptive capacity.

What does this all mean for international law, or for thinking about this 'crisis of authority' as a problem of metaphysics? It means that there are various structural impediments to today's public international law becoming anything other than a post-war vanity project. These are, as noted above: the dominance of Judeo–Christian cosmologies in the discursive imagination of international law texts; the masculinization of the state and the global economy; the creation of a humanness that is dependent upon a technology of the state and of international law; and the limitation of international lawyers' narrative scope to one of destruction and redemption.

For those of us invested in thinking about international law, the challenge then may be to think of ways in which international law can create the conditions for humanness that do not rely on these terms. The work of judgment, as I have noted earlier in this book, relies on an initial suspension of disbelief, in order for jurists to transform a finding that has implications for the material well-being of individuals into a story about something greater than those individuals. As we have seen from the *Nuclear Weapons* and *EC–Biotech* cases, this is usually a story about (the security of) the state; (the inviolability of) sovereignty; (the importance of) an ever-accelerating global trade; (the destructive and saving power of) technology, and (the inevitable, yet fragile status of) humanity. The art of judgment is imagined as having the power to reveal the truth of the world, and these stories make a particular truth that is compelling precisely because it allays our anxieties about what it means to be human in a desacralized, globalized world.

6.2 INTERNATIONAL LAW WRITING

When international law writing such as that in the *Nuclear Weapons* and *EC–Biotech* cases becomes 'hysterical' (as described in my foregoing analysis), it reveals another truth: that of the gendered and nihilistic metaphysics underscoring the ideas of what the international, human, and technology are. And while we cannot change this heritage of a history of ideas, we do nonetheless have a power to create a future role for scholarly analysis and of legal judgment, by reimagining *how* it should undertake the work of revelation. As I have noted in Chapter 3, post-structuralist feminist thinkers, in particular Luce Irigaray, Hélène Cixous, and Julia Kristeva, have been writing since the 1960s about ways of using language to subvert 'monophallic' linguistic structures. More recently, feminist legal scholars have taken up some of these strategies by rewriting significant (English and international) legal judgments.[1] These new writings, however, have focused more on the substantive aspects of the legal decisions (relying on socio-legal analysis) and less on the *form* of the decisions, which is what I have examined in this book.[2]

In order to demonstrate the potential of *écriture feminine* to tell a different story of international law, I have undertaken the following exercise, which recounts a formative moment in international law history: the signing of the Treaties of Westphalia, in 1648.[3] The legacy of the Treaty has been far-reaching, with

[1] There are several examples of feminist or feminine appropriation of legal judgments, including the *Women's International War Crimes Tribunal on Japan's Military Sexual Slavery* (2000), which was convened by NGOs throughout Asia to hear testimonies from women forced into sexual slavery by the Japanese Imperial Army during the Second World War, with a judgment delivered at The Hague; the *Feminist Judgments Project* led by Rosemary Hunter, Clare McGlynn, and Erika Rackley, to write alternative judgments of significant cases in English law (published as *Feminist Judgments: From Theory to Practice*, 2010); and the *Feminist International Judgments Project* led by Loveday Hodson and Troy Lavers, to write alternative judgments of significant international law cases (2013–2015).

[2] In my own work I have incorporated various forms of poetic writing into my analyses; see for example 'The Decision not to Prosecute the Emperor' in Yuki Tanaka, Tim McCormack, and Gerry Simpson (eds), *Beyond Victors' Justice? The Tokyo War Crimes Trial Revisited* (2010) 63–76 and 'The Gentle Cannibal: The Rise and Fall of Lawful Milk' 40 (2) *Australian Feminist Law Journal* 2015, 215–28.

[3] The Treaty of Westphalia (the Treaty) is a collective term for two peace treaties—the *Instrumentum Pacis Monasteriense* and the *Instrumentum Pacis Osnabrugense*—that were signed in the Catholic city of Münster and the Lutheran city of Osnabrück (both in Westphalia, Germany) on the 24 October 1648. These treaties marked the closure of the Thirty Years' War—a bloody conflict between Catholics and Protestants (carried out in its later stages between the rival dynasties of Bourbon and Habsburg) fought across large swathes of Europe. There were an estimated 300 representatives from around the region present at the signing of the treaties, with the notable exceptions of representatives from Russia, England,

references still made today to the 'Westphalian paradigm'[4] and to 'post-Westphalian sovereignty'.[5] While the Treaty was by no means the sole catalyst for the eventual universalization of the nation-state form, it nonetheless presented a significant claim by its princely signatories to jurisdictional independence from the Roman Catholic Church. It thus marks, if not a constitutive moment, at least a founding myth in the story of international law's emergence. At the time the Treaty was signed there were a significant number of politically active women in Germany. Some were Princess-Abbesses who had the right to collect taxes and tolls from their convent estates, and who held juridical rights, recognizing no ecclesiastic superior save the Pope. Others included powerful Regent Dowagers—figures such as Juliane von Hessen of Ostfriesland and Sibylle Christine von Anhalt-Dessau of Hanau-Münzenberg, who governed land and negotiated truces.[6] Despite their visibility in the public domain, these women ruled in the name of men (the Pope, in the case of the Princess-Abbesses; their underage sons, in the case of the Regent Dowagers). Their power was, therefore, limited in significant ways (for example, they could not pass on title to their daughters), and was also unusual in that women outside of a small feudal ruling class would not have had access to any such political influence.

The following account is an imagined one, in the voice of a woman, Maria von Helfenstein, who lived during the Thirty Years' War. I have tried to capture a sense of the time in which Maria lived by using English spelling conventions from the

Turkey, and of the Pope. The two treaties were signed on the same day: the one in Osnabrück was signed by Sweden and the Holy Roman Empire, and the other, the Franco–Imperial Treaty of Münster, was signed by France and the Holy Roman Empire.

[4] M.T. Franca Filho, 'Westphalia: a Paradigm? A Dialogue between Law, Art and Philosophy of Science' 8 *German Law Journal* 2007, 955.

[5] Ibid., 974: '[I]t is somewhat controversial to talk about a "Westphalian revolution", in the sense commonly attributed to the term "revolution". The non-revolutionary character … of the Westphalian paradigm, however, does not serve to detract any significance from it.'

[6] Thanks go to Martin K.I. Christensen for this information, collated with the biographies of other women who have held positions of power in the public sphere, on his website at http://www.guide2womenleaders.com.

mid-seventeenth century, and I rely on her voice of undomesticated anger to carry through a concern that is as transhistorical as it is transdisciplinary. The poem collages text from the treaties and some of the philosophical and literary texts discussed in earlier chapters. By gathering key metaphors of the sun, the voyage, and the body of woman, as they emerge again and again in literary and legal texts that deal with tensions between Church and State, the poem draws out what is at stake in the *Nuclear Weapons* and *EC–Biotech* cases.

[Münster, 24 October 1648]

Lady Landgravine, they call me. Madame the Landgravine.

They, numbering precisely hundreds. I, numbering more than one, Maria to my mother: born of Helfenstein, of Wernberg, of Leuchtenberg, of a hundred million matryoshkan names. They, men representing men with their Amities and Honours: Princes, Heirs, Successors, say: 'tis done.

'Tis done, pass'd and conclud'd, one sober Munster day they call, the 24th Day of October. Done a short day, for Westphalian Octobers are quick pass'd by the Sunne. A long negotiation with no beginning and at whose end there were fewer Men.

A drop of wax to seal a treaty. Red-spott'd sheets to guarantee, a Universal Peace.

The year is 1648. They, numbering precisely hundreds, are borne of these sheets.

★★★

Crouching, they were crouching. Calling to shadows cast by fire, upon the wall of a secret cave. That day they crawl'd through a narrow passage, up toward an October Sunne. Light, they thought, would show them Knowledge. Thirty years of hungry war, ended: so, it was done.

Will there be Mourning? No, no.

They can't turn back but call it dead, and seal the entrance with a stone. 'The body', they say, 'the ancestor and our saviour, lies bury'd there'. Bury'd in an unconscious place, the body with a Demonick face. A dream, a cave, created by they who know. Or invent a dream to be, and have been, to bear witness to it. I be the opening, the tomb or the mouth through which they crawl out.

Will there be Mourning? No, no. Oblivion, in perpetuum: through Amnesty or Pardon. They pardon and grant amnesty to forget this sad invention. They parasites, they treaty, they human.

Not even a shroud covers the ground cast open
They devour the sound of formless cries
Security found in sacrifice

★★★

Their Security has a neutral taste. A pharmakon ingest'd to Forget. Neutral, nothing, mouth-melting expiation for flesh-eating; tasting, wine once the colour of a woman's desire. An Outrageous Desire that drew the time between life and death, now reformed and shew'd as Property, which alone will save Manne:

Vassals; Subjects; People; Towns; Woods, Gold and Rivers shall, without reserve, belong to the most Christian King. Belonging, without Reservation, Hostag'd to a Christian crown. A Sovereign Crown to Guarantee, Unconditional Life. For this, Words, Writings, Outrageous Actions, are bury'd in Oblivion.

Such oblivion or courtly love is called Forgiveness, among Men.

★★★

Family Contracts must be observed; conserv'd and maintain'd entire. Men and the children of men will make their liquid Empire Form a good and Faithfull Neighbourhood, of Armies, Friends, Guests and Strangers. These are the Hosts who settle their debt by selling my body-pieces for the benefit of Peace.

Body-pieces beaten into golden Angels are stamp'd with Sovereign faces. With these metal memories of places we shall have full power to go and come, to trade and return, with Liberty of Commerce and secure Passages.

To go, and come. To trade, and come home.
To go without ever risking losing home,
for the law of the same
be guarante'd by property or its Proper Name.

In the Sovereign's likeness to Human lies a fiction within a fiction. The body dieth but the figure survives through the state circulation of labour and wives, staying the spectres of wolves, Fathers and paper Gods.

Let us note, however: passage secur'd is conditional, tho' they declare it unconditional.

★★★

Burial; sacrifice; consumption, exchange: rituals to protect against perpetual Silence. With civilis'd speech they cry out their laws who they imagine to echo 'gainst boundary Walls: those that enclose what they call, their Territories.

Their full Jurisdiction is authoris'd force: the power to kill within boundary walls. The architecture borne by this October archi-text, now appears and from here it shall never be alledg'd, allow'd or admitted, that:

Any Law, Decrees, Contracts, Privileges, Mandates, Oaths, Indulgences, Judgments, Appeals, Rescripts, Edicts; Commissions, Inhibitions, Suspensions, Adjudications, Capitulations, Protestations, Contradictions, Transactions, Renunciations—Any Concordats with the Popes, Dispensations, Absolutions or any other Exceptions
shall take place
against
this Contention.

***

It may be done, but Pope the most Innocent X doth retort that the treaty be null, void, invalid and unjust. Damnable! he calls it, reprobate, inane, empty of meaning and effect for all time. Not for my security condemns he the treaty but by reason of a more heinous crime.

For you see, the ink-tongue of Manne cleaves off a Perpetual, but Human, Time.

Natural law and Natural time; Divine law, Divine time. He stakes a Third, call it a Westphalian dream. He is pushed, or leaps. Air strokes wings ripp'd from the bodies of peace; he soars! Drip too near already to the sunne, drip. Reddn'd wax and tears claw down toward an Icarian Sea.

He be a Prosthetick Machine, this flight, this dream: a mask that mimics and reproduces the living. Not breathing, this Artificial Manne be orthograph'd, and as law scars the boundaries of his Sovereign State.

Binding no less the absent than the present, the Ecclesiastics than the Seculars, this be the site through which Religious time is displac'd and Natural time eras'd. It is sealed, 1648, a mythic time for a mythic place.

Law makes this place, exhuming its ghosts to determine cause of death and reburying them as the crumbs of faith. He be, in other words, a Prosthetic clock: a technology of forgetting. He pretends, in other words, to supplement ancestral loss, through the repetition of authority.

The Loss, however, of which they cannot Speak, is the Loss of Being before Time.

***

Being is time that be defin'd by the relation to time. A technical conjugation where time makes human and law marks time. Law-writing spools a clockwork. He be prophecy, memory and history.

His lines conjure a proof: the Existence of Sovereign Subject. A Subject of a many-bodied Manne, of a Father who sees—not me!—he draws the distance 'tween identical brothers. This Father is always already dead, but the Icon in his place keeps the Secret in the grave: their Secret, their first symbolic murder.

***

With such Guarantee they are free. Free to pursue Life by means other than Life. Law, as this means, be an erotic iteration that stands for the loss of Being before Time. Standing in-, for- as-, law erects a Symbolic order that, catching the light, mirrors a Religious Divine.

Erstwhile, the horizon of Intimate Time was disappearing before our eyes—

***

Returning to Law's Order that gestures toward a hidden sublime, we see how he needs Virtue, in order to keep time. A utopic Virtue, an entropic dream, that they call Universal Peace.

Will there be Mourning? No, no.

Virtue is called Justice, from just war, love of fatherland and its laws. Love for the sovereign who rules thro' fraternal force. The other end of Virtue is, of course, the name they give, to their guarantee of sole access to my security.

Can any orphan'd woman lose the name of Virtue and still live brand'd with shame? Can any woman claim his Universal Peace? This is an ectopic theme that haunts me in my sleep.

★★★

Manne, who looks too far beyond him in the care of future time, hath his heart all the day long gnaw'd on by fear of death; hath no repose nor pause of his anxiety but in sleep. And so he sleeps, and dreams dreams that seal o'er the yawning catastrophe.

To remain thus asleep he must set Law's time to administrate his clean and proper state. To slacken the pace of legal time would threaten his mandate, his power to decide and to procreate World as his Mirror Image. To delay the pace would threaten the turgidity and tranquility of territorialis'd debt.

So time is built out thro' Sovereign Law and without Delay. Didn't Hamlet say: 'For who would bear the whips and scorns of time, the law's delay, the insolence of office?' Who indeed, lest he could guarantee his Perpetual Peace?

Lady Landgravine, they call me. Madame the Landgravine. They gift me so they can guarantee Manne's humanity, Law's masculinity. Their passage to Life and Immunity seduces with promises of Security. But for me? What Virtue is left with no body to keep?

★★★

What I hope *écriture feminine* such as this can do is to destabilize international law's usual reference points by making explicit the homosocial ontological structure behind international law's story of origin, as well as show how the contest for the power to determine what is human plays out between Church and State.[7] The virtue to which the Lady Landgravine character alludes is a virtue that is defined by allegiance to a masculinized state, which itself is supported by an uncounted sacrifice of (feminine and feminized) bodies: a sacrifice of material bodies for an immaterial one. It is a virtue, as I describe earlier in this book, which is expressed in terms of a jurisprudence of necessity, rather than a jurisprudence of care.

[7] For a helpful elaboration of the relation between poetics and ontology, see Jennifer Anna Gosetti-Ferencei, *Heidegger, Hölderlin, and the Subject of Poetic Language: Toward a New Poetics of Dasein* (2004).

If we are to rethink what international law's virtues are, we can certainly move away from the idea that virtue is to be measured in terms of international law's ability to preserve the inviolability of the state or *its* bodies. We should also move away from the notion that making virtuous decisions requires international lawyers to buy into polarized discourses of purity and pollution, salvation and damnation (and just as damaging, the notion of equivalence based on a fraternity of states). Instead, we can invent an international law that is more self-aware of its epistemological context, and attentive to the historical, relational, material particularities of each deliberation. The following section reflects on three recent cases dealing with matters of trade, war, and the environment, showing how we can use the techniques of *écriture feminine* to go beyond the critique of *Nuclear Weapons* and *EC–Biotech* to create a normative vision for international law.

6.3 LAWS OF TRADE, WAR, AND THE ENVIRONMENT

Following the Second World War, the Soviet Union and the United States launched a military and economic rivalry that would see the further technification of war, and the rapid development of the intentional financial system. The vanquished nations of Germany and Japan had their economies restructured and flooded with money in order to draw them (and their technical and administrative expertise) into the new global economy. Today, we can clearly see the legacy of this post-war settlement in the form of Germany and Japan's economic dominance (and gradual remilitarization). But there are further unforeseen changes to our geopolitical landscape: the rise of the BRICS countries (in particular China);[8] a series of proxy wars in the Middle East dominated by military technology such as cyber surveillance/warfare and drones, and rapid global climactic change caused by fossil fuel consumption. This brave new world produces all manner of problems resonant with those discussed in this book: questions about technology, humanness, and the

[8] This popular acronym for the emerging economies stands for 'Brazil, Russia, India, China, and South Africa'.

international domain that international lawyers are poorly equipped to deal with.

In an extension of the analysis that I have undertaken in the earlier chapters, I offer here brief meditations on three recent international law cases that raise specific issues I imagine will occupy the discipline in years to come: the WTO decision in *China–Measures Related to the Exportation of Various Raw Materials*[9] (the *Raw Materials* case) and *China–Measures Related to the Exportation of Rare Earths, Tungsten and Molybdenum*[10] (the *Rare Earths* case); the ICJ case *Questions of Interpretation and Application of the 1971 Montreal Convention Arising from the Aerial Incident at Lockerbie Libyan Arab Jamahiriya v UK and US* (the 'Lockerbie case');[11] and the WTO decision in *European Communities–Measures Prohibiting the Importation and Marketing of Seal Products* (the 'Seal Products case').[12] Unlike the limit-cases of *Nuclear Weapons* and *EC–Biotech*, the decisions do not reveal the tenuous metaphysical foundations on which the authority of international law rests. These cases are, on their face, straightforward applications of blackletter law, reaffirming the inviolability of the sovereign body; the primacy of equivalence between state bodies; the central importance of humanness to the existence of the state; and the apolitical nature of the legal decision. They also, however, deal with matters that go to the heart of global politics today: consumption, militarization, and human/animal relations. As such, it is worth looking at them to reorient their centre of gravity.

Raw Materials and *Rare Earths* are two recent WTO disputes brought by the United States (and numerous third parties) against China in 2009 and 2012 respectively, for purported violation of

[9] WT/DS395 *China–Measures Related to the Exportation of Various Raw Materials* (2009).

[10] WT/DS432 *China–Measures Related to the Exportation of Rare Earths, Tungsten and Molybdenum* (2012).

[11] *Questions of Interpretation and Application of the 1971 Montreal Convention Arising from the Aerial Incident at Lockerbie (Libya v UK; Libya v US)* Provisional Measures, 1992 ICJ REP. 3; 114 (Orders of Apr. 14). My thanks go to Troy Lavers and Loveday Hodson for bringing my attention to this case, which we have discussed as part of their *Feminist International Judgments* project.

[12] *European Communities—Measures Prohibiting the Importation and Marketing of Seal Products*, Appellate Body Report, WT/DS400/AB/R and WT/DS401/AB/R, adopted on 18 June 2014.

obligations under the GATT 1994 rules, and more onerous obligations that accrue to China under its terms of accession to the WTO. In both cases, the WTO DSB examined the legality of China's export duties, quotas, and price and licensing requirements placed on materials important to various industries 'upstream' in developed economies.[13] China argued that restrictions on export were justifiable under GATT Article XX (b) and (g) (exceptions that allow WTO members to restrict trade in order to protect 'exhaustible natural resources').[14] The DSB Panel and the Appellate Body found in both cases that China had no recourse to GATT Article XX, and required China to remove the trade restrictions in question. *Raw Materials* and *Rare Earths* are discussed

[13] In the *China–Raw Materials* case, the complainants (the United States, joined by the European Communities, Canada, Mexico, and Turkey) alleged violation of DSU Article 6.2 and GATT 1994 Articles VIII: 1(a), X:1, X:3(a), XI:1, XI:2(a), XX(b), and XX(g). China had agreed to eliminate all export duties and export quotas upon accession to the WTO, exempting products listed in an Annex to its Protocol of Accession. The DSB Panel found that the wording of the Protocol did not allow China to rely on GATT Article XX exceptions, and that even if it did, China would still be unable to meet the Article XX requirements. The Appellate Body upheld the Panel's finding that China's Accession Protocol precluded China's recourse to Article XX, and by 1 January 2013, export duties and export quotas imposed on the raw materials in question had been removed. In the *China–Rare Earths* case, the United States alleged violation of Articles VII, VIII, X, and XI of the GATT 1994, as well as paras 1.2, 2(A)2, 2(C)1, 5.1, 5.2, 7.2, 8.2, and 11.3 of Part 1 of China's Protocol of Accession. Specifically, the United States (later joined by the European Union, Japan, and Canada) contested China's restrictions on the export of various forms of rare earths, tungsten, and molybdenum, as well as a number of published and unpublished export restrictions. All parties to the dispute appealed various aspects of the DSB's report. The Appellate Body found that the Panel had not erred in finding that China's export quotas were not justified under GATT Article XX(g), and on 20 May 2015, China informed that DSB that the measures had been removed.

[14] Article XX (also mentioned earlier in the book in the context of the *EC–Biotech* dispute) sets out general exceptions to the GATT rules, enabling trade-restrictive measures to be taken: 'Subject to the requirement that such measures are not applied in a manner which would constitute a means of arbitrary or unjustifiable discrimination between countries where the same conditions prevail, or a disguised restriction on international trade, nothing in this Agreement shall be construed to prevent the adoption or enforcement by any contracting party of measures: ... (b) necessary to protect human, animal or plant life or health ... (g) relating to the conservation of exhaustible natural resources if such measures are made effective in conjunction with restrictions on domestic production or consumption.'

by international law commentators as cases whose central concerns are the limits to sovereign power: how should states balance their various external obligations to free trade rules with their domestic obligation to protect their environment and increase economic development by controlling their natural resources?[15] The Panel and Appellate Body defer unsurprisingly to the restrictions imposed by China's Accession Protocol, reducing at the same time, scope for the interpretation of GATT Article XX. The realpolitik story of the two cases is that of an emerging economy that has a hold on resources vital for the Great Powers, and of international law ensuring that such emerging economies are not able to control the flow of resources by reference to environmental protection or conservation. Left out of the text is any consideration of the social and environmental impacts of extracting and consuming raw materials. Absent, too, is any reflection on what our desire for these materials means in symbolic terms.

Out of earth comes wolframine; out of wolf's froth comes tungsten. Dense, hard, it melts last of all metals. Dark grey, it takes its place in light bulbs and radiation shields. Glinting, it coats x-ray tubes and projectiles for military fields. The earth gives us another essential element: molybdenum. It is volatile, used for motors. Silvery grey, to strengthen alloys. And artillery has it in spades. Slivers return to earth as glistening fertilizer, shells and steel. Rare earths, raw materials: turned by new potters on their maker's wheel and churned up from the bowels. Bauxite, coke, fluorspar, magnesium, manganese, carbide, zinc. Upstream, downstream, duties and tax draw the matter from state to state—from corporation to conveyor belt, away from public minds. Digging; sloshing; shipping; smelting; grinding. They light our cold bodies, our soft bones.

Going back in time now: on 21 December 1988, Pan Am Flight 103 was bombed over Lockerbie, Scotland, killing all those on board and eleven residents in the town below. This was the latest incident in a long and violent struggle between Western powers (starting with Italy's seizure of Libya from the Ottomans

[15] See, for example, Manjiao Chi, 'Resource Sovereignty in the WTO Dispute Settlement: Implications of *China –Raw Materials and China –Rare Earths*' 12(1) *Manchester Journal of International Economic Law* 2015, 2–15; Brigid Gavin, 'Sustainable Development of China's Rare Earth Industry Within and Without the WTO' 49(3) *Journal of World Trade* 2015, 495–515; Julia Ya Qin, 'Judicial Authority in WTO Law: A Commentary on the Appellate Body's Decision in *China-Rare Earths*' 13 *Chinese Journal of International Law* 2014, 639–51.

in 1911) and rebel independence movements (with Muammar Gaddafi in power in 1988). Gaddafi's government was suspected of organizing the Lockerbie bombing, in retaliation for the killing of citizens and Gaddafi's adopted daughter in the bombing of Libyan residential areas by the United States (which itself was in retaliation for the Libyan bombing of a disco in Berlin frequented by US military personnel).[16] The United States demanded that Libya extradite two of their nationals suspected of carrying out the Lockerbie bombing, following which the UN Security Council passed a resolution imposing economic sanctions on Libya.[17] Libya requested provisional measures from the ICJ, on the basis that the US demand and sanctions were contrary to provisions in the *Montreal Convention* (that gave Libya jurisdiction to deal with the matter).[18] The ICJ found that it had jurisdiction to hear the dispute, but before it could award provisional measures Libya entered into an agreement with the UK to hand the Lockerbie suspects over to them. In 1999, the Lockerbie suspects were handed over and tried in the Netherlands under Scottish law, and one of the suspects jailed.

As with the *Raw Materials* and *Rare Earths* cases, commentators have analysed the ICJ decision as signifying a contest of power between two primary authorities of international law: the UN Security Council and the International Court of Justice.[19] In terms of realpolitik, this could be a story of politics (the UN SC) versus law (the ICJ) or about imperial/economically powerful states versus the post-colonial state. The decision, however, has neither been discussed in terms of the oil, arms, or investment deals being carried out in the background, nor in terms of the

[16] For an account of Gaddafi's rule, see Alison Pargeter, *Libya: The Rise and Fall of Qaddafi* (2012).

[17] UNSC Res 748 (31 March 1992) UN Doc S/RES/748.

[18] *Convention for the Suppression of Unlawful Acts against the Safety of Civil Aviation* (adopted 23 September 1971, came into force 26 January 1973) 974 UNTS 178 ('Montreal Convention').

[19] See, for example, Michael Plachta, *The Lockerbie Case: The Role of the Security Council in Enforcing the Principle* Aut Dedere Aut Judicare' 12(1) *European Journal of International Law* 2001, 125–40; Vera Gowlland-Debbas, 'The Relationship Between the International Court of Justice and the Security Council in the Light of the Lockerbie Case' 88(4) *The American Journal of International Law* 1994, 643–77; and Kamrul Hossain, 'Legality of the Security Council Action: Does

havoc wreaked on the Libyan population as a result of sanctions and civil war. In 2005, after the UN Security Council lifted sanctions in 2003, Libya auctioned oil and gas exploration licences to US energy companies. In 2010, BP confirmed that it was to begin drilling off the Libyan coast. In 2011, civil war in Libya (triggered in part by the Arab Spring) prompted the UN Security Council to pass a resolution authorizing military intervention.[20] In 2013, a leaked email revealed that the convicted Lockerbie bomber Abdelbaset al-Megrahi would be released as part of a prisoner transfer agreement, once Muammar Gaddafi's regime in Libya had fulfilled its promise to buy an air defence system produced by a manufacturer part-owned by BAE Systems. It also revealed that one of the UK's key objectives in engaging with Libya was to convince it to invest £80 billion of its sovereign wealth fund through the City of London.[21]

Out of the earth pipes black gold: the world's insides gush out. Thicker than water, we're drinking the sun. Squeezing it into our deep-sea pipes. Swallowing it into our cars and planes. We would die of thirst if it were to stop, if the world were to stop for the lack of oil. We're sell such lovely tungsten arms, made from time itself. Libya: glinting, volatile, vast. Faster, further, gliding, burning. Upstream, downstream, courts save public morality while the public pays in blood.

The *Seal Products* case was brought in 2009 at the WTO DSB against the European Communities by Norway and Canada, who challenged a ban on the importation of seal products into the European Union.[22] It marks the first time that the WTO has considered the place of public morality about cruelty toward animals (specifically, seals) within the international trade law regime. While it is not the story of technology or of the risk of harm to the environment exemplified by *EC–Biotech* and *Nuclear Weapons*,

the International Court of Justice Move to Take Up the Challenge of Judicial Review?' 5(17) *Uluslararas Hukuk ve Politika* 2009, 133–63.

[20] UNSC Res 1973 (17 March 2011) UN Doc S/RES/1973.

[21] Robert Mendick and Edward Malnick, 'Lockerbie Bomber Release Linked to Arms Deal, According to Secret Letter' 27 July 2013: http://www.telegraph.co.uk/news/politics/10206659/Lockerbie-bomber-release-linked-to-arms-deal-according-to-secret-letter.html.

[22] *European Communities–Measures Prohibiting the Importation and Marketing of Seal Products*, Appellate Body Report, WT/DS400/AB/R and WT/DS401/AB/R,

this case does bring up the problem of what it is to be human (and its relation to the animal) in this globalized world.

In this case, the Appellate Body upheld the WTO Panel's finding that the ban fell under Article XX(a) of the GATT (providing a provisional justification for the ban, on the basis of protecting 'public morals'). While Canada argued that this public concern over animal welfare would also extend to the killing of other species (for food and sport), the Appellate Body dismissed this, saying that general animal welfare concerns would fall under the GATT Article XX(b) and lent themselves to 'scientific or other methods of inquiry',[23] which could set standards for state intervention that were altogether different to those standards relevant for the protection of public morals. They therefore confirmed that WTO members have some discretion in designing measures intended to protect public morality. The Appellate Body also upheld the Panel's reasoning that the implementation of an alternative, less trade-restrictive measure such as the introduction of a certification system would not have met the objectives of the ban.

In their final determination, however, the Appellate Body found that the ban did not in fact meet the conditions of Article XX. This was, first, because the EU unjustifiably or arbitrarily discriminated against seal-product traders by allowing products from 'indigenous' seal hunts. The Appellate Body reasoned that, first, not only was this 'indigenous communities' exception ambiguous (opening it up to abuse), but it did not have to meet any welfare requirements. Second, the EU had given Greenlandic Inuit more support than Canadian Inuit to market their products under the ban's exception.[24] Some commentators have dealt with this case as a litmus test for the international trade regime

adopted on 18 June 2014. This concerned the European Parliament and Council Regulation 1007/2009 [2009] OJ L286/36 and its implementing Commission Regulation 737/2010, which prohibited the 'placing on the market of seal products' unless (i) they resulted from hunts traditionally conducted by Inuit and other indigenous communities; (ii) they resulted from by-products of hunting that is regulated by national law and conducted for the sole purpose of the sustainable management of marine resources, or (iii) they were bought into the EU exclusively for the personal use of travellers or their families.

[23] Above n. 22 [5.198].

[24] Above n. 22 [5.326–5.337].

to account for the heightened sensibilities of those populations that are adverse to the importation of certain offensive products (and the consequent right of sovereign states to determine the parameters of the trade in those products).[25] Other commentaries on this case revolve around the issues of animal welfare, looking in particular at the relevance of animal welfare-related international law to the WTO's GATT regime.[26] Both discourses rely on nineteenth-century notions of an English civility that abhors cruel treatment of 'innocent' animals and that legislates for their 'welfare'—a civility that has nonetheless been comfortable with the large-scale global industrialization of food animal production which slaughters around 60 billion land animals a year.[27] They also endorse a narrow notion of what the phrases 'public morality', 'public concern', and 'animal welfare' mean.

Onto the earth fall newborn seals: soft bodies, warm coats. Belting, smashing, grinding, skinning. Newborn blood churned up from the bowels, thicker than water and glinting on snow. Upstream, downstream, public morals are offended, the state is offended by these frightening men who wield machetes and do not pay tax and are unashamed. These are not artefacts in mumbling canoes; these are not artisans or soldiers. Europe does not deal in carnivals.

[25] Robert Howse and Joanna Langille, 'Permitting Pluralism: The *Seal Products* Dispute and Why the WTO Should Accept Trade Restrictions Justified by Noninstrumental Moral Values' 37 *Yale Journal of International Law* 2012, 367. There are also numerous commentaries online by non-governmental organizations pressing for the abolition of the annual seal slaughter and the trade in skins.

[26] See, for example, Katie Sykes, 'Sealing Animal Welfare into the GATT Exceptions: The International Dimension of Animal Welfare in WTO Disputes' 13(3) *World Trade Review* 2014, 471–98. Sykes argues that there should have been more consideration by the Appellate Body of how the emergent body of international norms regarding animal welfare interacts with WTO law. Sykes problematizes the 'public morality' exception by pointing out that while there is a growing international movement (against sealing), that movement is cosmopolitan and urbane, distanced from the traditional, rural cultures from whence the practice of sealing emerged. Tamara Perišin, 'Is the EU Seal Products Regulation a Sealed Deal? EU and WTO Challenges' 62 *International and Comparative Law Quarterly* 2013, 373–405 and Heather Cook, 'The EU Seal Products Ban Tests the WTO's Public Morals Exception' 81(4) *Journal of Transportation Law, Logistics and Policy* 2015, 311–34.

[27] See, for example, http://www.worldwatch.org/node/5443.

CONCLUSION

At the turn of the millennium some astrophysicists proclaimed that the universe would most likely expand forever, accelerating, without limit, and that approximately 96 per cent of outer space was unknowable 'dark matter' and 'dark energy'.[1] While in a century previous to this Joseph Conrad wrote about the fear of, and desire for, an uncolonizable continent in the world,[2] the scientific imaginary today conjures a vacuum beyond it: invisible, impenetrable, and infinite. To touch his lost origin man must now fly at the speed of light into the dark heart of technological singularity,[3] and to find his humanness he must make all traces of his material corporeality disappear. Such a paradox of omnipresence and invisibility is a dangerous story of escape, from the oblivion of mortality without origin to that of immortality without end.

Perhaps it was because Stanisław Ulam escaped from Poland on the eve of the Second World War; because his parents could not; because he was a brilliant mathematician; and because

[1] See for example Mario Livio, *The Accelerating Universe: Infinite Expansion, the Cosmological Constant, and the Beauty of the Universe* (2000); Centre National de la Recherche Scientifique, 'Confirmation of the Accelerating Expansion of the Universe', http://www2.cnrs.fr/en/45.htm?&debut=160xt/..

[2] Joseph Conrad, *Heart of Darkness* (1902; 2007 edn).

[3] Stanislaw Ulam was among the first to refer to the concept of 'technological singularity' in May 1958, as 'the ever accelerating progress of technology and changes in the mode of human life, which gives the appearance of approaching some essential singularity in the history of the race beyond which human affairs, as we know them, could not continue'. Stanislaw Ulam, 'John von Neumann 1903–1957' 64 *Bulletin of the American Mathematical Society* 1958, 1. This refers, I think, to the idea of a completion of humankind's expression through technology, which would entail both an end of invention, and of humanness, as we know it. This problem is helpfully described by Bernard Stiegler as follows: '[I]n the astral age, this world is now common to all humanity, it is "accomplished," culminated in its movement of planetary extension, insofar as this movement would have characterized it—"culminated" also means finished, terminated, disappeared or disappearing ("change of epoch").' Bernard Stiegler, *Technics and Time, 1: The Fault of Epimetheus* (George Collins and Richard Beardsworth trans, 1998 edn) [trans. of: *La technique et le temps, 1: La faute d'Épiméthée*, 1994] 90.

his fellowship at Harvard was not renewed that he joined the Manhattan Project and with others there invented the hydrogen bomb.[4] This was the first of two major inventions he worked on in his lifetime. The second, a theory of nuclear pulse propulsion imagined in 1947, was developed into what was known as Project Orion. Project Orion envisaged an 8 million ton interstellar ark the size of a city to be launched into space, which at top velocity would travel close to the speed of light.[5] Together they marked the cutting edge of technological invention in the twentieth century: the first designed to destroy human life, and the second, to save it.

The decade 1996–2006 witnessed the 'Human Genome Project': a mapping of human DNA.[6] It also bracketed the *Nuclear Weapons* and *EC–Biotech* cases. As I suggest in this book, not only did the turn of the millennium see an ever-greater shift in science *inwards* (towards control of human reproduction) but also a concurrent and increasing turn *outwards*, beyond the material confines of the earth. Bound by desire for a lost intimacy, the human power of invention now has to be figured, not in terms of access to other bodies but in terms of a metabolic *speed* of access. This is a speed at which man could escape the shrinking globe, through a generative body, guaranteeing his existential survival. Modern man crawls, he flies—toward liberation and an abyssal immanence. As the technology that precipitates this movement,

[4] 'Manhattan Project' was the codename of a research programme created by the United States to develop nuclear power to use in the Second World War. For the longer biography of this fascinating figure, see William G Matthews and Daniel O Hirsch, *The Adventures of a Mathematician: Stanisław Ulam* (1991).

[5] The *Partial Test Ban Treaty*, 10 October, 480 UNTS 43, 1963 is generally acknowledged to have ended this project. While in real terms science had not reached the capacity to fly objects in space at anything approaching the speed of light; it is science's reference to *light* as a measure of what is good which is interesting from a philosophical perspective. This is discussed in more detail in Chapter 3.

[6] The project began in 1996, and in May 2006 the sequence of the last chromosome was published in the scientific journal *Nature*. The purported aims of the project were to: identify all the approximately 20,000–25,000 genes in human DNA; determine the sequences of the 3 billion chemical base pairs that make up human DNA; store this information in databases; improve tools for data analysis; transfer related technologies to the private sector: on The US Department of Energy's Human Genome Program website: http://www.ornl.gov/sci/techresources/Human_Genome/project/about.shtml.

international law is haunted by the impossibility of producing or recovering a body *anywhere*. It is thus that while invention is indeed the condition of human life in the international domain, the various technologies it creates are unable to sustain the reproduction of that life.

Before concluding with some final thoughts I will first retrace the steps that we have taken up to this point. Focusing on the themes of 'technology', 'human life', and the 'international domain', the first part of the book introduced two case studies: one that pertained to the governance of genetically modified organisms and the other that pertained to the governance of nuclear weapons. What becomes evident from these case studies is that while jurists in both cases felt compelled to assume the necessity of technology's 'saving power', the potentially annihilating risks of technological proliferation led to findings that can be called hysteric, in both form and content. The decisions were characterized by (in turn) unusual refusals to decide; multiple delays; extremely lengthy opinions; calls for evidence subsequently not considered; and agonizing discussions about hierarchies of existence between international law, sovereign states, and human life. In the *EC–Biotech* dispute we see a preoccupation with speed and delay, and in the *Nuclear Weapons* case there is a preoccupation with silence and speech. In both cases there is a pervasive anxiety about international law's capacity to secure the protection of human life vis-à-vis technology.

To make sense of the key themes that recur through the two case studies, I turned to post-war philosophers who have thematized the role of technology in the determination of what it means to be human. Their engagements provide an interesting set of theological reference points with regard to technology, human life, and an emerging post-industrial secular political domain. Freud treats technology as a threatening entity that subjects humans to the universal forces of death and desire. Benjamin poses technology against the state. Schmitt argues that the sovereign is the force that should hold technology in check; while Heidegger and Stiegler argue that technological invention is itself a process of representing humanness. Each of these accounts resonates with the jurists' discussions in *Nuclear Weapons* and *EC–Biotech,* whereby nuclear and genetic technologies were posed against the state, or against international law, or against human life. I then brought in feminist critiques of the gendered metaphysics upon which the political economies of the (male) philosophers rely, arguing that such critiques enable us to think differently about the 'failure' of the international lawyers to decide on the legality of nuclear weapons and genetically modified organisms.

The remainder of my analysis looked at other historically significant texts (treaties and speeches) to see whether it is indeed theoretically convincing to think about international law as an invention that secures the 'humanness' of human life, in a global political economy separate from a religious one. Beginning with the unconditional surrender documents of Japan and Germany, nuclear weapons and international law alike were each imputed to have both a saving and a destroying potential for the state, or for humanness. An examination of those documents shows how the state makes a proprietary claim to land that is imagined in terms of the reproductive human body, which itself makes the individual human body part of a community across space (humanity) and time (human*ness*). Excerpts from the wartime speeches and declarations by officials and the heads of state of the United States, Germany, and Japan, as well as from post-war documents such as the *Atlantic Charter* and the *United Nations Charter*, show a new world dominated by the rhetoric of sovereign equality and the recognition of fraternity. While referring frequently to divine authority, the language of those texts proclaims the invention of a domain in which a universal humanity or humanness will be secured, independently of religious jurisdiction and through a ritual binding into a global economy.

Returning then to the *Nuclear Weapons* and *EC–Biotech* cases and placing these within a post-war context (looking in particular at the texts produced at the end of the Cold War), what emerges is a picture of a public discourse imbricated in a crisis of modernity, most visibly in the form of international law that as a human invention is confronted with the predicament of having to simultaneously account for its own existence (without transcendental authority), and the existence of humanness (a quality that attaches to a transcendental form of life). Following on from the analyses of the two case studies, we can see that while the public language of international law promises to guarantee humanness in a world without God, the decisions in *Nuclear Weapons* and *EC–Biotech* do not deliver. The terms 'risk' and 'unconditionality' referred to in the case studies are expressions of the eschatological tensions embedded in public language that deals with technology, and we see that the ICJ and the WTO DSB could not choose between the mutually constitutive bodies of the sovereign state and the biological human, nor between international law and other technologies that have a saving *and* a destroying power vis-à-vis human life. International law's order, in other words, is driven by a desire to produce and guarantee 'unconditional life': human life without condition, infinite and immortal. In the face of (genetic, nuclear) technologies that threaten to collapse the symbolic separation of self-authorized human existence from the originary force of 'nature' or the 'divine', jurists fail (or refuse) to decide.

The crisis of judgment displayed in the *Nuclear Weapons* and *EC–Biotech* cases is a crisis that can also be described as a manifestation of modern nihilism (here, a secular expression of the eschatological bind) most present in the uneasy tension between speed and delay that international law constitutes and navigates. As a technology, international law functions to keep a universal human time, but in striving to transcend the material conditions of human life it is confronted by its ambitions for a *timelessness* that would guarantee immortality. While the jurists and philosophers I have examined in the book have framed the relation between technology, human life, and the international in ways that enable us to name the problem, they, like our international law forefathers, are also beholden to the fantasy that human life *can* be unconditional: purely symbolic, or purely secular. This fantasy relies upon metaphysics akin to a house of cards: it reduces human life to something that is only reproduced symbolically, without any material conditions and with the imagined properties of a singular sex.

Rehearsing well-worn tropes of the brotherly/enlightened/active/visual subject versus the natural/ignorant/receptive/visible object, public discourse establishes the modern global economy as a masculine economy, and the ideal of the sovereign state as a *masculine* ideal. Human life—in terms of its humanity and human*ness*—is produced and preserved within a masculine discursive domain. The secular authority of international law, in other words, is not only based on a structural verisimilitude to the theological, but also on a valorization of 'masculine' virtues. The post-war thinkers Luce Irigaray, Julia Kristeva, and Adriana Cavarero show classical Western metaphysics to be premised on gendered tropes that are channelled through cultural, social, and economic discourse. An analysis of public discourse that draws on their critiques shows that the existential crisis symptomatic of international law cases dealing with questions of technology and risk has its basis not only in religious eschatology but also in the privileging of a masculine sex over others. I argue that the attempt (in international discourse and, specifically, in international law) to enact a human transcendence premised on the idea of a single sex, erases the material (coded feminine) conditions of reproduction.

Is technological invention a condition of human life in the international domain, and if so, how are we to live with it? In response to the question, technological invention *is* a condition of human life in the modern international domain. It is co-emergent with the idea of modern human life that is separate from the symbolic life of the Church. Indeed, as has been canvassed by various thinkers throughout the twentieth century, technological invention promises total knowledge and total power: the 'end of time', in the language of theology. As my analysis shows, we rely heavily upon the idea that a global human community can be produced entirely symbolically, without paying heed to the material conditions or experience of human life. And our symbolic production of this community is deeply gendered, risking international law's own paradigm. It is, however, in the very unsettling of the relation between the modern state and human life, in the very risk or danger of international law's collapse, where there lies a possibility for recognizing international law's fetishization of unconditional life and for engendering a more intimate understanding of what it means to be human, caring for our rootedness in the earth.

As both a product and constitutive technology of modernity, international law (if it is to have any future) therefore has the potential to prompt a radical rethinking of what it means to be human. The question that then remains is how we—humans, international lawyers—are to undertake this in our work. The final chapter in this book offers a vision of what such attentiveness might look like in relation to 'real' international law, with reference to three recent WTO and ICJ cases. As we enter a terrifying age of climate catastrophe, globalized food production, and drone warfare, it seems to me that international lawyers have a great deal to do in order to reorient our art.

Amaterasu, light of the sun
Scorching the ashes of a bunker nation
Drifting into her vermillion sky
Fragmenting images of stone
Her own temple caves
The echo of laughter shadows
Her jurisdiction of double flowers
Keeping in the early hours
Another time

EPILOGUE

Distr: General

RESOLUTION

The author,

1. *Reaffirming* that international law today faces new challenges in its quest for 'human security' in the face of unknown risks,
2. *Guided* by the work of feminist legal theorists and post-structuralist thinkers,
3. *Having* considered a range of international law texts produced since the Second World War,
4. *Proposes* that the work of international law to secure human life can be described as a work of modern technics,
5. *Expresses* deep concern that sovereignty is conditioned upon the designation of the sovereign state's speaking body as a masculine one, privileged over the conception of a hysteric feminine,
6. *Remains* concerned that the idea of the modern state is bolstered by an infinite acceleration of political economy in pursuit of unconditional life,
7. *Notes* that international law as a technology attempts to maintain the desire for unconditional existence by simultaneously marking the time of immanent human life while burying the material human body,
8. *Recognizes* that in the face of incalculable risk, the failure of international law jurists to guarantee the promise of unconditionality has led to a crisis of jurisdiction,
9. *Calls* for a re-evaluation and re-imagination of the technics of international law and its relation to the human,
10. *Urges* readers to embrace a poetics that resists the violent binaries engendered by existing forms of legal syntax, and
11. *Decides* to remain actively seized of the matter.

BIBLIOGRAPHY

Abbas, Ackbar (ed.), *The Provocation of Jean Baudrillard*, Twilight Books (1990)

Adam, Barbara, Beck, Ulrich, and Van Loon, Joost (eds), *The Risk Society and Beyond: Critical Issues for Social Theory*, SAGE Publications Ltd (2000)

Adorno, Theodor and Horkheimer, Max, *Dialectic of Enlightenment*, New York (Ian Cumming trans. 1998) [trans. of *Dialektik der Aufklarung*, 1979]

Agamben, Giorgio, *The Open: Man and Animal*, Stanford University Press (Kevin Attell trans., 2004 edn) [trans. of: *L'aperto: L'uomo e l'animale*, 2002]

Agamben, Giorgio, *State of Exception*, University of Chicago Press (Kevin Attell trans., 2005 edn) [trans. of: *Stato di eccezione*, 2003]

Alston, Philip (ed.), *Peoples' Rights*, Oxford University Press (2001)

Althusser, Louis, *Ideology and Ideological State Apparatuses (Notes towards an Investigation)*, Monthly Review Press (Ben Brewster trans., 1971) [trans. of: *Idéologie et appareils idéologiques d'État (Notes pour une researche)*, 1970]

Anderson, Luke, *Genetic Engineering, Food and Our Environment*, Resurgence Books (2000)

Anghie, Antony, *Imperialism, Sovereignty and the Making of International Law* (2005)

Anghie, Antony, Chimni, Bhupinder, Mickelson, Karin et al. (eds), *The Third World and International Order: Law, Politics and Globalization*, Leiden, Martinus Nijhoff (2003)

Arendt, Hannah, *The Human Condition*, University of Chicago Press (1958)

Arrighi, Giovanni, *The Long Twentieth Century: Money, Power and the Origins of Our Time* Verso (1994)

Badiou, Alain, *Being and Event*, Bloomsbury Revelations (Jon Roffe trans., 2006) [trans. of: *L'être et L'événement*, 1988]

Barthes, Roland, *Writing Degree Zero*, Hill and Wang (Annette Lavers and Colin Smith trans., 1967 edn)

Barthes, Roland, *A Lover's Discourse: Fragments*, Hill and Wang (Howard, Richard trans., 1978 edn)

Barthes, Roland, *Mythologies*, Vintage Classics (Lavers, Annette trans., 1993)

Bartlett, Robert, *The Making of Europe: Conquest, Colonization and Cultural Change 950–1350*, Princeton University Press (1993)

Bataille, Georges, *The Accursed Share: The History of Eroticism and Sovereignty* vol. I, Zone Books (Robert Hurley trans., 1993 edn) [trans. of: *La Parte maudite*, 1949]

Bataille, Georges, *The Accursed Share: The History of Eroticism and Sovereignty* vol. II and III, Zone Books (Robert Hurley trans., 1993 edn) [trans. of: *La Parte maudite*, 1949]

Beard, Jennifer L., *The Political Economy of Desire: International Law, Development and the Nation State*, GlassHouse Books, Routledge (2007)

Beardsworth, Richard, *Derrida and the Political*, Routledge (1996)

Beardsworth, Sara, *Julia Kristeva: Psychoanalysis and Modernity*, SUNY Press (2004)

Benjamin, Jessica, *Shadow of the Other: Intersubjectivity and Gender in Psychoanalysis*, Psychology Press (1998)

Benjamin, Walter, *Illuminations: Essays and Reflections*, Schocken (Peter Demetz ed., 1986) [trans. of: *Zur Kritik der Gewalt*, 1921]

Berger, John, *Ways of Seeing*, Penguin Books (1990)

Bernstein, Peter, *Against the Gods: The Remarkable Story of Risk*, Wiley (1996)

Bhabha, Homi, *The Location of Culture*, Routledge (1994)

Bix, Herbert P., *Hirohito and the Making of Modern Japan*, Harper Perennial (2001)

Blanchot, Maurice, *L'Entretien infini*, Gallimard (1969)

Bodin, Jean, *Six Books of a Commonwealth*, Harvard University Press (Kenneth D. MacRae ed. and Richard Knowlles trans., 1962 edn) [trans. of: *Les Six livres de la République*, 1576]

Boisson de Chazournes, Laurence and Sands, Philippe (eds), *International Law, the International Court of Justice and Nuclear Weapons*, Cambridge University Press (1999)

Botting, Fred and Wilson, Scott (eds), *Bataille: A Critical Reader*, Wiley-Blackwell (1998)

Breuer, Josef and Freud, Sigmund, *Studies on Hysteria*, Penguin Books (Nicola Luckhurst trans., 2004 edn) [trans. of: *Studien über Hysterie*, 1895]

Brownlie, Ian, *Principles of Public International Law*, Oxford University Press (2003)

Butler, Judith, *Bodies that Matter: On the Discursive Limits of 'Sex'*, Routledge (1993)

Cadava, Eduardo, Connor, Peter, and Nancy, Jean-Luc (eds), *Who Comes After the Subject?*, Routledge (1991)

Calarco, Matthew, *Zoographies: The Question of the Animal from Heidegger to Derrida*, Columbia University Press (2008)

Calarco, Matthew and Atterton, Peter (eds), *The Continental Ethics Reader*, Routledge (2003)

Cavarero, Adriana, *In Spite of Plato: A Feminist Rewriting of Ancient Philosophy*, Polity (1995)

Cavarero, Adriana, *Stately Bodies: Literature, Philosophy, and the Question of Gender*, The University of Michigan Press (Robert de Lucca and Deanna Shamek trans., 2002 edn) [trans. of: *Corpo in figure*, 1995]

Cane, Peter, Evans, Carolyn, and Robinson, Zoë (eds), *Law and Religion in Theoretical and Historical Context*, Cambridge University Press (2008)

Cheah, Pheng, David, Fraser, and Grbich, Judith (eds), *Thinking Through the Body of the Law*, NYU Press (1996)

Chinkin, Christine and Charlesworth, Hilary, *The Boundaries of International Law: A Feminist Analysis*, Manchester University Press (2000)

Chodorow, Nancy, *The Reproduction of Mothering: Psychoanalysis and the Sociology of Gender* (1978)

Chodorow, Nancy, *The Power of Feelings: Personal Meaning in Psychoanalysis, Gender, and Culture* (2001)

Cixous, Hélène, *Portrait de Dora* (1976)

Clack, Beverley (ed.), *Misogyny in the Western Philosophical Tradition: A Reader* (1999)

Collins, Ace, *Songs Behind the Hymns that Inspire America* (2003)

Conrad, Joseph, *Heart of Darkness* (1902)

Cormack, Bradin, *A Power to Do Justice: Jurisdiction, English Literature, and the Rise of Common Law, 1509–1625* (2007)

Corngold, Stanley, *The Fate of the Self: German Writers and French Theory* (1994)

Crawford, James, *Brownlie's Principles of International Law* (2012) 130

Crawford, James, *The Creation of States in International Law* (1979)

Deleuze, Gilles and Guattari, Félix, *Anti-Oedipus* (1977)

Derrida, Jacques, *Of Grammatology* (Gayatri Chakravorty Spivak trans., 1976 edn)

Derrida, Jacques, *Spurs: Nietzsche's Styles* (Barbara Harlow trans., 1978 edn)

Derrida, Jacques, *Dissemination* (Barbara Johnson trans., 1983 edn)

Derrida, Jacques, 'Letter to A Japanese Friend' in David Wood and Robert Bernasconi (eds), *Derrida and Différance* (1988)

Derrida, Jacques, 'More than One Language' in *A Derrida Reader: Between the Blinds* (Peggy Kamuf trans., 1991 edn)

Derrida, Jacques, *Of Spirit: Heidegger and the Question* (Geoffrey Bennington and Rachel Bowlby trans., 1991 edn) [trans. of: *De l'esprit*, 1987]

Derrida, Jacques, *The Other Heading: Reflections on Today's Europe* (Pascale-Anne Brault and Michael B. Naas trans., 1992 edn) [trans. of: *L'autre cap*, 1991]

Derrida, Jacques, 'Force of Law: The Mystical Foundations of Authority' (Mary Quaintance trans., 1992) in Drucilla Cornell, Michael Rosenfeld, and David Gray Carlson (eds), *Deconstruction and the Possibility of Justice* (1992) 3 [trans. of: *Force de loi: le fondement mystique de l'autorité*, 1989].

Derrida, Jacques, *Aporias* (Thomas Dutoit trans., 1993 edn) [trans. of: *Apories: Mourir-s'attendre aux limites de la vérité*, 1993]

Derrida, Jacques, *Specters of Marx* (Peggy Kamuf trans., 1994)

Derrida, Jacques, *The Gift of Death* (David Wills trans., 1995 edn) [trans. of: *Donner la mort*, 1992]

Derrida, Jacques, *The Politics of Friendship* (George Collins trans., 1997 edn) [trans. of: *Politiques de l'amitié*, 1994]

Derrida, Jacques, *Archive Fever: A Freudian Impression* (Eric Prenowitz trans., 1998 edn) [trans. of: *Mal d'archive: Une impression freudienne*. 1995]

Derrida, Jacques, *Resistances of Psychoanalysis* (Peggy Kamuf, Pascale-Anne Brault and Michael Naas trans., 1998 edn) [trans. of: *Résistances de la psychanalyse*, 1996]

Derrida, Jacques, *Monolingualism of the Other or The Prosthesis of Origin* (Patrick Mensah trans. of: *Le monolinguisme de l'autre: ou la prothèse d'origine* 1996]

Derrida, Jacques, *Of Hospitality: Anne Dufourmantelle Invites Jacques Derrida to Respond* (Bowlby, Rachel trans., 2000) [trans. of: *De l'hospitalité: Anne Dufourmantelle invite Jacques Derrida à répondre* 1997]

Derrida, Jacques, *Without Alibi* (Peggy Kamuf trans., 2002 edn) [trans. of: *Etats d'âme de psychanalyse*, 2000]

Derrida, Jacques, *On Cosmopolitanism and Forgiveness* (Mark Dooley and Michael Hughes trans., 2001 edn) [trans. of: *Foi et Savoir suivi de Le Siècle et le Pardon*, 2001]

Derrida, Jacques, *Rogues: Two Essays on Reason* (Pascale-Anne Brault and Michael Naas trans., 2005 edn) [trans. of: *Voyous: deux essais sur la raison*, 2003]

Derrida, Jacques, *Deconstruction Engaged: The Sydney Seminars* (Paul Patton and Terry Smith eds, 2006)

Derrida, Jacques, *The Animal That Therefore I Am* (Marie-Louise Mallet ed.) (David Wills trans., 2008 edn) [trans. of: *L'Animal que donc je suis*, 2006]

Derrida, Jacques, *The Beast and the Sovereign v I* (Michel Lisse, Marie-Louise Mallet, and Ginette Michaud eds) (Geoffrey Bennington trans., 2009 edn) [trans. of: *Séminaire Law bête et le souverain*, 2010]

Deutsch, Hélène, *Psychoanalysis of the Sexual Functions of Women* (Paul Roazen trans., 1991 edn) [trans. of: *Psychoanalyse der weiblichen Sexualfunktionen*, 1925]

Deutscher, Penelope, *A Politics of Impossible Difference: The Later Work of Luce Irigaray* (2002)

Diprose, Rosalyn, *The Bodies of Women: Ethics, Embodiment and Sexual Difference* (1994)

Diprose, Rosalyn and Ferrell, Robyn (eds), *Cartographies* (1991)

Doane, Janice and Hodges, Devon, *From Klein to Kristeva: Psychoanalytic Feminism and the Search for the 'Good Enough' Mother* (1992)

Dobb, Maurice, 'Capital Accumulation and Mercantilism' in Maurice Dobb, *Studies in the Development of Capitalism* (1946)

Douzinas, Costas, *The End of Human Rights: Critical Legal Thought at the Turn of the Century* (2000)

Dower, John, *Embracing Defeat: Japan in the Wake of WWII* (2000)

Dufourmantelle, Anne, *Of Hospitality: Anne Dufourmantelle invites Jacques Derrida to Respond* (Rachel Bowlby trans., 2000 edn) [trans. of: *Du l'hospitalité: Anne Dufourmantelle invite Jacques Derrida à répondre*, 1997]

Felman, Shoshana, *What Does a Woman Want? Reading and Sexual Difference* (1993)

Fletcher, John and Benjamin, Andrew (eds), *Abjection, Melancholia and Love: The Work of Julia Kristeva* (1990)

Ford, Boris (ed.), *Medieval Literature: Part One: Chaucer and the Alliterative Tradition* (1982)

Foster, Hal (ed.), *The Anti-Aesthetic: Essays on Postmodern Culture* (1983)

Foucault, Michel, *Madness and Civilisation* (1967) (Richard Howard trans., 1967 edn) [trans of: *Folie et Déraison: Histoire de la folie à l'âge classique*, 1964]

Freud, Sigmund, *The Interpretation of Dreams* (Angela Richards ed., 1992 edn) (James Strachey original trans., 1953 edn) [trans. of: *Die Traumdeutung*, 1900]

Friedman, Thomas, *The Lexus and the Olive Tree* (1999)

Fukuyama, Francis, *The End of History and the Last Man* (1992)

Gay, Peter (ed.), *The Freud Reader* (1995)

Gilman, Sander et al., *Hysteria Beyond Freud* (1993)

Girard, René, *Deceit, Desire and the Novel* (Yvonne Freccero trans., 1966 edn) [trans. of: *Mensonge romantique et vérité Romanesque*, 1961]

Girard, René, *Violence and the Sacred* (Gregory Patrick trans., 1977 edn) [trans. of: *La violence et le Sacré*, 1972]

Glendinning, Simon, *On Being with Others: Heidegger–Derrida–Wittgenstein* (1998)

Goodrich, Peter, *Reading the Law: A Critical Introduction to Legal Method and Techniques* (1986)

Gosetti-Ferencei, Jennifer Anna, *Heidegger, Hölderlin, and the Subject of Poetic Language: Toward a New Poetics of Dasein* (2004)

Grosz, Elizabeth, *Jacques Lacan: A Feminist Introduction* (1990)

Grosz, Elizabeth, *Space, Time and Perversion* (1995)

Grosz, Elizabeth, *The Nick of Time: Politics, Evolution and the Untimely* (2004)

Grotius, Hugo *The Free Sea* (Ralph van Deman Magoffin trans., 1609 edn) [trans. of: *Mare Liberum*]

Grotius, Hugo, *On the Laws of War and Peace* (2004) [trans. of: *De jure belli ac pacis*, 1625 (revised edn, 1631)]

Hardt, Michael and Negri, Antonio, *Empire* (2000)

Harootunian, Harry and Yoda, Tomiko (eds) *Japan After Japan: Social and Cultural Life from the Recessionary 1990s to the Present* (2006)

Hay, Dennis, *Europe in the Fourteenth and Fifteenth Centuries: A General History of Europe* (1966)

Heidegger, Martin, *Being and Time* (John Macquarrie and Edward Robinson trans., 1962)

Heidegger, Martin, *The Question Concerning Technology and Other Essays* (William Lovitt trans., 1977 edn) [trans. of: *Die Frage nach der Technik*, 1954]

Heidegger, Martin, *Nihilism as Determined by the History of Being* or *The Eternal Recurrence of the Same* (David F. Krell trans., 1984 edn) [trans. of: *Die seinsgeschichtliche Bestimmung des Nihilismus*, 1944–46]

Hobbes, Thomas, *Leviathan* (1651)

Hooke, S.H., *Middle Eastern Mythology* (1963)

Howes, David (ed.), *Empire of the Senses: The Sensual Culture Reader* (2005)

Hunter, Janet, E. *The Emergence of Modern Japan: An Introductory History Since 1853* (1989)

Hunter, Rosemary, McGlynn, Clare, and Rackley, Erika, *Feminist Judgments: From Theory to Practice* (2010)

Iacoboni, Marco, *Mirroring People: The New Science of How We Connect With Others* (2008)

Inoue, Kyōko, *MacArthur's Japanese Constitution: a Linguistic and Cultural Study of its Making* (1991)

Irigaray, Luce, *Speculum of the Other Woman* (Gillian C. Gill trans., 1985 edn) [trans. of: *Speculum de l'autre femme*, 1974]

Irigaray, Luce, *Je, Tu, Nous: Towards a Culture of Difference* (Alison Martin trans., 1993 edn)

Irigaray, Luce, *Thinking the Difference: For a Peaceful Revolution* (1994)

Irigaray, Luce, *Sharing the World* (2008)

Jameson, Fredric, *The Political Unconscious* (1981)

Jameson, Fredric, *Postmodernism, or, the Cultural Logic of Late Capitalism* (1991)

Janssens, Rudolf V.A., *What Future for Japan?* (1995)

Jessup, Phillip, *A Modern Law of Nations* (1948)

Johns, Fleur, *Non-Legality in International Law: Unruly Law* (2015)

Kamuf, Peggy (ed.), *The Derrida Reader: Between the Blinds* (1991)

Kapsalis, Terri and Litherland, Gina, *The Hysterical Alphabet* (2007)

Kelsen, Hans, *Principles of International Law* (2nd edn, 1967)

Kelsen, Hans, *General Theory of Law and State* (Anders Wedberg trans., 1999 edn) [trans. of: original unpublished, 1945]

Kerr, Heather and Nettlebeck, Amanda, *The Space Between—Australian Women Writing Fictocriticism* (1998)

Kojève, Alexandre, *Outline of a Phenomenology of Right* (Bryan-Paul Frost ed.) (Bryan-Paul Frost and Robert Howse trans., 2000 edn) [trans. of: *Equisse d'une phenomenologie du droit*, 1981]

Koskenniemi, Martti, *Apology to Utopia* (1989)

Krasner, Stephen, 'Westphalia and All That' in Judith Goldstein and Robert Keohane (eds), *Ideas and Foreign Policy: Beliefs, Institutions, and Political Change* (1993)

Kratochwil, F., *Rules, Norms and Decisions* (1989)

Kristeva, Julia, *Powers of Horror: An Essay on Abjection* (Leon S. Roudiez trans., 1982 edn) [trans. of: *Pouvoirs de l'horreur*, 1980]

Kristeva, Julia, *Revolution in Poetic Language* (Margaret Waller trans., 1984 edn) [trans. of: *La Révolution Du Langage Poétique: L'avant-Garde À La Fin Du Xixe Siècle, Lautréamont et Mallarmé*, 1974]

Kristeva, Julia, *Desire in Language: A Semiotic Approach to Literature and Art* (Leon Roudiez ed., Alice Jardine trans., 1980 edn) [trans. of (*inter alia*): *Polylogue*, 1977]

Kristeva, Julia, *In the Beginning was Love: Psychoanalysis and Faith* (Leon Arthur Goldhammer trans., 1987 edn) [trans. of: *Au commencement etait l'amour*, 1985]

Kristeva, Julia, *Tales of Love* (Leon S. Roudiez trans., 1987) [trans. of: *Histoires d'amour*, 1984]

Kristeva, Julia, *Black Sun: Depression and Melancholia* (Leon S. Roudiez, trans., 1989)

Kristeva, Julia, *Strangers to Ourselves* (Leon S. Roudiez trans., 1991)

Kristeva, Julia, *Time and Sense: Proust and the Experience of Literature* (Ross Guberman trans., 1994)

Kristeva, Julia, *Towards a Semiology of Paragrams* (Patrick French and Roland Lack trans., 1998 edn) [trans. of: *Semeiotike: recherches pour une sémanalyse*, 1969]

Kristeva, Julia, *The Sense and Non-Sense of Revolt: The Powers and Limits of Psychoanalysis* (Jeanine Herman trans., 2001 edn) [trans. of: *Sens et non-sens de la révolte: Pouvoirs et limites de la psychanalyse*, 1999]

Kristeva, Julia, *Live Theory* (2004)

Koschmann, J. Victor, *Revolution and Subjectivity in Postwar Japan* (1996)

Kuovo, Sari and Pearson, Zoe (eds), *Between Resistance and Compliance? Feminist Perspectives on International Law in an Era of Anxiety and Terror* (2011)

Kurokawa, Kisho, *The Philosophy of Symbiosis* (1994)

Lacan, Jacques, *Écrits: A Selection* (Alan Sheridan trans., 1977 edn, revised edn Bruce Fink trans., 2002 edn) [trans. of: *Écrits*, 1966]

Lacan, Jacques, *The Seminar of Jacques Lacan Book XI: The Four Fundamental Concepts of Psychoanalysis* (Jacques-Alain Miller ed.) (Alan Sheridan trans., 1981)

Lacan, Jacques, *The Four Fundamental Concepts of Psychoanalysis: The Seminar of Jacques Lacan, Book 11* (Jacques-Alain Miller ed.) (Alan Sheridan trans., 1998 edn) [trans. of: *Le séminaire, Livre XI: Les quatre concepts fondamentaux de la psychanalyse*, 1973]

Lacoue-Labarthe, Philippe, *Typography* (Christopher Fynsk ed., 1989 edn)

Lacoue-Labarthe, Phillipe, *Poetry as Experience* (Andrea Tarnowski trans., 1999 edn) [trans. of: *La poesie comme experience*, 1986]

Lauterpacht, Hersch, *Recognition in International Law* (1947)

Lawrence, Thomas, *The Principles of International Law* (1895)

Lechte, John and Margaroni, Maria, *Julia Kristeva: Live Theory* (2004)

Lee, Maria, *EU Regulation of GMOs* (2008)

Lingis, Alphonso, *Foreign Bodies* (1994)

Lispector, Clarice, *The Passion According to G.H.* (Ronald W. Sousa trans., 1988) [trans. of: *A paixão Segundo G.H.*, 1964]

Lyotard, Jean-Francois, *The Confession of Augustine* (Richard Beardsworth trans., 2000) [trans. of: *La confession d'Augustin*, 1998]

Mackay, James, *History of Modern English Coinage* (1984)

Marion, Jean-Luc, *God without Being* (Thomas Carlson trans., 1995 edn) [trans. of: *Dieu sans l'etre*, 1983]

Marks, Susan (ed.), *International Law on the Left: Re-examining Marxist Legacies* (2008)

Marx, Karl, *Capital: A Critique of Political Economy v 1* (Ben Fowkes trans., 1976)

McNulty, Tracy, *The Hostess: Hospitality, Femininity, and the Expropriation of Identity* (2007)

McVeigh, Shaun (ed.), *Jurisprudence of Jurisdiction* (2007)

Mitchell, Juliet and Rose, Jacqueline (eds), *Feminine Sexuality. Jacques Lacan and the École Freudienne* (1982)

Miyoshi, Masao and Harootunian, H.D. (eds), *Postmodernism and Japan* (1989)

Moi, Toril (ed.), *The Kristeva Reader* (1986)

Mooers, Colin, *The Making of Bourgeois Europe: Absolutism, Revolution and the Rise of Capitalism in England, France and Germany* (1991)

Morgenthau, Hans J., *Politics Among Nations: The Struggle for Power and Peace* (1993)

Mulhall, Stephen, *Heidegger and Being and Time* (1996)

Nancy, Jean-Luc, *Being Singular Plural* (Robert Richardson and Anne O'Byrne trans., 2000 edn) [trans. of: *Être singulier pluriel*, 1996]

Nancy, Jean-Luc, *Corpus* (Richard A. Rand trans., 2008)

Negri, Antonio, *The Savage Anomaly: The Power of Spinoza's Metaphysics and Politics* (Michael Hardt trans., 1991 edn) [trans. of: *L'Anomalia selvaggia: saggio su potere e potenza in Baruch Spinoza* 1981]

Nietzsche, Friedrich, *The Will to Power* (Walter Kaufmann ed.) (Walter Kaufmann and R.J. Hollingdale trans., 1968) [trans. of: *Der Wille zur Macht*, 1901]

Nietzsche, Friedrich, *Twilight of the Idols* (R.J. Hollingdale trans., 1990 edn) [trans. of: *Götzen-Dämmerung, oder, Wie man mit dem Hammer philosophiert*, 1989]

Nietzsche, Friedrich, *On the Genealogy of Morals* (Horace Barnnett Samuel trans., 2003 edn) [trans. of: *Zur Genealogie der Moral: Eine Streitschrift*, 1887]

Norris, Christopher, *Deconstruction* (1982)

O'Leary, Timothy, *Foucault and the Art of Ethics* (2002)

Oliver, Kelly (ed.), *The Portable Kristeva* (2002)

Orford, Anne, *Reading Humanitarian Intervention: Human Rights and the Use of Force in International Law* (2003)

Orford, Anne (ed.), *International Law and its Others* (2008)

Osiander, Andreas, *The States System of Europe, 1640–1900: Peacemaking and the Conditions of International Stability* (1994)

Painter, David S., *The Cold War: An International History* (1999)

Pargeter, Alison, *Libya: The Rise and Fall of Qaddafi* (2012)

Pashukanis, Evgeny, *Selected Writings on Marxism and Law* (P. Beirne and R. Sharlet eds) (Peter B. Maggs trans., 1980 edn)

Patton, Paul and Smith, Terry (eds), *Jacques Derrida: Deconstruction Engaged* (2001)

Plato, *Timeus and Critias* (Desmond Lee trans., 1972 edn)

Plato, *The Republic* (C.D.C. Reeve trans., 2004 edn)

Pearce, Lynne, *The Rhetorics of Feminism: Readings in Contemporary Cultural Theory and the Popular Press* (2004)

Von Pufendorf, Samuel, *On the Law of Nature and Nations* [trans. of: *De jure naturae et gentium*, 1672]

Von Pufendorf, Samuel, *On The Duty of Man and Citizen According to the Natural Law* (Michael Silverthrone trans., 1991 edn) [trans. of: *De officio hominis et civis juxta legem naturalem libri duo*, 1673]

Rabinow, Paul (ed.), *The Foucault Reader* (1984)

Ratner S.R. and Slaughter, A.M., *The Methods of International Law* (2004)

Rose, Jacqueline, *States of Fantasy* (1998)

Rose, Jacqueline, *On Not Being Able to Sleep: Psychoanalysis and the Modern World* (2003)

Rousseau, Jean-Jacques, *The Social Contract* (Victor Gourevitch trans., 1997 edn) [trans. of: *Du contrat social ou principes du droit politique*, 1762]

Rowlands, Mark, *Animals Like Us* (2002)

Said, Edward W. *Culture and Imperialism* (1993)

Sanders, N.K. (trans.), *Poems of Heaven and Hell from Ancient Mesopotamia* (1971)

Schmitt, Carl, *The Nomos of the Earth in the International Law of Jus Publicum Europaeum* (G.L. Ulmen trans., 2003 edn) 126–7 [trans. of: *Der Nomos der Erde*, 1950)

Schmitt, Carl, *Political Theology: Four Chapters on the Concept of Sovereignty* (George D. Schwab trans. and Tracy B. Strong contrib., 2006 edn) [trans. of: *Politische Theologie. Vier Kapitel zur Lehre von der Souveränität*, 1922, revised edn, 1934]

Schreiner, Olive, letter to Karl Pearson in *The Letters of Olive Schreiner* (Rive Richard ed., 1988 edn)

Sedgwick, Eve, *Between Men: English Literature and Male Homosocial Desire* (1985)

Simpson, Gerry, *Law, War and Crime* (2007)

Skinner, Quentin, *Visions of Politics: Volume I: Regarding Method* (2002)

Spivak, Gayatri Chakravorty, 'Can the Subaltern Speak?' in *Marxism and the Interpretation of Culture* (Cary Nelson and Lawrence Grossberg, eds, 1988) 296

Spivak, Gayatri Chakravorty, *A Critique of Postcolonial Reason: Toward a History of the Vanishing Present* (1999)

Steele, Jenny, *Risks and Legal Theory* (2004)

Stiegler, Bernard, *Technics and Time, 1: The Fault of Epimetheus* (George Collins and Richard Beardsworth trans., 1998 edn) [trans. of: *La technique et le temps, 1: La faute d'Épiméthée*, 1994]

Stiegler, Bernard, *Technics and Time, 2: Disorientation* (Stephen Barker trans., 2008 edn) [trans. of: *La Désorientation*, 1996]

Sophocles, *Electra and Other Plays* (Watling, E.F. trans., 1993)

Teschke, Benno, *The Myth of 1648* (2003)

Thomson, Iain, *Heidegger on Ontotheology: Technology and the Politics of Education* (2005)

Tuck, Richard (ed.), *The Rights of War and Peace: Political Thought and the International Order from Grotius to Kant* (2005)

De Vattel, Emerich, *The Law of Nations* (Joseph Chitty ed., 1858) [trans. of: *Droit des gens; ou, principes de la loi naturelle appliqués à la conduite et aux affaires des nations et des souverains*, 1758]

Virilio, Paul, *The Art of the Motor* (Julie Rose trans., 1995 edn) [trans. of: *L'art du moteur*, 1993]

Virilio, Paul and Lotringer, Sylvère, *Pure War* (Mark Polizzotti trans., 2008) [trans. of: *La guerre pur*, 1983]

Waldron, J. (ed.), *Nonsense Upon Stilts: Bentham, Burke and Marks on the Rights of Man* (1987) 137

Wallerstein, Immanuel, *Historical Capitalism with Capitalist Civilization* (1995)

Weber, Max, *From Max Weber: Essays in Sociology* (H.H. Gerth and Wright Mills trans., 2009 edn) [original publication 1946]

Weekley, Ernest, *An Etymological Dictionary of Modern English* (1967)

Whitford, Margaret, *Luce Irigaray: Philosophy in the Feminine* (1991)

Willems, Johannes and Beck, Ulrich, *Conversations with Ulrich Beck* (2004)

Wilson, Charles, *England's Apprenticeship 1603–1763* (1965)

Wittgenstein, Ludwig, *Philosophical Investigations* (G.E.M. Anscombe trans., 1957 edn) [trans. of: *Philosophische Untersuchungen*, 1953]

Wright, Elizabeth, *Lacan and Postfeminism* (2000)

Wolfe, Carey, *Zoontologies: The Question of the Animal* (2003)

Worton, Michael and Still, Judith (eds), *Intertextuality: Theories and Practices* (1990)

Yoda, Tomiko, and Harootunion, Harry (eds), *Japan after Japan: Social and Cultural Life from the Recessionary 1990s to the Present* (2006)

Zajko, Vanda and Leonard, Miriam, *Laughing with the Medusa* (2006)

Žižek, Slavoj, *On Belief* (2001)

Žižek, Slavoj, *The Sublime Object of Ideology* (2008)

JOURNAL ARTICLES

Amoore, Louise, 'Risk before Justice: When the Law Contests its Own Suspension' 21 *Leiden Journal of International Law* 2008, 847

Anghie, Antony, 'Colonialism and the Birth of International Institutions: Sovereignty, Economy, and the Mandate System of the League of Nations' 34 *NYU Journal of International Law and Politics* 2001–2002, 513

Beard, Jennifer and Pahuja, Sundhya, 'Divining the Source: Law's Foundation and the Question of Authority' 19 *Australian Feminist Law Journal* 2003, 1

Benvenuto, Sergio and Girard, Rene, in collaboration with Maurizio Meloni, 'Psychoanalysis and Sacrifice: Difference and Identity between Psychoanalysis and Mimetic Theory' 14 *Journal of European Psychoanalysis* 2002, 14

Butler, Judith, 'The Body Politics of Julia Kristeva)' 3(3) *Hypatia* 1989 104–18

Calarco, Matthew, 'Deconstruction is not Vegetarianism: Humanism, Subjectivity and Animal Ethics' 37(2) *Continental Philosophy Review* 2004, 175–201

Caldwell, Anne, 'Transforming Sacrifice: Irigaray and the Politics of Sexual Difference' 17(4) *Hypatia* 2002, 24

Charlesworth, Hilary, 'Feminists Critiques of International Law and their Critics' 13(1) *Third World Legal Studies* 1995, 1–16

Charlesworth, Hilary, Chinkin, Christine, and Wright, Shelley, 'Feminist Approaches to International Law' 85 *The American Journal of International Law* 1991, 613, 615

Chi, Manjiao, 'Resource Sovereignty in the WTO Dispute Settlement: Implications of *China–Raw Materials and China–Rare Earths*' 12(1) *Manchester Journal of International Economic Law* 2015, 2–15

Chinkin, Christine, 'Rape and Sexual Abuse of Women in International Law' 5 *European Journal of International Law* 1994, 326–41

Cixous, Hélène, 'The Laugh of the Medusa' (1) *Signs* 1976, 875–93 (Keith Cohen and Paula Cohen trans., 1976 edn)

Cover, Richard, 'Violence and the Word' 95 *Yale Law Journal* 1986, 1601

Davies, Margaret and Mack, Cathy, 'Legal Feminism: Now and Then?' 20 *Australian Feminist Law Journal* 2004

Derrida, Jacques, 'The Force of Law: The Mystical Foundation of Authority' 11 *Cardozo Law Review* 1990, 911

Derrida, Jacques, 'The Principle of Hospitality' 11(1) *Parallax* 2005, 6

Dorsett, Saunnagh and McVeigh, Shaun, 'The Persona of the Jurist in Salmond's *Jurisprudence*: on the Exposition of "What Law is …"' 38 VUWLR 2007, 771–96

Ellstrand, N., 'Gene Flow and Introgression From Domesticated Plants into Their Wild Relatives' 30 *Annual Review of Ecology and Systematics* 1999, 539

Engle, Karen, 'Feminism and its (Dis)Contents: Criminalizing Wartime Rape in Bosnia and Herzegovina' 99 *American Journal of International Law* 2005, 778

Filho, M.T. Franca, 'Westphalia: a Paradigm? A Dialogue between Law, Art and Philosophy of Science' 8 *German Law Journal* 2007, 955

Foucault, Michel, 'My Body, This Paper, This Fire' 4(1) *Oxford Literary Review* 1979 (Geoff Bennington trans.)

Gavin, Brigid, 'Sustainable Development of China's Rare Earth Industry Within and Without the WTO' 49(3) *Journal of World Trade* 2015, 495–515

Gowlland-Debbas, Vera, 'The Relationship Between the International Court of Justice and the Security Council in the Light of the Lockerbie Case' 88(4) *The American Journal of International Law* 1994, 643–77

Grbich, Judith, 'Tracing the Figure of the Native in Postcolonial Theory and Native Title Law: Enlightenment, Aesthetics and Charles Harpur' 22 *Australian Feminist Law Journal* 2005, 127

Halley, Janet, 'Rape in Berlin: Reconsidering the Criminalisation of Rape in the International Law of Armed Conflict' 9(1) *Melbourne Journal of International Law* 2008, 78

Herwig, Alexia, 'Wither Science in WTO Dispute Settlement?' 21 *Leiden Journal of International Law* 2008, 823

Hossain, Kamrul, 'Legality of the Security Council Action: Does the International Court of Justice Move to Take Up the Challenge of Judicial Review?' 5(17) *Uluslararas Hukuk ve Politika* 2009, 133–63

Howse, Robert and Langille, Joanna, 'Permitting Pluralism: The *Seal Products* Dispute and Why the WTO Should Accept Trade Restrictions Justified by Noninstrumental Moral Values' 37 *Yale Journal of International Law* 2012, 367

Janover, Michael, 'The Limits of Forgiveness and the Ends of Politics' 26(3) *Journal of Intercultural Studies* 2005, 221

Keating, Paula, 'The Conditioning of the Unconditioned: Derrida and Kant' 3(1) *Borderlands E-Journal* 2004, 36

Kennedy, David, 'Receiving the International' 10(1) *Connecticut Journal of International Law* 1994, 1

Kessler, Oliver, 'Is Risk Changing the Politics of Legal Argumentation?' 21 *Leiden Journal of International Law* 2008, 863

Lee-Koo, Katrina, 'Connecting the Dots: Feminist International Relations and Feminist International Law in Australia' 32 *Australian Feminist Law Journal* 2010, 21

Linklater, Andrew, 'Citizenship and Sovereignty in the Post-Westphalian State' 2(1) *European Journal of International Relations* 1996, 77–103

Loizidou, Elena, 'Flesh, Bones and Other Matters' 29 *Australian Feminist Law Journal* 2008, 33

MacKinnon, Catherine, 'Rape, Genocide, and Women's Human Rights' 17 *Harvard Women's Law Journal* 1994, 5–16

Meloni, Maurizio, 'A Triangle of Thoughts: Girard, Freud, Lacan' 14 *Journal of European Psychoanalysis* 2002, 27–56

Mertus, Julie, 'Shouting from the Bottom of the Well: The Impact of International Trials for Wartime Rape on Women's Agency' 6(1) *International Feminist Journal of Politics* 2004, 110

Moi, Toril, 'The Missing Mother: The Oedipal Rivalries of René Girard' 12(2) *Diacritics Cherchez la Femme Feminist Critique/Feminine Text* 1982, 21

Nagan, Winston P. and Hammer, Craig, 'The Changing Character of Sovereignty in International Law and International Relations' 43(1) *Columbia Journal of Transnational Law* 2004, 1

Orford, Anne, 'Muscular Humanitarianism: Reading the Narratives of the New Interventionism' 10(4) *European Journal of International Law* 1999, 679–711

Orford, Anne, 'Trade, Human Rights and the Economy of Sacrifice' (Working Paper, Jean Monnet Program, 2003/04) 14

Orford, Anne, 'International Law and the Making of the Modern State: Reflections on a Protestant Project' 3(10) *In-Spire: Journal of Law, Politics and Societies* 2008, 5–11

Orford, Anne, 'Jurisdiction Without Territory: From the Holy Roman Empire to the Responsibility to Protect' 30(3) *Michigan Journal of International Law* 2009, 981–1015

Otto, Dianne, 'A Sign of "Weakness"? Disrupting Gender Uncertainties in the Implementation of Security Council Resolution 1325' 13 *Michigan Journal of International Law* 2006, 139

Peel, Jacqueline, 'Risk Regulation Under the WTO SPS Agreement: Science as an International Normative Yardstick?' (Working Paper, Jean Monnet Program, 2004)

Plachta, Michael, 'The Lockerbie Case: The Role of the Security Council in Enforcing the Principle *Aut Dedere Aut Judicare*' 12(1) *European Journal of International Law* 2001, 125–40

Polat, Necati, 'The Same and the Similar: Nihilism and Mimetic Hostility' 5(2) *Law and Critique* 1994, 219–39

Qin, Julia Ya, 'Judicial Authority in WTO Law: A Commentary on the Appellate Body's Decision in *China-Rare Earths*' 13 *Chinese Journal of International Law* 2014, 639–51

Schildrick, Margrit, 'Transgressing the Law with Foucault and Derrida: Some Reflections on Anomalous Embodiment' 47(3) *Critical Quarterly* 2005, 30

Simpson, Gerry, 'Warriors, Humanitarians, Lawyers: The Howard Government and the Use of Force' 27 *The Australian Yearbook of International Law* 2008

Stevenson, Anne, 'The Hysterical Women's Movement' *Times Literary Supplement* (9 September 1983) 961

Threadgold, Terry, 'Book review: Law and Literature Revised and Enlarged Edition by Richard Posner' 23 *Melbourne University Law Review* 1999, 830, 838

Todorov, Tzvetan, 'In Search of Lost Crime' *The New Republic* 29 January 2001, 29, 30

Toscano Franca Filho, Marcilio, 'Westphalia: a Paradigm? A Dialogue between Law, Art and Philosophy of Science' 8 *German Law Journal* 2007, 10

Ulam, Stanislaw, 'John von Neumann 1903–1957' *Bulletin of the American Mathematical Society* 64 1958, 1

CASES

Legality of the Threat or Use of Nuclear Weapons, Advisory Opinion, ICJ Reports, 8 July 1996, 226

European Communities–Measures Concerning Meat and Meat Products (Hormones), WT/DS26/AB/R, adopted 16 January 1998

Japan–Measures Affecting the Importation of Apples, Report of the Panel, WT/DS245/R, 15 July 2003 as upheld by the Appellate Body Report, WT/DS245/AB/R, adopted 10 December 2003

European Communities–Measures Affecting the Approval and Marketing of Biotech Products, WT/DS291, WT/DS292, WT/DS293, adopted 21 November 2006

China–Measures Related to the Exportation of Various Raw Materials (2009), WT/DS395, adopted 20 May 2009

China–Measures Related to the Exportation of Rare Earths, Tungsten and Molybdenum (2012), WT/DS432, adopted 24 April 2012

European Communities–Measures Prohibiting the Importation and Marketing of Seal Products, Appellate Body Report, WT/DS400/AB/R and WT/DS401/AB/R, adopted 18 June 2014

INTERNET SOURCES

U.S. Department of Energy's Human Genome Program, http://www.ornl.gov/sci/techresources/Human_Genome/project/about.shtml (accessed 23 October 2006)

From 'Understanding the WTO: The Agreements – Standards and Safety' http://www.wto.org/english/thewto_e/whatis_e/tif_e/agrm4_e.htm (accessed 24 October 2006)

Treaty of Westphalia, 'Peace Treaty between the Holy Roman Emperor and the King of France and their Respective Allies' October 24, 1648, http://www.yale.edu/lawweb/avalon/westphal.htm (accessed 2 August 2008)

Livio, Mario, *The Accelerating Universe: Infinite Expansion, the Cosmological Constant, and the Beauty of the Universe* (2000); Centre National de la Recherche Scientifique, 'Confirmation of the Accelerating Expansion of the Universe', http://www2.cnrs.fr/en/45.htm?&debut=160xt/ (accessed 13 April 2009)

OTHER REFERENCES

Borges, Jorges Luis, 'The Analytical Language of John Wilkins' (2006) [originally published as: *El idioma analítico de John Wilkins* in *La Nacion*, Argentina, 8 February 1942]

Evans, James G., 'The US Japan Fleet. *Com.* Perry Carrying the "Gospel of God" to the Heathen. 1853'

Imperial Rescript on National Revitalisation (*Nentō, Kokuun Shinkō no Shōsho*)

Imperial Rescript on the Termination of the War (*Daitōa-sens-shūketsu-no-shōsho*)

SPEECHES

Maximillian Robespierre, *On the Moral and Political Principles of Domestic Policy* (1794)

Franklin D. Roosevelt, 'State of the Union Address to the Congress' (Speech delivered to the United States Congress, Washington, 6 January 1941)

Franklin D. Roosevelt, 'Radio Address' (Broadcast from the Whitehouse delivered 9 December 1941)

Joint Statement by President Roosevelt and Prime Minister Churchill, 14 August 1941

Harry Truman, 'Address to the Opening Session of the United Nations Conference on International Organisation' (Speech delivered to the Opening session of the United nations Conference on International Organisation at San Francisco, 25 April 1945)

Grand Admiral Karl Doenitz, President of the German Reich, 'Radio address to the German people on the unconditional surrender of Germany' (Speech delivered at Flensburg, 8 May 1945)

Harry S. Truman, 'Victory speech' (Speech delivered 1945) *The Public Papers of H.S. Truman* (1961)

Secretary of State George Marshall, 'Address to the graduating class of Harvard University' (Speech delivered at Harvard University, 5 June 1947)

United States Secretary of State J.F. Byrnes, 'Restatement of Policy on Germany' (Speech delivered at Stuttgart, 6 September 1946)

Franklin D. Roosevelt, 'Casablanca Conference radio address' (Speech delivered 12 February 1943) *The Public Papers of F.D. Roosevelt* (1969) 12

Reagan, Ronald, 'Address on Foreign Policy' (Speech delivered at Cabell Hall, University of Virginia, Charlottesville, 16 December 1988)

His Holiness Benedict XVI, 'Address to the United Nations General Assembly' (Speech delivered at the 62nd session of the United Nations General Assembly 95th plenary meeting, New York, 18 April 2008)

TREATIES

Covenant of the League of Nations (as agreed on 28 June 1919)

Charter of the United Nations 1 UNTS XVI (signed on 26 June 1945)

Partial Test Ban Treaty UNTS 43 (entered into force 10 October 1963)

Convention for the Suppression of Unlawful Acts against the Safety of Civil Aviation 974 UNTS 178 (adopted 23 September 1971, came into force 26 January 1973)

Agreement on Sanitary and Phytosanitary Measures, Final Act Embodying the Results of the Uruguay Round of Multilateral Trade Negotiations, General Agreement on Tariffs and Trade, Annex 1A, 15 April 1994

INDEX

The manufacturer's authorised representative in the EU for product safety is Oxford University Press España S.A. of El Parque Empresarial San Fernando de Henares, Avenida de Castilla, 2 - 28830 Madrid (www.oup.es/en or product.safety@oup.com). OUP España S.A. also acts as importer into Spain of products made by the manufacturer.
Printed and bound by CPI Group (UK) Ltd, Croydon, CR0 4YY
14/09/2026
02216308-0002